The International Plumber

The farcical, bizarre, and often unorthodox exploits during a professional life up to retirement (1941-2001)

by

Anthony Jessop Price MA (Oxon) CEng FICE FIWEM

Contents

Dedication

To my family, who have put up with my travel commitments and holiday sideshows (that always seemed to take in views of local impounding reservoirs, water treatment works, and water pollution plants) while remaining sane and growing up into normal, intelligent people.

Also, to Damodar Shirwaiker, engineer, for his skills in the drawing office, badminton court, and golf course, and for being a lifelong friend.

Acknowledgements

Lesley Blount. For her tireless work in correcting an engineer's English to improve the rational narrative for anyone who might wish to read what the author has written.

My daughter, Eleanor Price. For assisting me to understand 21st-century computer technology and formatting for this book, and forever kindly reminding me that I always write a dozen words when only one might do.

About the Author

Jessop Price was born in Truro, Cornwall, during the Second World War and is proud to call himself a Cornishman. After the war, his family returned to the City of London, which became his new home for the next 12 years, where his father was Headmaster of St Paul's Cathedral Choir School. His playground throughout this period was the war-torn bomb sites surrounding the cathedral.

Academic life started as a chorister at St Paul's Cathedral and ended at Magdalen College, Oxford, in 1963 with a degree in Engineering Science. Jessop then joined the respected consulting civil engineers John Taylor & Sons in Westminster and started his international career with an immediate posting to Ndola, Zambia, where he met and married Kay. Jessop's travels began during the early stages of commercial air travel. Modes of transport varied from long-distance flights to four-seater aircraft and from off-road Land Rovers to camels.

His work took him to many parts of the world, and he experienced moments that proved to be entertaining, unconventional, and eccentric. Many such incidents are the subject of this book.

On retiring in 2001, his life has been no less exciting. He has been treasurer for a 270-pupil primary school near Victoria Falls in Zambia, where the education provided has enabled the children to escape from the poverty trap into which they were born. Together with Kay, they built their own home from scratch and gardened to award-winning standards, opening their gardens for charity events and filming for TV programmes.

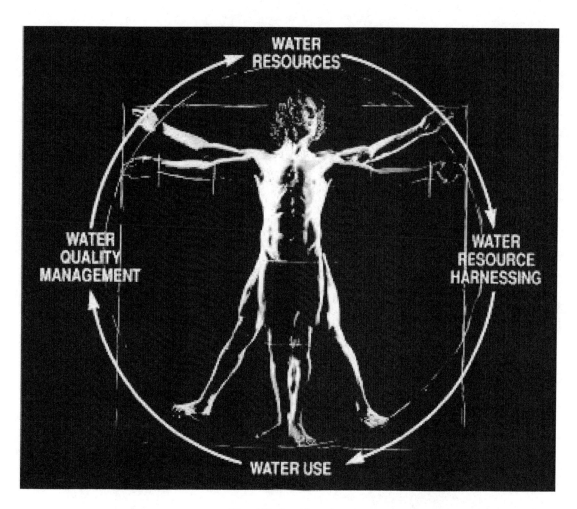

The Water Cycle

The Author

Prologue

"Water, water, every where, nor any drop to drink."
Samuel Taylor Coleridge Poet (1772 – 1834)

Leonardo da Vinci said, "water is the driving force in nature", and we all know without it, the human race could not exist. In Western culture, we assume water is instantly available at the turn of a tap in quantities we require. We become indignant if this 'luxury' is constrained. Other cultures are not so lucky. There are countries with plenty of natural water resources but with an ingrained philosophy that water is a gift from our 'Maker' and freely available to everybody. Such situations often allow the minority, with authority and influence, to secure supplies while the majority go without. It is appalling to discover, also, there are several billion people on our planet who spend the whole day collecting water of dubious quality from watering holes, returning with a full pot on their heads for the very survival of their family.

My working life as a civil engineer has been focused on providing safe drinking water to men and women across all six continents, bar Antarctica. Events have often proven to be farcical, bizarre, and regularly unorthodox through the people I met, from prime ministers to teaboys. The way this has been done, though, has changed over the centuries. For instance, Victorian engineers based in London had to travel by boat to advise clients across the world; and may have been 'out of office' for three months or more just to attend meetings in places as far away as India, St Petersburg, and Shanghai. By the time I started my career, commercial air travel was relatively new, but it did allow me to leave the office on one Friday evening, travel to Dar es Salaam on a night flight, meet with government officials on Saturday and Sunday, travel back to London on a night flight and be in the office first thing Monday morning.

As a graduate trainee, calculations were undertaken on slide rules and log tables. Computer development was vigorous during my career, and by the time I retired in 2001, laptop and mainframe computers had become every engineer's tools. Designing and drawing by computer were beginning to be the norm. This change in the working environment is truly beneficial both for the engineering profession and for the clients we serve. By 2020, with the regular adoption of 'video conferencing' by my successors, travel away from home will be considerably reduced.

My experiences are part of social history, and I believe it right to record the way water engineering was undertaken during my working life across the last four decades of the twentieth century. We took decisions then, based on technology and environmental considerations available at the time, that might be frowned on by engineers of the twenty-first century - thanks to effort and research undertaken during my career. I have written this book, therefore, as a testament to what was achieved within the constraints of tools at our disposal.

Preparation for my career began as a St Paul's Cathedral chorister, singing at Queen Elizabeth II's Coronation in 1953 and undertaking a two-month tour of the USA (billed as part of the Coronation Choir), performing six concerts a week. Music enabled me to receive further education at Lancing College and Magdalen College, Oxford, before settling down in 1963 to a profession with a respected consulting engineer, John Taylor & Sons, in Westminster.

Rather than dwell on a synopsis of engineering treaties, which might bore the pants off non-engineering readers, I have used my engineering experience as a skeleton to hang extraordinary events that happened to me during my work.

I became a successful marketeer for the firm, winning mega wastewater projects for Tehran and Athens against the host Government's will, National potable water projects for Egypt and Mauritius, purchasing a US consultancy for $1 and securing annual consultancy fees for the firm of over £60m by 1997 – twice that of any other UK competitor.

The book describes how I unwittingly gave a lift to a convicted poisoner in Zambia, graciously refusing an offer of a boiled sweet, and visited the Congo, where passports were 'confiscated' by Congolese Immigration Authorities until our return.

Working in communist states was 'different'; in PDR Yemen, the firm became embroiled in the civil war in 1986, with staff rescued off Aden by the Royal Yacht Britannia before flying into Heathrow and being met by Lynda Chalker, the UK Minister for Overseas Development,

Employed by the Wali of Dhofar in Oman, in the aftermath of cross-border insurrections, my wife and I were invited to dinner with the client at his home when Kay was made an 'honorary man' and then invited later to meet the 'wives' in their hareem.

Experiences were not all tortuous as we spent ten years providing a water supply to all inhabitants of Mauritius, which was, without a doubt, the catalyst for today's tourism industry across the nation.

My autobiography concentrates on these and similar hilarious incidents throughout my career to provide wholesome supplies of water where none existed and to enable those for whom I worked to live a broader, healthier life.

Image acknowledgements

Page iv	The Water Cycle	Acer Consultants Ltd
Page 18	Aerial View Lancing College	Lancing College
Page 31	Aerial View Magdalen	www.flickr.com
Page 41	Avonmouth SWW	www.google.com/maps
Page 48	Map of Zambia	www.geology.com
Page 59	Norman Carr	www.africansafaris.com
Page 88	Athens Treatment Plant	Hyderconsulting.com
Page 89	Map of Egypt	www.google.com/maps
Page 99	John W Boyer Jr	Philadelphia Suburban Water Co.
Page 102	Dubai Twin Towers	Emirates Towers Hotel
Page 118	Map of Saudi Arabia	www.worldometers.info
Page 126	Map of Aden	www.wikipedia.org
Page 144	Map of Mauritius	www.nationsonline.org
Page 163	Sir Veerasamy Ringadoo	www.wikipedia.org
Page 172	Map of Oman	Magellan Geographix Atlas
Page 182	Map Ethiopia	www.mappr.co
Page 198	Map of Pennsylvania	www.gisgeography.com
Page 206	Patapsco WTP	Hyderconsulting.com
Page 209	Map of SE Asia	www.nationsonline.org
Page 212	Malaysia Dam	Acer Consultants Ltd
Page 228	Map of India	www.nationsonline.org
Page 238	Chandrababu Naidu	www.editingworld.in
Page 246	Rajiv Luthra	www.vccircle.com

Chapter 1: The Early Years

"Water is the driving force in nature."
Leonardo da Vinci, Italian Painter & Engineer (1452-1519)

My Genesis

To begin at the beginning My launch into this world coincided with war-torn Britain. My father had been appointed Headmaster of St Paul's Cathedral Choir School in 1937 at the young age of thirty-three. He arrived in London from the Barchester-esque Chester Cathedral precincts and was thrust into a quasi-Dickensian existence, where St Paul's Cathedral clerical staff had to wear frockcoats, gaiters, and top hats to attend Cathedral services.

Father addressing the School Monitors in his Carter Lane Study

In 1938, there was more than a hint of war with Germany. Father focussed the Dean and Chapter's mind on the development of modern warfare and advised it would be far too dangerous for the Choir School to remain in the City as they did in the 1914-18 Great War. Having convinced them, he was dispatched to the provinces in search of a suitable location for the school should a major European conflict become a reality. By the time war was declared in 1939, the Dean and Chapter had

Father as Fire Warden

already decided the choristers at this London choir school should be 'billeted' with the much bigger Truro Cathedral School in Cornwall to meet their education requirements. The boys would then sing services in Truro Cathedral. Father was to share an office with Mr Mischler (the other headmaster), who was also appointed in 1937 but at the even younger age of twenty-seven. The 'marriage' of the schools must have had difficulties, but I understand it was well managed. St Paul's Cathedral choristers who spent their time in Truro have reminisced fondly to me of their schooldays and of my parents in

1

particular, even though Father was a disciplinarian – but much respected, nonetheless.

St Paul's Cathedral Choir Boys 1945
Photo taken on the caged roof of Choir House

The siblings I had three older brothers, all born before the Second World War. My brother David died in 1940, aged two and a half. Dr Orchard encouraged my Parents to have another child. Was my arrival just a happy 'mistake' or more of a planned event? I neither enquired about my parents nor had any interest in knowing. I was born in September 1941 at Woodlands in Old Falmouth Road, Truro. The bungalow still stands today, virtually untouched. Four pleasant years passed, spent in Cornwall like any other true Cornishman. But, at the end of the Second World War, I was whisked up to Choir House in Carter Lane EC4 and became a Londoner. My memory of these first four years remains sparse, except for when I fell into a pond in the field below the bungalow. Rumour has it I swallowed a tadpole and was heard to remark, "it tasted like plum pudding". This, together with my Parents' insistence I should never leave food on the plate (because it would be an insult to those starving Africans) ensured I was called 'dustbin' at school. Even today, I am known to hoover up my grandchildren's leftovers in case my Parents might be watching. I grew up with two elder brothers, Richard, born in Chester in 1936, and Martin, born in 1939, within the sound of Bow Bells.

Academic career

Dulwich College Kindergarten/Preparatory School

Was I a difficult child? My first encounter with education was achieved travelling on Southern Railway from Blackfriars to Dulwich, back in the days when there were 'No Smoking' and 'Ladies Only' carriages. This 'excitement' of visiting the school was made in the company of my brother Martin, Canon Knight's two sons, Canon Collins' son Andrew (*now Sir Andrew, a judge*) and Minor Canon Charles Moxon's son Michael (*who became an honorary Chaplain to the Queen and Dean of Truro Cathedral until his retirement in 2004*). We all travelled on the same train. Apart from Michael Moxon, I was younger than the others and was accompanied by a Swiss au pair who we called Mamsey One. My early morning entertainment was to race towards the edge of the platform as a train approached but, with judicious judgement, always stopping clear of disaster. This daily charade totally overwhelmed my 'controller', who reported me to Mother. As a result, I was put on reins and manoeuvred safely in and out of carriage compartments.

Early achievements I was never destined to become an academic 'livewire' (*unlike my brothers, who went on to secure scholarships to Queens College, Cambridge, and first-class degrees*). Throughout my school career, I fought ferociously for one of the bottom five places in the class – in the belief, I was going to be a 'late developer'. Fortunately, I was good at sports and generally sympathetic to my peers, so I managed my school time with effective but benign enthusiasm. My first report in 1946 said I was

> "*An intelligent and happy little boy with a good social sense .... enjoys making things and is very clever with his hammer .... good memory for music and loves playing his drum .... powers of concentration are well forward for his age .... pleasing development in every way*".

My Parents would have believed this was a good beginning to the next fourteen years of academic life.

My first brush with medicine 1950 saw me in hospital with acute peritonitis at the age of nine. This was a serious condition in those days, which had nearly caused the death of King Edward VII and did delay the royal pomp of his Coronation. Dr Potter (the Choir School's Consultant Paediatrician) rushed me to hospital in his car at 7.00 am on 27th June; he just happened to be the senior paediatric Consultant at the West London Hospital in Hammersmith. A subsequent letter from the Hospital to the Choir School doctor, Dr Dorran, says I was:

> "*.... suffering from acute abdominal pain and vomiting and found to be acute appendicitis. He was operated on by the Resident Assistant Surgeon, Mr Morris, who removed an almost gangrenous appendix, and there was evidence of general peritonitis. After the operation, he developed a swingeing temperature with a high leucocyte blood count and evidence of pelvic abscess. He was treated with penicillin and streptomycin, and his temperature subsided without further operation. He was discharged on 17th July 1950, very well indeed.*"

I spent three weeks in Hospital, enjoying the attention. This meant I missed most of my last summer term at Dulwich but spent a luxurious existence with Aunt Rosemary and Uncle Eric (Mother's younger brother) in Winchester, breathing country air and not the London smog. Mother came to visit, clutching my new school outfit. I had mysteriously secured a place at St Paul's Cathedral Choir School without a voice trial.

Choir House, Carter Lane EC4

Familiar sights and smells I remember evenings at Choir House in the late 1940s; the man with a pole to light the London street gas lamps which provided a dim yellow illuminated mist; commercial horses with their nose-gays standing on Ludgate Hill's wooden block surface waiting while their rider carried out his duties in the local shops; the sound of the Cathedral clock as it went through the quarters; candle smells on special evenings, and the methods used to prolong Mother's stay in my bedroom at night before lights out (a trick learnt by observing what happened at St Paul's Cathedral High Altar on Sundays). I created a mini-altar out of orange boxes and covered it with a white sheet, put on a cope-like dressing gown, and could be relied on to recite the whole of the communion service if it meant a few extra minutes of light and life before being tucked up in bed. I remember Mother's sigh of polite exasperation and resignation when I went from reading the epistle to the gospel and then back again for a very long special epistle for the day, followed by prayers for the clergy, the King and his subjects, Africans, and all other peoples I had learnt about in school. *Some of these antics continue to be well rehearsed in a modern idiom by my grandchildren today.* My mother dined out for many a year on one slight dyslexic rendering of Job Chapter 38, a Chapter chosen by me for its 41 verses. My misreading of verse 3, projected with every confidence and conviction I could muster to get my voice to the far end of the imaginary cathedral, came out as "Grind up now thy lions like a man ..." (*ed. Gird up now thy loins like a man*). This illuminating 'performance' took Mother by surprise and nearly caused instant death by convulsions of silent laughter in the quiet of my bedroom and probably brought a slight smirk to Job's face as well.

St Paul's Cathedral Choir School, London

Introduction There are references to boy choristers at the top of Ludgate Hill stretching back to Roman times. Throughout the ages, boys have been singing in the Cathedral, taverns and Drury Lane until Maria Hackett, a formidable Victorian lady, appeared on the scene. After many years of persistence, she persuaded the Dean and Chapter to construct a purpose-built school to house the St Paul's choristers in Carter Lane, next to the Deanery. The structure still exists today although, since 1965, it has been leased to the Youth Hostel Association, whose website describes the location as:

"Re-purposed after nearly 100 years as a school for choirboys, this remarkable building is steeped in history, this hostel includes old-school choirboy graffiti (in a wood-panelled classroom, no less), atmospheric spiral staircases and an elaborate exterior. And, of course, there's nothing quite like waking up to those cathedral bells. The hostel's central location is also great for exploring London on foot, with many of London's famous attractions close by......."

In the 1950s, a weekly cocktail of small classes, sports, and 26 hours of music, produced special schooling. This helped instil a sense of self-discipline and personal responsibility in 38 little choristers as an important building block for life. My stay at the Choir School coincided with some 'occasions' which, when cementing the component parts together, realised a robust education. Performing at the Royal Festival Hall's opening concert in 1951 during the Festival of Britain was the start of things to come. I remember being at the midday morning service in the cathedral when Great Tom[1] began to toll on two separate occasions; first, on Wednesday 06th February 1952, to broadcast to the City of London that King George VI had died; and then again, a year later, on Tuesday 24th March 1953, for that of his mother, Queen Mary. We were privileged to be some of the first in the land to hear about these important events. It was rare to have a funeral at St Paul's Cathedral, but in 1955, we sang at that of Sir Alexander Fleming, credited with having discovered penicillin in 1928 (*and I had good reason to be grateful for his breakthrough*).

The Queen's Coronation The whole of our Cathedral choir was part of the 1953 Coronation Choir. We had to attend a dozen rehearsals in St Sepulchre-without-Newgate and present a registration card on each occasion, which was formally stamped to record our attendance. Absence from just one rehearsal resulted in non-participation on the day of the occasion. (*This, unfortunately, happened to Alfred Deller, the world-renowned St Paul's Cathedral countertenor who had recording and performance commitments elsewhere*). Father had a very beautiful bass voice. He told the Authorities if he wasn't included in the Coronation Choir, they couldn't have the St Paul's choristers! His request was granted. Each choir member was given a 183-page book containing the Form and Order of Her Majesty's Coronation, the content of which was mostly the music we had to sing. There were the 'old favourites' such as '*I was glad when they said unto me*' by Hubert Parry and Vaughan Williams' Holy Communion Service in G minor, as well

---

[1] Great Tom was cast in 1706 by Richard Phelps, master of the Whitechapel Bell Foundry, and weighed over 5 tons

as a selection of well-chosen anthems from across the ages. Several pieces were written especially for the occasion by the great and the good in the UK music world; Herbert Howells, William Harris, George Dyson, Healey Willan (*Canadian*), Vaughan Williams and what I remember as being a very difficult Te Deum Laudamus by William Walton. The rehearsals concentrated on these modern works because most of the other pieces were already in our regular Cathedral repertoire.

The Great Day for us began with a six o'clock bell at the Choir School to stir us into action. Matron had decided we should have sustenance in Westminster Abbey. A banana sandwich and various other items of nourishment were placed in our cleaned-out sponge bag, which was then tied around the waist and hidden from view eventually by our surplice. A coach took us from the quiet City streets, over Blackfriars Bridge and along the South Bank, crossing the River Thames again at Lambeth Bridge to approach Westminster Abbey from the Abbey Precincts of Dean's Yard.

By now, it was eight o'clock. We were ushered into the Abbey through a side door and made to climb a staircase encompassed by structural scaffolding. This temporary edifice was erected all the way to the Abbey roof. Our place for the service was immediate to the east of the organ screen, high up in the building, almost touching the Abbey ceiling. St Paul's Cathedral choir were all on Cantoris (the right side when looking at our conductor mounted on the organ screen), with the Abbey choir on Decani (the left). The rest of the 400-strong choir was equally spread out on either side of the building and at the same height above the Abbey floor. Today's Health & Safety Executive and Fire Regulations would never allow so many people into such an enclosed space with so few effective 'escape' routes.

The Coronation was due to begin at 11.30 am, so there were three hours to kill. Our entertainment was to peer down (with difficulty) to watch 8,000 invitees as they dribbled into the Abbey. These included the full complement of the Aristocracy plus Heads of State and senior officials from across the Commonwealth, all in their fine regalia. While this was going on, an ad hoc orchestra conducted by Sir Adrian Bolt performed from the top of the organ screen. The musicians were drawn from UK-based orchestras. (I secured autographs of the two leading violinists, Paul Beard, *leader of the BBC Symphony Orchestra* and George Stratton, *leader of the LSO and a member of the Aeolian Quartet*.) This orchestra performed to keep the waiting congregation from being bored and played 15 well-known English pieces before the Service, from Thomas Tallis through Henry Purcell and Edward Elgar to William Walton.

The Organisers had given each piece a code letter A, B, C, etc., to ensure good communication with the orchestra under these unusual conditions. Sir Adrian would hold up a card as the morning progressed, displaying a single code letter to inform the orchestra which piece they were then to play. For some reason, the Organisers had swapped the letter allocation for two of the pieces without informing everyone of the changes. When the time came to play one such piece, Sir Adrian held up his card in all innocence, causing half the orchestra to perform one piece while the rest played another score! He was appalled to hear his 'team' creating cacophony and was quick to stop the orchestra. A verbal instruction from the conductor allowed proceedings to continue. In retrospect, I can't help but think maybe a little chorister might have been the instigator of this debacle.

Dr William McKie, Organist of Westminster Abbey, conducted the music during the Service. Not all the choir could see him, so sub-conductors were placed on each side of the Abbey, Dr John Dykes Bower, Organist St Paul's Cathedral on Cantoris and Dr William Harris, Director of Music at St George's Chapel Windsor Castle on Decani.

The whole ceremony was carried out with military precision, managed by the Earl Marshal, the Duke of Norfolk. Proceedings got off to a rousing start with *I was Glad* as the Queen entered the Abbey at 11.20 am. We used to sing this regularly at St Paul's, but on Coronation Day, we were to hear the Queen's Scholars of Westminster School 'sing' the two lines "*Vivat Regina! Vivat Regina Elizabetha! vivat! vivat! vivat!*" that are normally omitted whenever we sang the piece as an anthem at evensong. It is, and was, a shout but followed by the whole choir repeating the words in music treble forte – an amazing sound that will remain with me 'unto the grave'. The ceremony was solemn with the occasional outburst of sound, such as Handel's *Zadok the Priest*, and all led by the Archbishop of Canterbury, Geoffrey Fisher, who (as Bishop of Chester) had married my Parents some twenty years earlier. We did our duty and sang our hearts out for the rest of the Service. The Queen was Anointed, Invested, Enthroned, Princes and Peers paid Homage, she received communion, and then she was gone, out into a wet London day to be greeted by hundreds of thousands of people who had come from all four corners of the globe to witness the occasion. We had to wait, perched up in the rafters of the Abbey, while the coroneted congregation ambled out as best they could. After a couple of hours or so, we were allowed down and bussed home to the City. It felt a bit of an anti-climax when we arrived back in Carter Lane. All was made good in the evening, though, when we climbed up the Cathedral to the Stone Gallery and watched a magnificent firework display before the headmaster ordered us to bed.

We all received a foolscap envelope through the Royal Mail at the end of term containing a small box and a declaration. Mine read:

"By Command of HER MAJESTY THE QUEEN, the accompanying medal is forwarded to Anthony Price to be worn in commemoration of Her Majesty's Coronation 02nd June 1953".

The American Concert Tour Canon John Collins arranged for the St Paul's Cathedral Choir to go on a Concert Tour to perform across the whole of the eastern half of the United States of America. This extraordinary event had two foci; it advertised our choir as having taken part in the Queen's Coronation, and it was to remind the American people there is a Chapel in St Paul's Cathedral dedicated to those UK-based American servicemen who lost their lives during the Second World War. This 'adventure' started on 24th September 1953. We were seen off by Dean Matthews at Waterloo Station, bound for Southampton to embark on the RMS Queen Elizabeth. It took five days to journey to New York.

We performed six concerts a week throughout the Tour. Commercial air travel had not yet developed, so our daily travel routine of about 150 miles was undertaken by silver Greyhound-style buses or by train (often overnight) if the distance was too great. The Concert Tour was managed by Columbia Artists Inc., and two of their organisation, Mr Jupp and Mr Hortop, accompanied us wherever we went. We had two buses, one for the boys and School staff and the other for the 18 vicars choral and the New York management staff.

St Paul's Cathedral Choir

Whole choir entourage on the QE 2

The Concert Tour started in New York and took us to New England and as far north as Ottawa and Montreal in Canada, west to Chicago, down the centre of the country to Memphis and New Orleans and then back to New York. Concerts were held at universities including Yale, Harvard, and Purdue, but we also performed in local school concert halls, professional concert halls like Carnegie and the cathedrals of Washington and New York. Mother came with us as 'wardrobe mistress'. She produced a detailed 100-page diary of the Tour describing her first-hand impressions and included postcard pictures and press cuttings. This record is very personal as to what went on over the weeks we were away. There is another diary written by George Hulland (Deputy Headmaster), which has been lodged with my school friend Peter Chapman. The two diaries make an excellent record of what happened during the Concert Tour, so there is little point in repeating events ad nauseam except to refer to my own special memories.

8

with best wishes
Dwight D Eisenhower

Father was determined to engage our minds on the school's normal curriculum. He decided to hold lessons on the coach as we travelled from one concert venue to another. This may have seemed a good idea on paper. Our teaching 'team' included Miss Brenner (trained nurse and Father's secretary), who taught French, George Hulland, our history and geography teacher and Father, who taught maths and divinity. Lessons in a moving bus were a nightmare for the teachers, and the headmaster soon caved into reason and told the school to treat the whole experience as "one big geography lesson". This relaxation of duties was not without some success, for later on (in my professional career), I was able to know the precise location of certain cities and towns on the North American continent. We performed in Boston (*where later my firm designed and project managed an immersed tube tunnel as part of the City's transportation system*); in Lancaster, Pennsylvania (*where I was Chairman of Philadelphia Suburban's consultancy*); and in Baltimore (*where we were specialist Consultants for their wastewater treatment plant on sludge treatment and odour control*).

Key memories of the Concert Tour for me were:

- Our first concert was in St John the Divine, New York's Cathedral, where the doors were closed when the audience reached over 10,000.
- Performing in Washington, first to President Eisenhower in the White House (I was chosen to formally present him with our Concert Tour Programme) and then, later that day, in Constitution Hall
- Visiting the Niagara Falls
- Seeing parts of New Orleans's old town; and staying at the Memphis Peabody Hotel, where ducks from the foyer fountain travelled up in the lift to the roof each night and down again in the morning (*I believe their offspring are still performing this ritual*).
- Hearing one of our choristers on a local radio station in some mid-west small town, who had been Shanghaied to give an interview while we were all out for a walk. What he actually said was not particularly significant except he signed off with "...byee, Julian Rogers, twelve". I can't explain why, but this became a catchphrase for the rest of my days at the Choir School.

- Seeing three drinking fountains side by side in Alabama, one for "whites", another for "blacks", and the third for "dogs". This appalling vision made me sit up, particularly as Canon Collins was a champion against apartheid[2]
- Performing on US TV with Alistair Cooke (of 'Letter from America' fame), when all our surplices were dyed light blue because the pure white was too bright for black and white television technology to handle at the time
- Our final concert was at Carnegie Hall, New York.

The itinerary was impressive, and I list it as follows:

St. Pauls Cathedral Choir Tour of the United States of America and Canada 1953

24 Sept	Embark on the Queen Elizabeth
29	Arrive in New York
30	St John the Divine, Cathedral (doors closed after 10,000 seated)
1 Oct	Concert in Baltimore, Maryland
2	Travel to Washington DC
3	McCaskey High School Auditorium, Lancaster Pennsylvania
4	Travel to Washington DC and Bristol, Virginia by night train
5	Tennessee High School Auditorium, Bristol, Virginia, then night train to Washington DC
6	Perform in the White House to President Eisenhower, the First Lady and newly elected Chief Justice Warren Constitution Hall, Washington
7	Concert in Philadelphia
8	Pottsville High School Auditorium, Pennsylvania
9	Travel to Newhaven, Connecticut
10	Milford High School Auditorium, New London, Massachusetts
11	Symphony Hall, Boston Massachusetts
12	Hartford Cathedral, Connecticut
13	Woolsey Hall, Yale University, Connecticut
14	Wellesley College, Harvard, Massachusetts

[2] Another champion of apartheid was Trevor Huddleston, an old Lancing boy who first came to prominence as a parish priest in Soweto, Johannesburg, and I was to meet him five years later at Lancing when he stayed with us for three months after he was deported by the South African Government.

15	Travel to New London, Connecticut
16	Concert in Oneonta, New York State
17	Travel to Montreal, Canada
18-20	Rest in Montreal
21	Notre Dame RC Church, Montreal
22	Travel to Sherbrooke
23	Kingston Cathedral, Ontario
24	Cinema in Hamilton, Ontario
25	Day Off – visit Niagara Falls
26	Concert in Buffalo
27	The Schwab Auditorium, State College Pennsylvania
28	Travel to Akron, Ohio
29	Travel to Lansing, Michigan
30	Day – off in Lansing
31	Concert in Chicago, Illinois
1 Nov	Music Hall, Purdue University, West Lafayette, Indiana
2	Day – off at Purdue University
3	Concert Hall, Indianapolis, Indiana
4	Concert in Cincinnati, Ohio
5	Memorial Auditorium, Louisville, Kentucky
6	Travel to Nashville, Tennessee
7	Travel to (*Peabody Hotel*) Memphis, Tennessee
8	Train to New Orleans, Louisiana
9	Concert in New Orleans
10	Baton Rouge High School Auditorium, Louisiana
11	Alexandria High School Auditorium, Virginia
12	Concert, Shreveport, Louisiana
13	Concert, Vicksburg, Mississippi
14	Travel to Gadsden, Alabama
15	Travel to Chattanooga, Tennessee
16	Memorial Hall, Chattanooga, Tennessee
17	Lexington Auditorium, Kentucky

18	Travel to Huntington, West Virginia
19	Concert in Huntington, West Virginia
20	Ramsey Junior High School, Bluefield, West Virginia
21	Virginia Polytechnic Institute Auditorium, Blacksburg, Virginia, then night train to New York
22	Omnibus Programme, New York TV Studios, interview with Alastair Cook
23	Sing at the Annual Dinner of the English-Speaking Union, Waldorf Astoria
2 Dec	Arrive in Southampton, UK

The 'adventure' finished when we returned to London, following the reverse route to our outgoing journey, ready to perform the Advent and Christmas music in the Cathedral. The term finished on Sunday, 04th January 1954.

Cricket on Choir House roof with AJP fielding at silly point'

Sport I was a natural ball player and, at the age of ten, bowled out all 10 of Westminster Cathedral Choir School 2nd XI and then proceeded to make more runs with the bat than the whole of the young papists put together. At the end of the match, I was held aloft back to the pavilion on David Backhurst's shoulders. It is useful to have a Father for your Headmaster because you end up being Captains of Cricket, Football and Head Boy! Nonetheless, I did have to earn my spurs and was awarded the Victor Ludorum at the School's Annual Sports Day at Bellingham playing fields (*maybe thanks in part to Peter Chapman breaking his leg in the long jump before all the events were complete*), the cricket bat for the season's best batting average (*subsequently won also by Alistair Cook, later to become Captain of the England Test side*) and the Bowling Shield twice for the season's best bowling figures. In my last year, we won all our football and cricket matches against other schools and, most importantly, we beat our arch-rivals over at Westminster Abbey Choir School.

PE on Choir House roof

One of our choral duties in the Cathedral was to sing Handel's Messiah each year under the Dome on the first Tuesday in December. In 1955, we had just played the Abbey Choir School at football on the previous Thursday, with a convincing win of 4-1 in our favour. I have to admit that year (little choristers being little choristers), we slightly changed the words of the chorus "For unto us a Child is Born" to 'Four one to us a child is born!' Ever since, that chorus has brought a smile to my face – yes, we did beat them at football that year 4-1!

Play To aid and abet our visits to Bellingham on Monday mornings and Thursday afternoons, we were helped by having enough space on the Choir School roof for two cricket 'nets'. The roof was caged so that balls did not inadvertently fly off into Cater Lane or the Deanery. We also played a serious game of fives, not Eton fives or Rugby fives but a five-aside game of throwing a cricket ball into a wooden slip catch cradle. The intent was to throw the ball towards the top edge of the cradle so the ball would skim off at odd angles to make it difficult for the opposing team to catch. This was not only a very enjoyable pastime but also engendered team competition and brilliance in fielding technique.

They say little girls can be nasty, but boys can also be mentally vicious, particularly when targeting those younger than themselves. Two 'tests' were designed to scare new probationers when they arrived at the Choir School aged 8 or 9. Their elders told them that, to become a chorister at the age of 9 or 10, they first had to jump down the flight of five stairs inside the school front door; a practice which went un-noticed by teachers until a probationer broke his leg and Father banned the practice forthwith. The second was much more 'mental' in every sense of the word; it was necessary for a probationer to throw himself off the Golden Gallery at the top of the Cathedral, slide down the Dome and (the requirements were very specific about this) land on a Number 11 bus as it was travelling around St Paul's Churchyard.

We enjoyed roller-skating, and Cater Lane's very smooth tarmac surface was perfect for this fun. Choristers were often seen travelling at speed after evensong between Mr Fosters, the hairdresser at the corner with St Andrews Hill, and the AA restaurant at the corner with Dean's Court.

The Choir School basement housed the kitchens, the stoke-hole and boiler, a play area for table tennis and communal lavatories and washbasins. The smell of whitening cricket boots and pads with blanco in the basement washroom remains with me to this day.

There was a terrific game that the more senior boys used to play in the Day Room once those in the junior dormitory had gone to bed. Two teams of five or six; one boy stood with his back to the wall (legs astride) while the other four or five team members bent down to form a long 'bridge', with the first boy's head in between the legs of the boy standing against the wall, etc., etc. The other team would then take a running jump onto this 'bridge'. The first to go were the lighter boys, whose job it was to hurdle as far as they could along the line of this 'bridge' to secure enough room for all his teammates to land on the 'bridge'. The last to jump tended to be the heavyweight. The principle of the game was to cause the 'bridge' to collapse, but if there was not enough room left on the 'bridge' for the final jump to land, then the 'bridge' team was the winner.

Academical Life Achievement in the classroom was not my 'finest hour' during primary education. The Choir School of 38 boys was divided into four forms, so there were never more than ten in a class. One of my best friends (Francis Saunders) and I vied for the bottom of the class. School Reports record my abilities and start off in the Autumn Term of 1950 with:

> *"When he can write and spell, he will get a better position – he does not know his tables – apt to be untidy."*

This kind of comment prevailed over the years. Some were more complimentary than others.

> My history master, George Hulland, wrote, "knowledge good, but the ability to transfer it to paper not so good"; while in Maths, I was advised, "not to get upset when there is thinking to be done but see the fun in tackling things which are not immediately obvious".

I cannot understand what Father thought when he wrote his Headmaster's comments to himself and my mother at the bottom of my School Report. In the early 1950s, his Comments started with:

> *"Works well in school and cathedral. Well bowled"; later, "everything he undertakes is done with the utmost enthusiasm", and in my final report, he wrote kindly ", The school has been disciplined but happy, the highest tribute possible to a Head Boy. Had a very good cricket season, owing to his ability with bat and ball". I noticed there is no reference to my abilities in Latin, French, History or Maths, but he finished with, "He has been an ideal Head Boy, and the School has been very happy under his leadership."*

Was this to be my best academic accolade, or was there more to come? Why shouldn't I record these little bits of nepotism for posterity?

14

Choir in St Paul's Cathedral conducted by Dr John Dykes Bower

Musical life Singing in the Cathedral for five whole years was an awe-inspiring activity. Thursday was the only day in the week we didn't sing, but this was made up with two services every Wednesday and Friday and four on Sunday, plus the 8.00 am (said Holy Communion) once we were confirmed. Cathedral life seemed to attract eccentricity. There are plenty of anecdotes, but the following three typify those that I remember.

Father preached in the Cathedral two or three times a year and, on one occasion, was led by the verger to the base of the pulpit steps. They bowed to one another, and as Father climbed, he saw a little man crouched in the pulpit who rather beseechingly said,

> *"I have a message"*. My Father had to think quickly and replied, *"So have I, and it is my turn now"*. A truly headmaster's comment for which there is no logical response.

A lady who regularly came to week-day evensongs (and was one of about six in such congregations) sadly had elephantiasis. She sat in the front row dressed in virgin bridal white and believed she was the reincarnation of Mary, the mother of Jesus. As we all processed in, she was close enough to the Canon-in-Residence to pop a boiled sweet in his mouth as he passed.

Mr Hamp, a verger and ex-policeman, regularly had to remove people from the Chancel and, on one occasion, was accosted by a man in the Bishop's stall who thought he had a right to sit there quietly as he was Jesus.

All choristers had to play at least one musical instrument and practice for 30 minutes every day. Half of us practised from 7.10 am while the rest went for a walk along the Embankment through the London smog, touching Waterloo Bridge and returning for breakfast at 8.00 am. The rest practised their instruments in the evening after evensong while we had free time. The first half swapped over the next day so that we all got the benefit of walking by the River Thames in the early morning because the Headmaster and Matron believed we should get fresh air into our lungs. The London smog continued until the 1956 Clean Air Act (*passed only as a result of London's Great Smog of 1952*).

Price Minor in a studio pose

I tried to learn the piano but could not coordinate my left and right hands. The violin seemed more to my liking, and I was fortunate enough to have Mrs Eluned Chappell as my teacher. She taught me musicianship, to play in tune, and that genius is only 10% talent and 90% blood, sweat and tears. There were plenty of tears when she knew I hadn't practised because sport also played an important part in my growing up. Father came into a legacy and very kindly suggested I go and choose a good violin. With £50 in my pocket, I went with Mrs Chapple to the specialist violin shop of John & Arthur Beare (just off Wardour Street at the time) and chose a fine instrument made in 1869 by George Craske, all for the price of £45 10s. This lovely violin, Mrs Chappell, and a bit of hard work enabled me to get a music scholarship to Lancing College that would pay for all my school fees, so long as I passed Common Entrance. This was when Mother came into her own, insisting I learnt so many French and Latin words each day; she tested me rigorously in the holidays, wherever we happened to be. Father kept giving me mental arithmetic to understand numbers and their relationship with one another. This parental push seemed to work, and in January 1956, I was bundled off to the cold, cold South Downs to learn how to become a man.

Holidays in my early years Father was a man of habit. Year after year, our holiday schedule was enjoyable but never showed much propensity for change. We always escaped the London smog.

In January, we visited my grandparents, Joseph Nathaniel (Bapa) and Mary Ann (Nana) Moxon, in Ashby-de-la-Zouch. In the late 1940s and early 1950s, we travelled by train from St Pancras (*on the London, Midland, and Scottish Railway*), changing in Leicester onto the Burton line. We always seemed to arrive in the dark, with the engine belching out steam and smoke. A taxi took us to my grandparents' house, called Glen Roy, on the Burton Road. My uncle Harold and Aunty Ann lived next door with my four cousins, Jennifer, Wendy (who was my age), Gillian and Christopher. There always seemed to be heavy falls of snow, and with no central heating, we were always sent to bed with stone-hot water bottles that were too hot to touch initially and as cold as ice in the morning.

I took my violin to practice and played Handel Sonatas with Nana's chiropodist. It was definitely a mutually enjoyable experience. Food at Glen Roy seemed to follow a pattern of a joint of ham, which is something I had never seen before, and other cold meats such as tongue, all with a salad. The dining room table had a second purpose as, covered in black cloth, it represented a football pitch for tiddly-winks football. Every year, we went to the pantomime in Leicester, which was always an enjoyable family occasion.

In the Easter holidays, we took a yacht on the Norfolk Broads. Father considered himself a good sailor, and we embarked at Wroxham on a six-berth vessel heading downstream on the River Bure to Horning, then upstream on the River Ant to Barton Broad, as well as along the River Thurne to Potter Heigham and Hickling Broad. I hold two specific memories. One year, we met up with an old St Paul's chorister with a shipmate who was the Royal Philharmonic Orchestra's principal trumpeter. He needed to keep his lip muscles in trim, so he rowed off into the reeds every evening to play his instrument. The melodic sounds wafting in the half-dark across the water were magic. The other memory is far from an illusion. There is a very low bridge at Potter Heigham that requires mariners to moor and take down the ship's mast before attempting to 'sail' underneath. We were in the process of this manoeuvre when one of the sheets (ropes controlling the sails) looped over a stationary motor cruiser's windscreen. Alas, our yacht continued to float onto its mooring, bringing the cruiser's windscreen with it as an unnecessary attachment. We soon found out the motor cruiser's owner was the local Chief of Police - in Norwich. I never did learn how this catastrophe panned out, except to say my father was saved from the indignity of a prison sentence.

In the five-week summer holidays, we went to stay at Benenden School in Kent. During the Second World War, Benenden School was evacuated to Newquay, and the three headmistresses (*the Founders, Miss Shelden, Miss Hindle and Miss Bird*) required a priest to prepare their 'girls' for confirmation. They approached the Dean of Truro, who offered Father the task. He continued this duty after the War going down to Benenden every Friday in term time on his day off and returning to the Choir School for Saturday morning lessons after Matins. As a thank you for his role in these pastoral duties, his family was rewarded by absorbing the pastoral environment of the Kent countryside, with all the benefits of a school setting to ourselves – swimming pool, tennis courts, croquet, etc. The headmistresses were often there for part of their holiday and taught me the intricate techniques of the school's form of croquet (vicarage lawn rules!).

Lancing College

Aerial view of Lancing College, Upper Quad and Chapel

Early days Lancing College was founded in 1848 by Nathaniel Woodard to educate the sons of the clergy. It was not noted for its academic excellence but rather for being an all round school of excellence. Past pupils have become novelists (*Evelyn Waugh and Tom Sharpe*), musicians and actors (*Geoffrey Bush, Steuart Bedford, Jamie Theakston, and George Baker*), playwrights and singers (*David Hare, Christopher Hampton, Tim Rice, and Peter Pears*), priests and diplomats (*Trevor Huddleston and Christopher Meyer*) and judges and politicians (*Robert Megarry, Nicholas Browne-Wilkinson and Tom Driberg*). The College ambience was frightening to begin with, but over time, it was possible to find your purpose in life without too much difficulty. I was in Seconds House, made up of Mr Brand (a crusty old bachelor Housemaster about to retire) and 50-odd tough boys with no particular focus on excellence in any direction. By week two, I found myself boxing for the house in some bantamweight or other. This scared me, but once in the ring, only you can determine your survival path; it is a good lesson for life, but not one I wished to repeat if it could possibly be avoided. I had to win and did, but, alas, it meant the following week, I found myself in a bus travelling up to Charterhouse to box for the College. My opponent met me off the bus, and we went to his School House for lunch.

> *"How long have you been boxing?"* he asked
> *"A couple of weeks,"* was my honest reply.
> *"Oh, I have been boxing for two years now."*

I could not wait for this horrible episode to unfurl so I could get back to the comfort of Seconds House and my bed. I didn't win, but I didn't totally disgrace myself either (or the College) and managed to secure my desire of never being asked to put on a pair of boxing gloves again. Cricket, football, and athletics were opportunities for me, and I went on to represent the College in all three. I won my school colours for Athletics and captained the Football 2nd XI, who were unbeaten throughout my final year, even against the 1st XI, which annoyed them intensely.

Education - the results Today, specialist educators would say I was moderately dyslectic. I was fortunate enough to have many good teachers, and it is interesting to record their comments throughout my school career.

Terry Kermode (Maths) was a strong, quiet type housemaster and played the flute in the school orchestra. He started by saying my work was:

> *"Rather variable: at best good"* (*Summer 1956*); this changed two years later, when I was studying for my 'A' Levels, to, "*I think he has been trying lately, but finds calculus considerably difficult"* (*Christmas 1958*) and as a final shot of exasperation he thought I was "*too amiable, without actually being idle. He has still got a lot of improvement to make in geometry"* (*Easter 1959*).

One of my other Maths teachers, Dennis Day, was more to the point:

> *"His written work has been adequate but never distinguished or penetrating"* (*Summer 1957*); "*It would be nice if he would explain his absence or lack of work before the event, rather than being pleasantly amiable after it"* (*Lent 1960*) and, with a flourish hoping he would never see me again, "*His intelligence has often produced reasonable, yet extraordinary mathematics demanded of him by his having declined to learn easy methods in the past. He has not finally cleared from my mind earlier impressions of charm unmatched by any real effort"* (*Summer 1960*).

In the end, I passed both Pure and Applied Maths 'A' Level – what a relief! Our paths did cross later when he taught my son, Nicholas. Any memories of what my former teacher thought of me were not said or may have been quietly forgotten without "any real effort".

My science teachers all thought I was a little more than backward. Mr Dar (an exchange teacher from India) and Lewis Brown taught me physics and thought early on I had:

> *"Made excellent progress during the term (second out of 27) but did not like his behaviour in the examination hall"* (*Christmas 1956*).

What was all that about? I seem to remember placing a Bunsen burner under something that caught alight in the end-of-term exam.

By Easter 1958, I was top of the form, but my enthusiasm was quashed by Lewis Brown's following words:

"His work has always been good, but it is in no way outstanding."

But outstanding enough to grab an 'A' Level.

My exploits in chemistry were derided by Bill Dovell, who referred to me as "a charming person but will have to do some work if he is to make any progress".

As regards Biology, "he contributes little to the work of the class and is weak in ability and effort".

I hate to think what my parents must have made of this regular litany of being told their son is nothing more than a charming but idle ne'er-do-well.

Is it any wonder my Headmaster, John Dancy, made a comment:

"Is he really cut out to be a Scientist, and wouldn't it be better if he did an arts subject after "O" Level?"

Later, he commented not on my academic work but on my unbeaten 50 runs on the 1st XI pitch in a House match against 'Sandersons', the eventual winners of the inter-House competition,

"I think (mainly on the evidence of the innings I saw in a House match) that he is toughening up somewhat".

Were my abilities in the arts subjects demonstrably better? My English teacher, 'Monkey' Chamberlain, said I was:

"An intelligent boy who is backward in his powers of comprehending what he reads and of expressing himself".

Robert Lockyer, a history teacher, wrote he had been:

"Most favourably impressed by my work, which is competently planned and quite well written" (Summer, 1956). He was obliged to modify his opinion nine months later to *"I think he is a conscientious worker, but his spelling and style are atrocious."*

**School Sacristans with
Rev Cuthbert Shaw, Chaplain**

The Rev. Cuthbert Shaw, School Chaplain, took me for divinity. He was a nice kindly man and co-incidentally was a colleague of Father at Westcott House, the Cambridge Theological College.

"He has worked well and should pass 'O' Level fairly easily". I failed! A year later, when I was more mature and in the Sixth Form, his comment to my Parents was, *"He is serious and interested and ready to think."* Was there a sting in the tail of his statement?

My Art master, Graham Collyer, recorded my "ceramic cat, unfortunately, exploded in the biscuit firing, but it was a strange brassbound creature from fairy talk and deserved to live."

Music was a major part of my life at Lancing, and it was good to have two strong supporters to look up to. Mrs Eluned Chapple (Violin teacher who started at Lancing the same term as I did) wrote:

"A good term's work. Intonation is improving. Sight-reading could be more accurate. He is to be congratulated on getting into the National Youth Orchestra. It will be a good experience".

Johnny Alston (Music Director) was also encouraging,

"He has a quick brain musically and, of course, a lot of talent".

I was given every opportunity to perform in front of the school and parents each term, both singing and on the violin. I remember singing the spiritual "I wonder where my mother has gone?" in Great Hall and miraculously seeing her in the audience.

Memory can sometimes eradicate the truth, but not when you play Bach's Double Violin Concerto in a concert and start the beautiful slow movement with an F♯ rather than an F natural. Johnny Alston smiled at the audience and said, "Let's start again"! He took me to music theory. My set works at 'A' Level were all a huge eye opener: Brahms 4th Symphony, Sibelius 3rd, Holst's Hymn to Jesus and Dvorak's Dumky Trio. A strange combination, but I was obliged to listen to the other three Brahms symphonies and as much Sibelius as was recorded on vinyl in 1959 – sometimes on '78s'. It all helped me to enjoy classical music and pass the exam. I was lucky to play and regularly sing with Steuart Bedford (who was a brilliant pianist and later became a recognised conductor of Britten, once the great man had died) and Nicholas Kraemer (who played the second violin in my school string quartet and has subsequently made a career as a harpsichord player and conductor of baroque music).

Other boys in Seconds House had different musical preferences. Pop music was evolving from the tuneful "How much is that doggie in the window" of the early 1950s into a culture of its own that was either loud or very loud. As a house prefect, I was obliged to regularly tell Tim Rice to turn down his 'very loud' pop music in the Fives Pit.

Father thought I might read music at Cambridge. As a trial run for my further education, I was sent up to St John's College in December 1958, where George Guest was the Music Director (Father had taught him as a boy at Chester Cathedral Choir School). The music exams were tough, but I played my violin with confidence. However, brother Martin (who was at Queen's College at the time) discovered, with a certain degree of amusement, I had scored 'nil points' in my associated French test, which promptly ended this particular opportunity.

If music is the food of love, play on The following year I was deemed choral scholarship material. Father arranged for me to have singing lessons with Gordon Clinton, a former St Paul's Cathedral vicar choral back in 1946, before taking up solo singing and a Professorship at the Royal College of Music. I visited him in his rooms behind the Albert Hall and showed him my chosen party piece for the voice trial – the bass solo in Bach's Magnificat, which I loved.

> "*Too easy,*" he said immediately and recommended I change to one of the bass arias in Bach's St Matthew Passion ("*Gladly would I take upon me, Cross and Cup, and all His burden, Could I follow Christ my Lord*").

This is a fiendish piece with long phrases requiring superb breath control and with notes that would show off (or not) the high and low registers. He was right, of course, but it meant ratcheting up my whole practising process. The voice trials were in March 1960. I auditioned first for Oxford (Academical Clerkship at Magdalen) one week before the Cambridge trials. This was a shrewd move by Magdalen as most of us 'young things' were trying for both Universities. Dr Bernard Rose, Informator Choristarum (organist and master of the choristers), offered me a scholarship. I am sure it was because I had the gall to try such a difficult piece, so I cancelled my voice trial for the following week in Cambridge. (Simon Carrington was not so lucky. He was obliged to wait another week before being offered a Choral Scholarship at King's College Cambridge; he read Music and then went on to become a founder member of The King's Singers. Another candidate for Magdalen was Michael Moxon, from my Dulwich school days.)

Down with the French I had failed French 'O' Level in 1957 and two years later had disgraced myself at a Cambridge trial by getting fewer marks in French than was thought humanly possible. Oxford University required me to have passed 'O' Level French before acceptance to read whatever subject, with or without a scholarship. I had reached a crossroads in life where reality was beyond reason. Between March and June 1960, I focussed on this chink in my armour. To hedge my bets, I was organised to sit two French 'O' Level exams. The first exam was set by the Oxford and Cambridge Board, which I took at Lancing with all the 15-year-olds taking their regular batch of subjects. For the second, Father had arranged for me to sit for the London University Board exam at Benenden Girl's School (me, the only boy in the examination hall). I passed 'O' Level French twice and could march onward to my university, head held high (I never thought to enquire how the Benenden girls faired that year).

The College Chapel

College Chapel

Lancing College hosted the largest private chapel in the world which was originally designed on a French chapel with 13th-century principles. It is one of the tallest interior vaulted churches in the UK. No pupil could be but influenced by its sheer wonder and grandeur. The whole school (400 boys) had to attend choral evensong daily and sing holy communion on Sunday. For my first year and a half, I was still singing treble in the college choir. My voice then 'broke', and I joined the congregation for a year before returning to sing bass. The evensong liturgy was identical to that at St Paul's, except instead of singing the psalms with the Anglican chant, we performed them in plainsong, which added to my musical education.

The College choral society performed a major choral work each year in the chapel. During my five years at Lancing, we sang Bach's B Minor Mass, Bach's Magnificat/Mozart's Requiem, Handel's Messiah, Brahms' Requiem, and Benjamin Britten's St Nicholas, which was composed for the College's centenary in 1948. We also performed Britten's Noyes Fludde (premiered in 1958 at Aldeburgh) with a host of local kindergarten school children to the animals. I was in the orchestra, banging bells of all sorts and sizes. Much later, I was invited in 1965 to sing the bass solos in Haydn's Creation, for which I had copious singing lessons. I met with Mrs

Eluned Chapple, my violin teacher who was leading the orchestra – I think she was a little disappointed that I had chosen to pursue a musical career with voice rather than violin. (Michael Windross, who had been at St Paul's and Lancing with me, sang the tenor solos.)

Valete My second Housemaster, Donald Parsons, watched my development as a teenager and started

> "I am sorry to report a certain lack of thrust and a dreamy quality about him which is apparently noticeable in his maths".

This improved by the end of 1957 with "*He is a very civilised person in the House and consequently a very useful influence*" and a term later, "*I now regard him as a mature and responsible member of the House on whom I may have to lean shortly.*"

As a terminal comment, he told my parents, "*We shall all miss Anthony, and the musical life of the House and the School will be impoverished by his leaving*".

So ends the chapter of my adolescence.

Home life in Benenden, Kent

Harvest Festival Father arrived in Benenden in 1958. His parishioners were definitely divided into two 'social sectors'; the village wealthies and those who worked the land. A former chairman of the merchant bank C. Hoare & Co (founded in 1672 and still operating today with head office in Fleet Street, London), Sir Geoffrey Leonard Hoare, lived in the village with his wife, Lady Alma, who was of Irish stock and blessed with a fiery temperament. Lady Alma's sister-in-law, Molly Hoare, lived in Church Cottage adjacent to the Church at the top of the very picturesque Village Green. She was different in every way from Lady Alma. When I first met her, she must have been in her late 70s. Each year, she put a notice outside her house "Figs for Sale – 10d (old pence) or £1 10 shillings a dozen". Rumour had it she had been a nurse in the Boer War; she never married and had a heart of gold. There was one flaw in her character, mutually shared with Lady Alma; the sisters-in-law were in permanent 'family hate' mode. The harvest festival comes around once a year, the culmination of which is the harvest supper at the 'Bull', an occasion attended by most of the village, including Lady Alma and Molly. Father resided over these happy occasions and decided one year, in order to keep the peace between these two 'genteel' aristocratic ladies, they should sit on either side of him on the top table. The evening was going well; good food,

24

good company, and chatter across tables. The evening ends with a brief speech by the vicar to thank God for the year's harvest and a special thank you to all those kind people who have made the evening so enjoyable. My father rose to his feet and started his yearly rhetoric with, *"What a wonderful evening we have had. Do you know ...."* he then looked down to his left and then to his right, *"I think this is the first time I have ever sat between two Hoares. ...."*. His short valediction did not phase his chosen guests, and his speech continued as though nothing had happened - but Mother's face was a picture.

Benefits of being a Vicar's son The 'village wealthies' believed it necessary to invite the vicar and his family to dinner every so often, even if they were not 'believers'. When at home, I was included in this generous gesture. The village supported several 15th-century hall houses built originally by the affluent farmers of the day. Colonel White lived at the Paper Mill located at the edge of the parish on the way to Hawkhurst. From the outside, you see an impressive black and white timber frame building with one roof sloping from the top of the two-storey house to nearly ground level. Inside, you immediately enter a vast room with a double height rising to the pitched roof, supported by its aged timber roof trusses, rafters and longitudinal purlins. The upstairs corridor is one-sided, overlooking the hall with bedrooms off to the side. Very impressive. I once bumped into Colonel White at Magdalen College, where he was attending a meeting of the British Antarctic Survey. We both had made our way into Hall for breakfast. Extraordinary to think that my path should cross with this ex-military man living in the Weald of Kent who had travelled to Oxford for a retirement interest regarding serious research on the Antarctic continent.

One of my favourite and regular visits was to Pympne Manor, the home of Pat Thoburn and her father Hugh, who had been chairman of the Abbey National Building Society. This highly desirable residence was out near the Benenden Chest Hospital on the back road to Rolvenden. In the 1930s, Hugh had converted three farm cottages (Pump Farm) into a magnificent Tudor mansion. All the beams and struts dated from 1475, and you would never have guessed this was a conversion and not the rehabilitated homely house that it represents today. Pat was a very talented artist and had won the prize for the best student of her year at the Slade School of Art in London. At an all too young age, she gave up her artistic aspirations to look after her ageing father – very honourable, but how unfortunate not to realise her natural gift.

No invitation was received from Sir Geoffrey Leonard Hoare (*chairman of the Merchant Bank*), so I was never to visit the Hoare's house.

Benenden School One of the joys of being Benenden's vicar was that he had the responsibility not only of preparing the girls at Benenden School for confirmation but also of teaching maths up to 'O' Level. One year, he agreed to teach the not-so-clever girls and found four princesses in his class; two Jordanians, an Ethiopian and HRH Princess Anne, who came to the School in September 1963. It was only shortly before that I joined John Taylor & Sons. I was in my drawing office with six other graduate engineers, nose to the grindstone when a colleague came rushing in with a huge grin on his face and thrust a copy of that morning's Daily Mirror under my nose. The headline, in extra bold type, was

"Vicar tells Princess Anne Sex doesn't Matter".

Oh dear, what has Father done now? The facts were that, as usual, the whole School descended on Benenden Village Church for Morning Service. It was Princess Anne's first Sunday, and, unusually, her detective and a mass of press reporters and photographers were in the congregation. When I questioned Father, he said he had been misquoted! His actual words, as a throwaway line at the end of his sermon, were:

"Sex is insignificant when compared to the glory and wonder of God".

The Fleet Street hacks were clearly economical with the truth to score a cheap headline and help sell their Newspaper. It taught me a lesson (alas, at my father's expense) to be careful when talking in public or amongst people other than direct family members.

'Cherry' Ingram On the other side of the Village Green were two large houses set back from the road. Lady Legard lived in 'Ashlawn' and was, by all accounts, a recluse. It was rumoured she had been trodden on by a camel in Egypt in the 1930s and had never been the same since. Every day she would appear from her drive to walk around the Village Green and return to the safety of her home. The other house was 'The Grange', home to Captain Collingwood Ingram. His family founded and owned The London Illustrated News. He was fascinated by the cherry tree and became well-known to the Cherry Association of Japan. He was invited to present a paper to them at their annual meeting in April 1926. Although cherry blossom was (and is) a Japanese national emblem, for whatever reason, the specimens being cultivated in Japan were on the decline. Collingwood Ingram began his speech:

"Why is it that your flowering cherries often seem to do better in England than in your native country? ...".

This headline must have caught the attention of his audience, but it was a rather headstrong statement for this diminutive Englishman to be made about such a sacred artefact of the Japanese nation.

Later on, he was shown a picture of a Taihaku (the Great White Cherry) and told this was now extinct in Japan as a result of natural disasters such as tsunamis and volcanic eruptions. Collingwood believed he had seen this species in an old country garden on the Kent/Sussex border and rushed home full of enthusiasm to prove his memory correct. Yes, he was right and immediately took scions (cuttings), bundled them up and sent them off to Japan by boat. Alas, on arrival, they were ex-scions. He repeated this process, and again they 'failed'. His explanation was that the cuttings had to go through temperature extremes as they travelled from the UK, down past the Cape of Good Hope and back up to Japan. To change tack, he decided to put each stem in a potato and carry them personally, not by boat, but by travelling due east to Japan via the Trans-Siberian Railway. Success. The little stems were all alive as they arrived in Toyko. He carefully handed them over to the Cherry Association of Japan with much trumpeting. This pioneering English gentleman had re-introduced the Great White Cherry into Japan. From then on, Captain Collingwood Ingram was known as "Cherry" Ingram, and he regularly exhibited at the RHS Flower Shows in his own right.

Cricket on the Village Green During the summer holidays, I regularly played cricket for the Village team on both Saturdays and Sundays. The team had some very credible players who lived in the village and had been to Cranbrook School (the local grammar school in those days). Some of the local farmers were handy with the bat. I enjoyed hitting a six at both ends, one going straight through Lady Legard's upstairs window. We regularly played 'away' to nearby villages, and every time was a good social occasion as well as entering into some serious play. One year, we even won the Kent Courier knock-out competition.

Orchestral courses

When I was fifteen, my parents decided it would be good for my education if I were to attend a residential orchestral course for a couple of weeks during the long summer holidays. They discovered maestro Ernest Read, nearly in his 80s at the time but who had an unequalled reputation for helping young amateur musicians, having founded the London Junior Orchestra in 1924. The ERMA (Ernest Read Music Association) ran summer courses which I attended for three years, first at Sherbourne Girls School, then at Wycombe Abbey Girls School and lastly at the Royal Academy in London. The number attending spawned four reasonably sized orchestras. The first year I was in the Second Orchestra conducted by Leslie

Regan, and who should I meet there but Francis Saunders (bosom friend from my St Paul's days) clutching his cello. I was in the top orchestra for the last two occasions, conducted by Ernest Read himself. He was small in stature, with always a mischievous smile on his face. He would bounce up and down on his rostrum giving huge encouragement to us all. Herr Maestro had the annoying habit of stopping the orchestra when there was a particular, technically difficult part to play. He would turn to the leader of the orchestra, who was always a highly competent performer and ask him to show the whole orchestra how that bit should be played. Usually, he got it right, and we would move on. However, if he did bungle the demonstration, Herr Maestro would turn to the other person at the front desk of the 1st violins and say, "Now you", and so on, until someone got it right. I was sitting at the fifth desk, enjoying the anonymity, and so was not perturbed by this charade. However, we had got to the 3rd movement in Beethoven's Fifth Symphony, the Scherzo. There is a tricky bit of rhythm, which makes the conductor stop the orchestra to show off the ability of the leader of the orchestra (or to show up, in this case). This particular charade went its usual course from the first to the second desk and then on to the third. By this time, my heart began to start pounding. These chaps in front of me were much better technicians than me, and by now, six of them had failed, and so did the two on the fourth desk. It was my turn. I couldn't say, 'sorry, but I have a medical chit saying I don't have to play solos today.' I started with all the bravado I could muster, counting like hell so I could manipulate the rhythm to something like Beethoven's original. I got it right!

"Come up and lead the orchestra, young man," said Mr Read.

I led the orchestra, but only until the session ended, and then I retreated back to the safety of the fifth desk to mind my own business.

The course expanded my musical appreciation of the classics, and I get a really good feeling today whenever I listen to the pieces we performed, including Kodály's Háry János Suite, Berlioz Le Carnaval Romain, Mozart's Piano Concerto in A (Ernest Read always encouraged the more senior attendees to offer themselves as a soloist for a concerto to be played by the First Orchestra), and of course the Scherzo of Beethoven's 5th, knowing I heard them first from the fifth desk of the 1st violins.

Education excellence in two generations

Father did not appear to me at the time to be particularly interested in my day-to-day activity at school. In retrospect, I believe he probably was and certainly moved mountains at crucial stages of my adolescence to progress me up the academic ladder. This belief became more focused when, fifty years later (2010), I received an email asking if I was related to the Rev Albert Jessop Price. The sender was Deborah Elliot, the daughter of a first cousin (granddaughter of Father's brother Herbert). As children, we never knew my father's side of the family as they lived up in Wallasey. My Grandfather, Albert Price (born 1863), had died before I was born. I never knew my grandmother, Eleanor Mary Price, and only once did I meet Father's three brothers Norman West, Herbert Hargrave, and George Edmund. Father had always told us he was Welsh and was christened Jessop because that was his mother's maiden name (who was from Yorkshire, and it was a Yorkshire tradition to christen children with their mother's maiden name). Later, Father christened all his four children Jessop, I christened our three children Jessop; and Eleanor and Nicholas have since also called their children Jessop.

Cousin Deborah was later to drop an unexpected bombshell. She had undertaken considerable research into the Price family tree and told me Grandma Price's maiden name was not Jessop but West and the Prices come from Ruddington in Nottinghamshire, an important centre of the hosiery industry in the 19th century, not Wales - Father had often proudly explained Wales was from where his forebears came. In fact, the family had been framework knitters for generations, and Luddites into the bargain. The men folk had two things in common, they had good bass voices and enjoyed cricket (one of them, Walter Price, having played for the MCC in 1870). Life was harsh in Ruddington, and Great Grandfather Samuel Price (born 1820) was persuaded to move across in the 1850s to Holloway in the Derbyshire Peak District to carry out his 'knitting'. Children in England were to benefit from the 1870 Education Act, which enabled all working-class children to be given primary education. Grandfather Albert Price wanted to be a teacher and, by the age of 14, became a pupil-teacher at Lea School near Holloway (1877-81) and then went on to Saltley Teacher Training College in Birmingham (1885). Father twice called on Florence Nightingale (whose family home was in Holloway) to give him a 'testimonial'. She was generous in her words of support, suggesting he was:

> "Kind and gentle with the children and very popular with them, both boys and girls – while at the same time has a firm control over them. He is a youth of pure and good morals and may be cited as an example of good conduct … it may be added his musical talent is considerable … my good wishes for his success in life - mental, moral and practical and spiritual and in that which is beyond."

With that blessing, he secured a teaching post in Cheshire and by 1894 was headmaster of St James National School in New Brighton, where he stayed for 37 years. My Father secured a free place at Wallasey Grammar and then a scholarship to Christ's Hospital School in Horsham (which had recently moved down from the City of London), from where he went on to Fitzwilliam House, Cambridge. It is surprising, therefore, that not only was he proud of his sons Richard and Martin winning scholarships to Queens College, Cambridge, but also, he was determined for his ne'er-do-well youngest son to read something at a 'proper' university. Within two generations, this Price family had escaped the poverty of framework knitters and became Oxbridge material (and wouldn't Samuel and both the Albert Prices have been delighted to know my daughter Anna would not only be head of maths at an impressive girls' school in High Wycombe but much of her married working life was spent at Eton College, where husband Nicholas was both teacher and housemaster).

Epilogue

Tragedy struck in 1957 while I was taking my 'O' level exams. My brother Richard had just gained a double first in Classics at Queens' College, Cambridge and had won a travelling scholarship to study in Greece for a year. He was hitchhiking all the way with a friend from his Marlborough school days. While in Yugoslavia, the car in which they were travelling hit a tree and all were killed instantly. Lancing College authorities were not going to tell me about this until I finished my 'O' level exams, but there was a small article in the Daily Telegraph reporting the incident and referring to Richard Jessop Price. My Housemaster, Donald Parsons, immediately called me in and very diplomatically told me the news. I immediately went into the School Library to read the article and cried my eyes out, which is not something I had really ever done before or since. I passed three out of ten 'O' level subjects. Father was reluctant to bring Richard's body back to the UK for some reason or other (and I never thought to ask him why), so he is buried in the new Miroševac cemetery at Dubrava on the outskirts of Zagreb.

Richard and Mother with two of her paintings - The King's School Canterbury and the discovery of the Roman Mithras Temple in 1956 among the bomb damage

Chapter 2: University Life. Is a Degree a Professional Qualification?

"I believe that water is the only drink for a wise man."
Henry David Thoreau, American author (1817-62)

Introduction

William of Wayneflete, Bishop of Winchester and Lord Chancellor, founded Magdalen College Oxford in 1458. Most of the buildings, such as Cloisters, were constructed in the late 1400s. Among the alumni are Thomas Wolsey, Oscar Wilde, and Sir John Betjeman. The Senior Common Room at the time I went to Oxford from 1960 to 1963 included Rupert Cross, blind from birth who was a brilliant teacher of law (and was tutor to the 2015 Attorney Generals in the US, the UK, and Australia), A.J.P. Taylor who was a 19th- and 20th-century European historian, Geoffrey Warnock, philosopher married to Mary (later Baroness Warnock) and two medieval historians Kenneth McFarlane and Alan Bennett. My time at Oxford

was dominated by listening to and performing the music of British composers (whether they were William Byrd, Thomas Tomkins, and John Taverner of the sixteenth-seventeenth century, or Benjamin Britten, Vaughan Williams, and John Tavener of the twentieth). However, I was not to study music but rather to enjoy the fruits of my labours at school in physics and maths by reading Engineering Science, whatever that might be.

Magdalen College Oxford with Cloisters and New Building beyond

My main reason for attendance at the University, therefore, was to focus on some future career so I might earn a reasonable living and be able to bring up a Price family that could look forward to the 21st century.

Academical Clerks

Academical Clerks with Dr Bernard Rose, Chaplins and Mr Tallboys

Duties All twelve of us Academical Clerks were busy singing for our supper throughout the year. Looking back at my experiences, sixty years later, I remember performing madrigals at 6.00am on May Morning three years running from the top of Magdalen Tower (even when it was snowing in 1963); performing the Tallis Lamentations (Parts I & II) live on the BBC Third Programme for an Invitation Concert in their London Maida Vale Studios; making gramophone records under the Argo label in the College Chapel; performing with the choir of New College Oxford, who had only one choral scholar (James Bowman, counter tenor) plus two tenor and two bass lay clerks - one of their basses Mr Pountney (*coincidently, I was later to marry a Miss Pountney*) was small, past retirement age and drowned out the four of us young Magdalen bass academical clerks, whether we were supposed to be singing double forte or pianissimo; entertaining the Fellows on Christmas Eve (after a sumptuous feast in Hall), the second half being Christmas carols timed to the nearest second to finish just as the College Clock struck midnight; and singing Evensong at 6.00pm every day in the College Chapel. This was a rigorous discipline, particularly for someone reading engineering science, which involved compulsory lectures and practicals.

Keeping the Academical Clerks sane Evensong came with unscheduled entertainment for the Clerks. The choir would process in at 5.55 pm, then sit and wait for the college clock to strike the hour. Our 'sitting down' was the cue for the verger (Mr Tallboys) to undertake a series of manoeuvres in the intervening three minutes or so. He would move visitors in the congregation from the pew in which they were sitting comfortably to somewhere else. There was no time or place for these stunned worshippers to engage in argument because Mr Tallboys was very much in charge, having been given authority to act in whichever way he pleased by wearing a verger's gown. This 'process' never ceased to amuse us, particularly on a Sunday when the Chapel was full and moving people required considerable insider knowledge of how many people you can squeeze into each pew.

Fellows We were reminded of a true story, which describes how Magdalen saw itself during the first part of the twentieth century when compared with the rest of the world. Dr Varley Roberts (Bernard Rose's predecessor as Informator Choristarum from 1882 to 1918) was known to have often lent over the organ screen and yelled, "Shut up" to any member of the congregation who might be so presumptuous as to sing along with the choir. On one occasion, the gentleman concerned protested, saying:

"This is, after all, the House of God!"

"True," responded Dr Varley Roberts, *"but it is also Magdalen College Chapel, and I will thank you to hold your peace, Sir, and let us get on with the psalms!"*

There were several distinguished Fellows at Magdalen during the early 1960s, the majority of whom were agnostics or atheists and saw little point in having a College Chapel, particularly in such a prestigious real estate located adjacent to the High Street.

A.J.P Taylor recommended the Chapel be turned into a swimming pool. Alan Bennett had been brought up as a good Catholic. He was a tutor to one of my fellow Academical Clerks, David Watson. Not much historical theory was divulged in his tutorials, but many versions of Alan's humorous sermon sketch 'Take a Pew' were performed in front of David, who had the responsibility of suggesting improvements until true perfection was achieved. We rarely saw Alan in college, except on Sundays. During the rest of the week, he was performing at London's Fortune Theatre in *Beyond the Fringe*, a satirical comedy revue with Dudley Moore (another Magdalen man and former organ scholar) and two Cambridge graduates, Peter Cook and Jonathan Miller.

Status in the University Academical Clerks were all given the status of demi (senior scholar), which meant we wore long black gowns to lectures, tutorials, and dinner. The impression given of an undergraduate cycling up the High with full gown fluttering in the breeze behind him was he was 'double-first' material. This amused us because most of the Academical Clerks were not academic high-fliers at all. Quite the contrary, I remember one Academical Clerk who had failed his first-year engineering exams in 1960 and was about to be sent down. He was a really nice guy and had a superb tenor voice, perfect for a collegiate choir. Bernard was determined to keep him at Magdalen and persuaded Tom Boase (College President) to let him stay, but only if he changed his course and read music instead. Mere 'commoners' were obliged to wear the short gown that only came down to the waist. Seeing them on a bike, you felt their presence at Oxford was only because of historical dependence, came from a less fortunate background, or were just going through university because they couldn't think of what else to do.

Singing lessons Gerald English came up from London every Tuesday to give singing lessons in New College. He had been one of the six St Paul's Cathedral Tenor Vicars Choral in my day and also sang with the Dellar Consort. I was dreading my first lesson with him because I knew he would remember an incident, which I recall to my utter shame. It was the autumn of 1953 when the St Paul's Cathedral Choir was touring the eastern half of the United States. I was not a good traveller and on one occasion was sitting near the back of the bus – not a good idea. The symptoms of carsickness crept up on me without much prior notice. As I was rushing to the front of the bus to open the door and throw up, I could constrain myself no longer, and the complete contents of my stomach ended up in Gerald's lap. He was a nice man with rimless spectacles who looked very dapper, which made this whole catastrophe even worse. I can't begin to imagine what Gerald's immediate thoughts were then: and now (eight years later), I was at his mercy to tear my singing prowess to shreds. I needn't have worried. I discovered he was a true gentleman, and as he took me through my scales and tried to make me sing 'through my eyes' (a technique which helps to focus the whole register with a uniform sound without tightening the throat muscles), he didn't mention the incident once.

Engineering Science

Theory My degree course failed to engage in anything remotely practical and was focused on academia. Mr Bialokoz, my tutor, who seemed to make a profession of collecting doctorates – having five from five separate universities, but not from Oxford (which is why he was called Mr and not Dr) advised me to attend every lecture because only then would I experience the whole syllabus. That meant attending four lectures or practicals in the morning and two in the afternoon every weekday, and morning lectures on Saturday. (This compared with one or two English lectures a term for my friend James Bowman, the choral scholar at New College!)

Time off Bernard Rose frequently wrote a polite letter to Professor Thom, or my tutor, asking if I could be excused from this lecture or that exam because I was needed on choir duty either in Oxford or down in London. This seemed to be a perk at the time, but it came to sting me when I was to take my Finals. In summer, I often used to walk from the Engineering Labs after morning lectures through The Parks to Magdalen. Invariably, a sport of some kind was going on, such as the University Cricket XI playing one of the County teams. I was fortunate to stay and watch the Nawab of Pataudi score a century for the University before lunch – a feat unequalled and a forewarning that he might strike fear into the England cricket team when eventually he would play for (and captain) India.

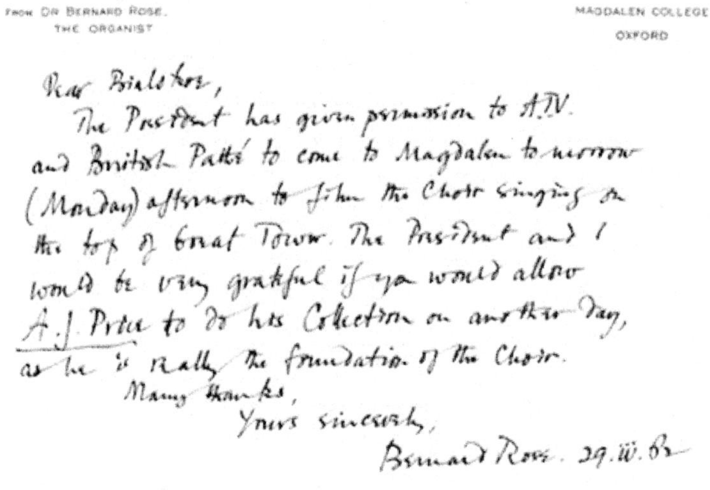

[Handwritten letter:]

Dear Bialehos,
The President has given permission to A.T.V. and British Patté to come to Magdalen tomorrow (Monday) afternoon to film the Choir singing on the top of Great Tower. The President and I would be very grateful if you would allow A.J. Price to do his Collection on another day, as he is really the foundation of the Choir.
Many thanks,
Yours sincerely,
Bernard Rose. 29.iii.62

***Typical Request from Bernard Rose when Choir
Duties overruled Academical necessities***

Finals I contracted pneumonia a month before I was to take my Finals and was whisked off to Oxford's Slade Isolation Hospital for the next three weeks. Mother came with a friend from Benenden, Pat Thoburn, who kindly brought a case of half bottles of champagne (medicinal), which was much appreciated. When Finals Day arrived, Tom Boase arranged for me to sit my exams in the private rooms in College of Dr James Griffiths' (*he was then Magdalen's Senior Dean responsible for undergraduate welfare*). As a result, I did not join all the other University undergraduates in the Examination Halls. James was a tall but rotund, friendly man who had become a physics lecturer in the 1920s. He used to travel across Europe in a Rolls Royce during his summer vacation, buying wine to put down for the Senior Common Room cellar; he much enjoyed the choir and was a reasonable cellist. His sitting room was large, tidy, and housed the most expensive commercial loudspeakers money could buy (in the early '60s), through which he played the classics as though a full orchestra was resident in College, much to the annoyance of his neighbours. Each morning of my exams, I would enter his rooms and see a large writing desk placed in the middle of his drawing room with an upright chair to one side. James would stand opposite, looking majestic in his long black doctoral gown, and with an earnest smile on his face, beckoned me to enter. Carefully placed on the writing table was a plate inscribed with the College crest. An apple and a fruit knife stared out at me as if to say,

"If you consume me, you will get a First."

35

James always greeted me with the same question, "*Sherry?*" whether it was a morning or afternoon session; what a pleasant way to undertake my finals and to throw off the mantle of 'undergraduate.'

The examiners gave me marks that could have been put down to intoxication, just plain incompetence, or to post-pneumonia stress syndrome. My main achievement, however, was that Tom Boase saw fit to write a "To whom it may concern" letter for me. This letter explains that, but for my illness, I should have obtained a higher-class degree. I doubt it, but fortunately, in my career as an 'international plumber,' I never met anybody who was in any way 'concerned.'

Lodgings

College cloisters I had rooms in College Cloisters for my first two years, looking outwards to gardens and a castellated 17th-century building that had been converted into communal lavatories for the 'young gentlemen.' One hot summer's day, I overheard an American tourist comment as he came out of the building:

"Gee, that is the most beautiful comfort station in the whole wide world!"

This plumbing facility had been part of an achievement by the Senior Common Room some sixty years earlier. Prior to 1900, Magdalen had no internal plumbing except in the kitchens, possibly the Master's Lodgings, and one or two other places of priority. At a specific meeting of crusty old dons to discuss how the College might be redeveloped to meet the needs of the twentieth century, someone suggested piped water should be brought into College to serve the undergraduates and dons who lived in. It seemed like an avant-garde proposal at the time. Several of the dons thought the whole issue would be unnecessary and far too expensive. A long and heated debate took place, with pros and cons being well made by intelligent but inward-looking men. After a while, one don, clearly fed up with the way the argument was progressing, stood up and, with true theatrical panache so that his point was well met, said:

"But the young gentlemen are only up for eight weeks at a time."

Once delivered, he promptly sat down. Maybe there were some dons with a taste for what was going on in the real world outside, for this outburst changed the flow of argument, and a modest pipe reticulation system was installed throughout College, with one tap serving each 'staircase' for the 'scout' (college servant) to use, together with two communal bathhouses and the communal lavatories opposite my rooms in Cloisters.

Longwall

My fellow lodgers For my third year, I moved across the road in Longwall to a house of a lady called Elsie, where there were lodgings owned by New College. The house was three storeys high at the end of a terrace (not by design, but thanks to Hitler's work some twenty years previously). The end wall and front door leaned comfortingly, but fortunately not beyond an angle of repose to cause catastrophic failure. I shared these lodgings with two altos, David Wulstan (a fellow Academical Clerk and mature student who later became Music Professor at the University of Wales, Aberystwyth) and James Bowman (the only choral scholar at New College, who was the UK's leading countertenor in the 1970s to 90s and made a CBE in the Queen's 1997 birthday honours). Elsie was a legend among Oxford landladies; small in stature, probably less than five feet tall, with a ruddy wizened face (thanks to the Guinness). She loved her 'boys,' whoever they were. Rumour had it she was brought up by an aunt who had been a previous tenant in the building. She would probably be described in today's parlance as having severe learning difficulties.

Plumbing facilities I had the ground floor room that was slightly down from the Longwall pavement. It was damp, and Mother was convinced it was the cause of my contracting pneumonia. There was a common front sitting room upstairs, with a bedroom behind and another bedroom at the top. The house had no running water, and Elsie would bring a jug of hot water into our bedrooms every morning for us to wash and shave. The winter of 1962-63 was particularly cold, and I remember that having poured cold water into a tumbler, by the time I finished brushing my teeth, there would be a thin film of ice on the meniscus. Whenever I needed a thorough scrub, I went to the College bathhouse, which housed ten over six-foot baths and had the resonance of the Sistine Chapel.

The only lavatory at the lodgings was in a lean-to shed at the top of the garden, hard up against the City Wall, lit and 'warmed' by an oil lamp flame, which allowed you to study various heirlooms stuck to the walls while you were 'engaged.' Elsie lived in a ten-foot square single-storey outhouse structure (behind the main terraced house) with a single water tap and a tin bathtub, which she used – sometimes. You were obliged to pass her lair when visiting the loo. When 'nature called' at night or when Elsie was having a bath in her tub, there would be a very audible giggle emanating from within her den, letting me know she was there and that she knew where I was going. This is where Elsie spent all her time when not down at the bar in the Eastgate and is where she cooked for her boys, giving them all a full English breakfast every day and a roast on a

Sunday lunchtime. Such meals were renowned throughout Magdalen and New College.

Music at the University

University orchestra Apart from singing in the Magdalen College Choir, there were many opportunities to engage in other musical activities. I joined the University Orchestra conducted by The Heather Professor of Music, Jack Westrup. We gave concerts in the Holywell Music Room, the oldest custom-built concert hall in Europe, having opened its doors to the public in 1748. It has the most phenomenal acoustics and was restored and refitted the year before I went up to Oxford. We played the classics and, in 1960, were the orchestra for the University Opera Club's performance of The Men of Blackmoor by Alan Bush, which expresses his Marxist views through the history of mining in Northumbria and Durham during the early 1800s.

The Clerkes of Oxenford My fellow Academical Clerk, David Wulstan, set up The Clerkes of Oxenford as a 'men-only a capella' group of about eight singers. We were all Academical Clerks from Magdalen, except James Bowman (*countertenor*) from New College, and performed early English choral music, some of which had not been heard for several hundred years. I found myself transcribing music, under David's direction, from individual 'part books' found in Oxford college libraries, including Magdalen. Sometimes a 'part book' was missing. David would make up that line using his musicological brain to guesstimate what might have been the original composer's intentions to achieve full four-part harmony. I was secretary of The Clerkes of Oxenford and became concert organiser and promoter until I left these shores in 1966. We sang mainly in Oxford college chapels, sometimes venturing south to perform in London churches such as St Georges Bloomsbury and The Holy Cross Church St Pancras, and in Hampton Court Chapel.

There was no other group of this type around in the UK at the time, or indeed anywhere else. David insisted on us all producing what he called 'white tone,' i.e., no vibrato, to sound like musical string or wind instruments. It is very pleasing today to see that the Clerks of Oxenford spawned brilliant groups such as The Sixteen, The Tallis Scholars, The Cardinall's Musicke, and many others.

Chapter 3: Training for a Professional Qualification

"Human nature is like water. It takes the shape of its container."
Wallace Stevens, American poet (1879-1955)

The real world

It is no bad thing being surrounded by excellence, but it wasn't until I joined John Taylor & Sons (JTS) in September 1963 on the Second Floor of Artillery House, Artillery Row, Westminster SW1, as a trainee graduate engineer (on a salary of £800 per annum) that I began to see the real world and meet real people. The Firm was founded in 1869 and moved into Artillery House in 1940. The main entrance to the second-floor office was oak-panelled to give the feeling of longevity, stability, and a sense of pride.[3] When I arrived, the workplace consisted of many individual drawing offices, each with six or seven budding engineers beavering away at their drawing boards. Senior engineers were each given their privacy in separate cubby holes, while Associate Partners had slightly grander private spaces. The four Partners were housed in oak-panelled offices.

The powerhouse of the drawing office

First impressions: **London, centre of the Universe** The whole feel of the Office reflected a profession that had, for over a century, provided Parliament with advice on whether or not to implement specific public works across the Nation; and (in some cases) across the World, particularly in those areas marked pink on the map. Closing my eyes, I could well envisage designers sitting in these very

Artillery House, Artillery Row SW1P

offices on high stools, quills in hand and ink pots by their side, designing conceptual plans for the Lambeth and Chelsea Waterworks Company or for overseas in the colonies at Singapore, Bombay, Karachi, Port Elizabeth, and in St Petersburg, Shanghai, and Baghdad and elsewhere. They would have been wearing top hats and had unshaven beards, a 'team' best described as veritable frock-coated Dickensian workaholics. That was indeed my first impression of the Firm to which I was now wedded. Opening my eyes, and there was Jim Robinson designing large-scale tunnel sewers for Coventry City, Richard Satchell engaged in talking

---

[3] In the 1970s, when I was responsible for re-designing the oak-panelled foyer, I discovered this grandeur reflected the previous tenant, Esso, the oil company. JTS had retained the oak-panelling as the least costly option.

about veteran Italian racing cars, Jerry Karaganjo (a Ugandan student working at JTS for three years as a post-graduate) deeply involved with a first-time village sewerage scheme for Petworth Rural District Council, Peter Keys working on the Riverside sewage treatment works serving 400,000 population for Dagenham Borough Council and Nouri el Hakim (an Iraqi) still sorting out the remnants of the Baghdad drainage scheme that had kept the Firm busy over the previous twenty years. That is quite a cross-section of engineering accomplishment and geographical non-sequitur, all in one room just off Victoria Street.

The workload of a graduate What was I up to on the adjacent drawing board? Nothing that I could remotely understand! The Firm was Consultant to the West Hertfordshire Main Drainage Authority and was involved with a complete rehabilitation of Maple Lodge Sewage Treatment Works at Rickmansworth, serving 600,000 population in and around Watford and St Albans in the upstream catchment of the River Colne (a tributary of the River Thames). A generator had vibrated its concrete plinth to total failure in one of the existing blower houses. My job was to determine the behaviour pattern of these vibrations and then come up with a concrete foundation design to combat failure in the future. There were plenty of dusty old technical books in the Firm's library, but none of them seemed to relate to my particular problem, as they all focussed on new design and not on what to do in the event of failure after forty years of oscillations! This was all way beyond my competence, and I can't remember how I got off this assignment and onto something more basic. In the summer of 1964, I was sent to Tenterden in Kent. JTS had designed and implemented the Town's first-time sewerage system during World War 1 as a combined rainwater and foul sewerage system.As the Town expanded, more impervious areas became connected to the system, which resulted in flooding after heavy rains in the lower-lying urban areas. JTS recommended separating rainwater from the foul sewage, thus creating two separate pipe systems. The Borough Engineer had made a big conceptual faux pas when instructing his own engineers and his Consultants. There were about 5,000 people living in Tenterden in the early 1970s. When I arrived, a contractor was laying pipes in every highway and byway according to alignments and gradients designed by JTS to secure two separate hydraulic systems. The new pipes were designed to accept foul sewage from the Town. This would then allow the existing pipework to be free of such water and only accept rainwater run-off from the urban area. The surface water would then eventually discharge into the River Rother system at the bottom of the hill and eventually flow out into the English Channel at Rye. Or so they thought! However, rainwater from all roof guttering in the town mixed immediately with domestic waste before the flow left each property. 'Somebody' had lost the plot and not thought about how to separate the two flows before they reached sewers in the public highway. As a result, my duty was to visit every house in town. I had to draw up individual house plans on A4 graph paper to locate the source of rainwater and domestic waste for every property; propose new pipework on each property to separate

40

rainwater from domestic waste, and design new house connection pipework both to the new surface water sewer and the existing sewer to ensure never the twain would meet again. I learnt a lot about diplomacy by chatting up local ladies to advise how their driveways, paths and lawns were to be dug up.

Tenterden is only about five miles from my parent's house in Benenden, so I lived at home all summer and played cricket on the village green every Saturday and Sunday.

Design project for 'Civils' qualification To secure associate membership of the Institution of Civil Engineers (AMICE, *the ultimate professional qualification*), you have to spend a minimum of three years of post-graduate training in engineering, one year of which must be on a construction site. You also have to prepare a detailed design of a significant engineering project, including the presentation of all calculations and drawings. Once eligible to become a member, you sit a 'professional interview' with a Fellow of the ICE and write an essay in the afternoon on a topic chosen by the invigilator.

Avonmouth Secondary Sewage Works

On my return to Artillery House, I became involved in designing a secondary plant at the existing Avonmouth Primary Sewage Treatment Works for the City and County of Bristol. This was more interesting, believe it or not, as I was engaged in new technology (including the first UK installation of an Archimedes screw pump to lift activated sludge to the head of the Works). The whole exercise was to ensure the final secondary effluent quality was acceptable as cooling water for the adjacent Aluminium Smelter. I was to be in at the birth of an environmental damascene awakening – the acceptance of using purified sewage effluent for industrial purposes. John Haseldine was the project Partner, and he was, as they say today, my line manager (although John never saw himself as a manager, more an owner). He was a tall, imposing and very kind man with a neat military moustache (having served in the Royal Engineers in India during the Second World War) and was one of two great-grandsons of John Taylor, leading the Firm in the 1960s. He made me learn the basics of sound engineering drawing principles, what you must include on a drawing and what to leave out when it might be considered either irrelevant or misleading. I had basic drafting competence inherited from my Mother, who was a very skilled artist in oils. My expertise, though, relied on a ruler, set square and compass rather than free hand. I intended to use the Bristol design calculations and associated drawings as my 'Design Project' for when I eventually got around to sitting my Professional Interview for the Institution of Civil Engineers and thus claim my professional qualification (CEng AMICE). Although I am not known for blowing my own trumpet, the reinforcing steel drawings for the circular settlement tanks were a work of art (thank you, Mother). It showed the outline of the circular structure with the reinforcing steel members super-imposed, each bar clearly defining its necessary overlap with the next, so the contractor could not misinterpret the instruction. I took some pride in preparing these drawings and believed they could have been 'accepted,' if not hung, at the Royal Academy's 1965 Summer Exhibition! The Firm had a rule that every drawing prepared by engineers and technicians in the drawing offices had to be traced onto linen by the Tracing Department located on the seventh floor above Binnie and Partners (a very reputable firm of consulting engineers). This policy ensured the Firm would always produce a unified standard of excellent presentation for clients and contractors alike, one of which the Partners were justifiably proud.

The Tracing Department was managed by two ladies in their sixties, May Stark and Joan Cunningham, who had both worked for the Firm since my Parents were 'young things.' They filled me with fear whenever I was obliged to visit, as I was confident they would find fault with my measly inexperienced pen and ink drawings. However, when I took up my Bristol drawings, they gave one look at them and said they were good enough to go straight to the client and needn't be traced. I gather this was a first at JTS and from then on, I became known as the Firm's most expensive 'draughtsman.'

In 2020, a fatal explosion occurred at the Avonmouth Sewage Treatment Works when the roof of a sludge digester ripped apart. Fortunately, this structure was not part of the design commitment entrusted to JTS, and the structure was in place long before any of our works were designed.

John Taylor & Sons wining Cricket Team

ACE cricket JTS was a regular participant in The Association of Consulting Engineers Cricket League. Most of the UK consulting firms still had their offices in, or around, Victoria Street when I started with JTS. (The reason for this was that in the 'old days,' Consultants promoted public works projects as they passed through Parliament. A Barrister would often ask the Consultant at the end of the Morning Session to produce a calculation or drawing ready for the Afternoon Session – hence the need for their offices to be close to the House of Commons.) During the Summer, on a Wednesday, we used to skive off work at 4.15 to play against one of our fellow members in a twenty-overs match. The grounds in which we played were in and around London, and we regularly travelled to Battersea Park, Regents Park, Dulwich, or Croydon and played until the game was over or dusk overtook our ability to see the ball. The JTS captain was Colin Johnson, one of our experienced draughtsmen. Nick Paul, a fellow graduate engineer, was handy with the bat, and I used to keep wicket. Gwilym Roberts, a Partner, was always very supportive. The regular weekly matches were friendly until we reached the final when the thought of winning the competition overtook our normal approach, and battle lines were drawn to ensure victory. I played in three finals, winning once over our arch-rivals Mott, Hay, and Andersen, who had an Australian engineer working for them who had played for his country against the MCC.

Time off from the office

Home base All the time I was 'training' for my professional qualification, I lived in a flat in Shaftesbury Avenue on the top floor of an office block, with the added advantage of eyeing up the nurses across the road at the French Hospital[4]. I shared the flat with Francis Saunders, whom I had known since St Paul's days and who was a cellist at the Royal Opera House, Covent Garden. This spot was chosen for ease of access to both our places of work. I had to travel to Victoria Street, either on a No. 24 bus or, if the morning was bright and sunny, a walk down St Martins Lane, across Trafalgar Square and St James Park through the tube station, and onto Artillery Row. Francis only walked a couple of hundred yards to the Opera House.

Musical chairs. Violin or voice I was leader of St Thomas' Hospital Orchestra thanks to Judy Kellett, a girlfriend from Benenden who was both a nurse and flautist. There were great 'medical' parties at the Hospital, which is where I was first introduced to the music of the Beatles. However, during a chance meeting with Dick Gamblin, a fellow Magdalen Academical Clerk, I was encouraged to join the Elizabethan Singers conducted by Louis Halsey (ex-King's Choral Scholar). This was the amateur choir to join in London in the 1960s, full of Oxbridge ex-choral scholars. Unfortunately, rehearsals clashed with my orchestral duties; voice won over violin, and I embarked on a semi-professional vocal career for the next three years. Sir John Dykes Bower auditioned me to become a deputy Vicar Choral at St Paul's Cathedral (weekends only). This coincided with one of the permanent basses, Michael Rippon, winning a contract to sing hymn tunes live on the BBC Home Service at 10.00 am on a Sunday. I served as his permanent deputy every Sunday morning and usually sang for the afternoon service as well. The company

---

[4] The French Hospital was at 172-176 Shaftesbury Avenue, set up in 1876 for 'the benefit of distressed foreigners of all nations requiring medical relief'; today the building is part of the Covent Garden Hotel

I was to mingle with was unusual for a young graduate engineer. The permanent bass Vicars Choral included Maurice Bevan, who had been there when I was a chorister (*and much later when my son Nick was a chorister*) and was a member of the Deller Consort, David Thomas, a former chorister with me who was at the beginning of a great singing career and Geoffrey Shaw who, like Maurice, was the 'perfect' choral bass. This was all a good experience for me. I was 'performing' with the best voices in town and, with no rehearsals for the deputies, my sight-reading just had to improve to near perfection. In order to ensure my vocal instrument was as good as I could make it, I invested the money earned singing by having private lessons from Roy Hickman (Professor, Guildhall School of Music, and Drama) at his flat in Barons Court, near Hammersmith.

Performing monkey I earned more singing at weekends than I did at JTS for the rest of the week! A Cathedral bass would often lean over to me during the sermon and ask if I was available for some future performance. On one occasion, the request was for a Wednesday evening assignment as the after-dinner entertainment at the Worshipful Company of Vintners in Lower Thames Street (*first chartered in 1363*), one of the twelve senior City of London livery companies. Just four of us, all from the St Paul's Cathedral choir, were to sing madrigals and Victorian ballads. I took my dinner jacket to work that day, changed in the office at Artillery House, and went by tube to Blackfriars. We had a quick rehearsal before the guests arrived. While we were relaxing, I asked to see the menu because we ate the same as the 100 or so guests as a perk of being a performer. The food looked good, and my mouth began to salivate as I turned over to the back cover of the menu. The page started with a list of that year's Livery Company hierarchy, including the Master Vintner, the Upper Warden, the Renter Warden, and the Swan Warden, a list of the toasts for the Queen with the various replies: and then my heart stopped a beat. To my horror, I saw in the largest capital letters that would fit on the page:

THE VINTNER'S SONG
sung by
ANTHONY JESSOP PRICE

I was more than speechless, but when I came to my senses, I asked in total amazement:

> "*Help! What is the Vintner's Song, and why do the officials think I have something to do with it?*"

The resident pianist, whose appearance suggested he had just survived the Blitz, told me not to worry,

> "*They all know the tune.*"

44

"Not to worry! I am scared out of my wits. Where is the music, and is it by Schoenberg?" I didn't think to ask why I hadn't been informed about this beforehand.

"Here it is."

The resident pianist produced a well-dog-eared manuscript half torn at the edges that had clearly seen both world wars.

"Don't you worry," he said. *"It's an old German drinking song in three verses, easily remembered, and with a pause on the high note at the end of the penultimate line to each verse. They all join in during the singing of the last verse and will play a little game with you. When you get to the pause on that penultimate line, they will hold on to it longer than usual, in fact, much longer than usual. I have this white handkerchief."*

He pulled it out of his pocket – not the cleanest I had seen that winter.

"When you have held that top note for a very long time, I will surreptitiously wave the handkerchief in your direction so that only you can see it. This is your cue to come off the high note and continue to the end. The assembled dignitaries of bishops, financiers, bankers, and other city gents would then come off their high note in the knowledge that, yet again, they had beaten the professional and restored pride and justice to the Livery Company!"

Was I hearing this correctly? Was I to be the performing monkey to one hundred of London's ablest and best who apparently regularly perform this charade?

"Let me see the music."

I think in my confusion, I forgot to say 'please.' A quick scan of the sheet suggested I might get away with the first two verses. The last verse, however, was one still to be experienced. Dinner was served, our quartet performed, the speeches were endless and all irrelevant in my predicament, and all the time, I was worried about this 'challenge,' particularly as one of Father's friends, the Rev RO Fulljames, was sitting close to where we were singing.

My turn came. The first two verses were performed to the best of my ability. But when we came to the last verse, the Hall erupted into what could politely be called 'song,' so I joined in the fun. The pause went on forever. I took two, if not three breaths on the long breve because nobody would have noticed. At long last, the handkerchief was produced with a discrete flurry in my direction. The pianist and I continued the song to the end, leaving a few inebriated guests to finish at their own pace. I slept well that night.

Serious extra mural activity I performed in a one-off all-professional LSO Chorus in 1965, conducted by István Kertész, to sing Debussy's Jeanne d'Arc at the Royal Festival Hall. The performance was very moving, but rehearsals were a nightmare; a large chorus practicing in small rooms with each tenor believing he was Gigli; result, total cacophony. Performances with the Elizabethan Singers took me to the V&A, the Queen Elizabeth and Royal Albert Halls and the Aldeburgh Festival. One performance at the Royal Festival Hall was with Michael Flanders in the first performance of his cantata Captain Noah and His Floating Zoo, with music by Joseph Horovitz; difficult stuff but enjoyable with an element of inevitable humour in the libretto. Louis Halsey was very kind to four or five of us and encouraged us to perform in Kingston Parish Church with his all-professional Thames Chamber Choir. I found myself singing with my old chums David Thomas and James Bowman, as well as some new ones such as Geoffrey Shaw, Chris Keyte, Nigel Rogers, Ian Partridge, and Bob Tear. Some of my most memorable musical experiences were with that august group of singers, performing works such as JS Bach's motet Komm Jesu Komm and Britten's Rejoice in the Lamb, to name but two.

Back to school

The City of London Corporation had produced several post-war reconstruction plans for the City following the devastation caused by Hitler's bombs. Detailed designs were received from Charles Holden and William Holford in 1947 to improve traffic flow around St Paul's Cathedral, and another, referred to as the Beaux-arts layout promoted by the Royal Academy to create a piazza to the west of the Cathedral á la St Peter's Rome. All plans seemed to have one thing in common, to demolish buildings in Carter Lane, including that of the existing Choir School. Maurice Bevan (Vicar Choral) was extremely generous to me. Knowing Father had been approached by the Dean and Chapter in 1951 to search for a new site for the school "as a matter of urgency," he let me be his Deputy for a Tuesday lunch-time open-air service in November 1965 to sing with the rest of the St Paul's Cathedral Choir. The occasion was the laying of the Foundation Stone by Dean Matthews for the new Choir School building in New Change. As the Dean was blessing the Foundation Stone, the Corporation took the decision to cancel any thoughts of demolishing Carter Lane (including the Choir School). The City Corporation had already agreed, however, to compulsory purchase the old Choir School building in Cater Lane (*under false pretences, as it so turned out*) and had entered into a 50-year lease with the YMCA.

Chapter 4: Zambia – Where is it?

"Filthy water cannot be washed"
African Proverb

Foreign challenge

Joining the colonial experience Before I started to work for a living, my early travels abroad had been by boat and limited to three expeditions; first to France in 1949, a parental holiday to St Brevin Les Pins south of St Nazaire, the summer home of Alain de Vendière de Vitrac (Mother's charge when she was an au pair in the 1920s); secondly, to the US in 1953 for three months with the St Paul's Cathedral Choir as part of the line-up of who 'performed' at the Queen's Coronation; and thirdly, a trip down the Rhine in 1960 with Peter Cousins (school friend at both St Paul's and Lancing) to visit his mother's German relations. I was well travelled, therefore, when compared with many English children brought up after the Second World War. I did not subscribe to the Flat Earth Society but was seriously ignorant of what went on beyond Europe and the oceans.

The year was 1966, and England had just won the Soccer World Cup when I found myself responding to one of those small professional adverts in the Daily Telegraph:

> "Water Engineers wanted in Ndola, Zambia, Central Africa – please respond to Brian Colquhoun & Partners (BC&P), Upper Grosvenor Street, London W1."

Why did this little insignificant ad shout at me to respond? Was it the posh address? Did I think I had lived too sheltered a life, or was I just naïve? Hugh O'Donnell interviewed me. I must have been the only applicant. Without much small talk, he told me I would first go to Salisbury for an induction (why send me to Wiltshire – yes, my naivety was beginning to ooze out of every pore – Salisbury, Rhodesia) and then on to Ndola where I would be working for Leslie Hall. (50 years later, almost to the day I got around to visiting Salisbury, Dorset, singing the week-end services in the Cathedral with an ad hoc semi-professional choir.)

Decision time Francis Saunders was married by then, and I had a new flatmate, Damodar Shirwaiker, a respected engineer at John Taylor & Sons. I confided in him as to whether I should take this job or not. The pay was less, but then the cost of living there could be significantly lower; I would not return home for three years; what about my 'career'; where on earth is Zambia? My early days as a philatelist gave me that answer – formerly Northern Rhodesia, a British colony which had gained Independence two years earlier in 1964. Damodar had given up all he had and moved from Goa to London, so maybe I was asking the wrong person for an unbiased opinion.

Exodus It was a September evening, and Damodar accompanied me to the BOAC Terminal in Victoria. I checked-in my flight to Salisbury, we said our goodbyes, and then I started my journey into the unknown, firstly by bus taking me to Heathrow via Hammersmith and the A4 (a route I became familiar with in the 21st century). The rest of the journey to Rhodesia is now only a very faint memory. In future years, air travel has become a way of life, something I try to forget as it represents lost hours on this earth.

The history of Zambia

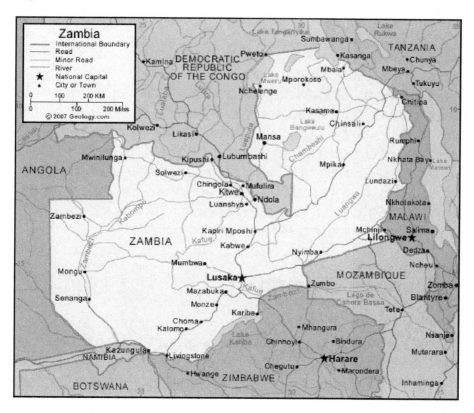

A human skull was found in Broken Hill (now Kabwe) in 1921 that has been carbon-dated as over 200,000 years old. The earliest known modern humans were thought to have been hunter-gatherers who lived a nomadic life collecting fruit and nuts and hunting antelope and other animals. Around the 4th century, Bantu tribes migrated from the north. They were farmers, had iron and copper tools and weapons, made pottery, and lived in self-sufficient villages growing their own sorghum and beans and keeping cattle and goats. By the 11th century, long-distance trade was beginning to enable the Bantu to export copper, ivory, and cotton textiles. Because the territory was landlocked, direct contact with non-

Africans did not occur until about 1800 when Arabs and Portuguese traders came up from Mozambique (from settlements across the River Luangwa, a tributary of the great River Zambezi).

The first Briton to set foot on Zambian soil was David Livingstone in 1851. His expedition travelled up the River Zambezi, and he was the first European to see the Mosi-oa-Tunya, which he renamed Victoria Falls (after his Queen). He died in 1873 in the Samfya swamps of the upper Congo River. Cecil Rhodes acquired mineral rights concessions from local chiefs in 1888. Northern Rhodesia (Zambia) and Southern Rhodesia (Zimbabwe) were formed, and The British South Africa Company (Cecil Rhodes' little fiefdom) administered both territories. In 1923, the British Government granted these two territories self-governance, although, in 1924, the administration of Northern Rhodesia was transferred to the Colonial Office in London as a protectorate, with Livingstone as its capital.

Significant copper deposits were found in 1928, transforming Northern Rhodesia from a prospective land of colonization for white farmers to a copper exporter. In 1953, the two Rhodesias joined with Nyasaland (Malawi) to form the Federation of Rhodesia and Nyasaland. Northern Rhodesia was the generator of copper revenues, most of which went south to Southern Rhodesia to fund new infrastructure. This translated into African unrest in Northern Rhodesia and, with it, a potential crisis. At the core of the controversy were African demands for greater participation in government, resulting in European fears of losing political control. After democratic elections in 1962, the Federation was dissolved, and Zambia was granted independence in 1964 without bloodshed.

Salisbury, Rhodesia (Zimbabwe)

Introduction I was put up in the Meikles Hotel, probably the best hotel in town, very colonial and where 'service' by staff was well understood and performed with an honest smile. Apart from visiting the BC&P's office, my brief stay was spent walking around the city centre. Two 'visions' of my first encounter with Africa remain burnt into my memory. The first is of colonials playing bowls – Father bowled for Benenden, where they played with sleeves rolled up and sporting braces. Here it was all so Edwardian; men and women dressed in whites, with hats to shade them from the sun, and not a black face to be seen among acres of rinks in this African capital city (not that Rhodesia was an apartheid state). The players were all serious as though they were professionals, motioning long sweeps of the arm before releasing their bowls, then running up the rink, stopping, and then walking, as though such a ritual would influence the bowl's final destination. Such ostentatious behaviour would have been frowned on at Benenden.

My second memory is of a concert I attended in City Hall. The Salisbury Municipal Orchestra was performing, and I was mesmerised by the cellist; they only had one. He was small in stature, and his instrument looked as though it had been in the African Bush for many a year. However, the volume he produced drowned out the rest of the ensemble. It reminded me of my Magdalen days when sometimes we performed with the New College Oxford choir, and Mr Pountney, their bass, secured the same result as the cellist I heard that night.

Abu Dhabi wastewater design The one thing I remember during my brief induction in the Salisbury office was my meeting with the senior Partner for Africa, Harry Lister, and his chief water engineer, Ron Marks. They were mulling over a model of Abu Dhabi Island, which was laid out on a coffee table; this seemed strange to me, knowing we were sitting in the centre of Southern Africa. Oil had been discovered off Abu Dhabi in the Arabian (Persian) Gulf eight years before. The indigenous population on the island was less than 20,000, but expatriates of all political persuasions were flocking to the State. BC&P had been instructed to design a first-time sewerage scheme for the Emirate. Their London office had no expertise in water engineering, so they handed the work out to Harry. As I entered his office, I could see they were both excited at the prospect of undertaking this prestigious (and no doubt profitable) assignment. Conceived in Salisbury, Rhodesia, the BC&P scheme was eventually built. The Firm lacked experience in dealing with sewage in very hot and arid climates. As a result, the BC&P scheme soon created an odour problem that pervaded the whole island. Whatever techniques they tried failed to resolve the issue.

This embarrassing nuisance incurred the insuperable displeasure of the Ruler, Sheikh Zayed Bin Sultan Al Nahyan. Unknown to BC&P, in 1974, the Ruler invited one French and five British Consultants to submit proposals to solve the odour problem and then to produce a master plan to treat wastewater from a future population of 600,000. Gwilym Roberts (who for 20 years had been in charge of the Baghdad main drainage scheme, with a 1,200,000 design population – and was later to become senior Partner at John Taylor and Sons) impressed the most. JTS signed an agreement with the Abu Dhabi Government that is still in place today, some 45 years later. BC&P were then 'relieved of their duties.'

Hugh O'Donnell was livid and reported JT&S to the Association of Consulting Engineers (ACE) for having 'stolen' work away from another Association member, strictly against Association rules. The ACE heard their complaint and listened to Gwilym Robert's argument as to why his firm was now instructed by the Sheikh. The complaint was quietly dropped.

Little did I realise in 1966, the BC&P model I was looking at, with such awe in the middle of Africa, was to be dramatically rehabilitated, revised, and rebuilt by JTS in the 1970s. For a brief period during the 1990s, I was to be the JTS supervising engineer with ultimate responsibility for this continuing project.

Future meetings I used to meet Hugh O'Donnell at least once a year after 1974 at the ACE Annual Dinner. I could tell that, on the one hand, he saw me as his protégé, but on the other, he was embarrassed that I was working for the firm that kicked BC&P out of Abu Dhabi for good.

Ndola

Adventus Leslie Hall met me at Ndola International Airport. He was a man in his late forties who gave you the impression he <u>was</u> Brian Colquhoun and Partners (Zambia). The airport has the infamous reputation of being the location where, just five years earlier, Dag Hammarskjöld, Secretary-General to the United Nations, failed to arrive. It was put about that his plane crashed into Ndola Hill, 15 miles from the airport. This is the only hill for four hundred miles in every direction. The theory was that the pilot had mistaken the airport runway lights for charcoal burners fires along the very straight Ndola-Mufulira road. This speculation has since been questioned, and I watched a revealing BBC 4 documentary on UK television in 2019, Murder in the Bush – Cold Case Hammarskjöld, which implied this was no accident but a South African attack on Dag Hammarskjöld for his hard-line approach at the UN to share the wealth created in Africa with the indigenous population. It was suggested that powerful South African businessmen organised the assassination of the UN Secretary-General with a three-pronged plan of attack. First, to detonate a bomb on-board his advertised flight from Kinshasa to Ndola; secondly, to hire an RAF fighter aircraft to shoot his plane down as it approached Ndola; and thirdly, to mobilise a team on the ground to obliterate the evidence. The visual evidence, and interviews with those still alive after 58 years since the event, were all convincing. The docudrama implied this was no tragic accident but a successful assassination of an honest and good international politician and diplomat.

Leslie took me to the Rutland Hotel, which had seen better days. It had no running water in the rooms (just like my Oxford days), but it was September, and the Jacaranda trees were in full flower to create a mauve haze throughout the hotel's so-called grounds[5]. It was a Friday evening, and Leslie suggested I call in at the

---

[5] *This image is one of my most memorable impressions of Zambia. It forgave many an imperfection in my comfort facilities. I felt a bit homesick, for the profusion of mauve flowers on these mature trees reminded me of Captain Collingwood Ingram's cherry orchard at The Grange, Benenden. That great orchard had many different varieties of cherry, including the Great White Cherry, 'Tai Haku'. Mother's oil on canvas painting of this orchard in springtime, painted in the early 1960s, is all that remains of this national treasure, as I understand the orchard was grubbed up in the 1990s.*

office on President Avenue in the morning, after which he would take me to the Lowenthal Theatre Club bar for lunch.

Introduction to the Lowenthal Theatre As I have explained in Chapter 3, I had spent much of the previous three years singing in semi-professional choirs performing Tallis to Schoenberg in places like the V&A, St Paul's Cathedral, the Royal Albert Hall and on the BBC. My introduction to the Lowenthal Theatre Club on that Saturday was met with the question

"Do you act?" to which I replied, *"Definitely not …. but I sing".*

A barrage of *"Hey, this new man sings"* rang out along this long bar.

"We are doing an Old Time Music Hall next Saturday; what can you sing for us?"

Had I said the right thing? My musical education was seriously lacking in anything that remotely sounded like old time music hall. My reticent response was

"If you show me the music, I'll have a go."

An old timer, who turned out to have a lovely bass-baritone voice, said, *"Come to lunch tomorrow, and you can thumb through my music".*

It was a strange entrée to the world of theatre in Central Africa. After a good Sunday roast with my new-found friend, I chose 'The Sergeant Major' and 'When I come up from Somerset'. I hurried back to the Rutland, scared of the notion that by the end of the week, I would have to memorise these songs and perform them solo - in public.

The Ndola office team I discovered the Ndola Office consisted of Leslie, myself, Mrs Mitchell (Leslie's American secretary) and 'little' Banda, the office boy. I say 'little' because, even though he was twice my age, he was small in stature, which appeared to be a characteristic of many Zambians in the 1960s. There was a story shared with all newcomers that the land now called Zambia had no indigenous population because the territory was sick with tsetse fly, malaria, etc., and all the adjacent tribes from the Congo, Angola, Rhodesia, Mozambique, Malawi, and Tanzania used to banish the runts of the family into this central 'space'. I don't think for a moment there is any truth in this theory, but there is no doubt there were a lot of small African people in Ndola – hence 'little' Banda, whom we loved dearly. (*Zambians were often influenced by Western people and things when choosing first names for their children. We met one of the Banda families who had Christened their son Elastic, another was named Hitler, and so on!*)

Leslie pointed out that BC&P had suddenly taken on a lot of municipal water engineering work, and I was the first arrival of "his team". Sure enough, a senior engineer, Dick Skinner, who had worked for Binnie and Partners in Artillery House, appeared about two months later. We must have rushed up and down the same staircase many a time without realising our paths would converge in darkest Africa. I understand now how Stanley felt when he asked: "Dr Livingstone, I presume?" Other young graduates soon appeared, Tom Chapman and Brian Kidd. Tom eventually became a client of mine when he worked for Southern Water in the UK; and I employed Brian in Abu Dhabi in the 1980s as a supervisory engineer. Dick eventually went to work in South Africa, where I assume he is now retired.

Mrs Mitchell saw us all as her 'boys' and, with a true mid-west drawl, used to give us advice about how to behave in the bush – always have your snake kit with you; wear gum boots and stomp through the bush because the snake's sensitive belly will feel the vibrations of your footfall and slither off the path into the undergrowth as they are not generally masochistic. There were some old-handers around who frightened the living day lights out of us young graduates by describing three snakes to avoid at all costs; the boomslang, coloured green, hangs in trees to drop down and bite you to death; the black mamba whose bite will not let you make more than five steps towards your Land Rover before you're a dead'un; and the gaboon viper, a slow-moving snake which, when you tread on it, injects so much venom that you will never know what hit you! In the 1960s, there was little antidote for these venomous snakes, so irrespective of the attitude of our friendly jokers, they were definitely to be avoided.

First encounters The workload in the Office was interesting and varied for a young engineer. I would soon visit Luanshya Mine Township, Mufulira, Broken Hill (later called Kabwe) and South African Breweries in Ndola, where I was instructed to sort out their industrial effluent problem. A map of the African continent in my old school atlas identified two names only in Northern Rhodesia, Lusaka, the capital and Kapiri Mposhi. Leslie was proud to show me the eggcup-shaped water tower he had designed and built there. As a piece of art, it was not bad because it is not easy to put a large concrete tank up in the air and make it look nice. It was only when I passed through on my way to Kabwe that I realised Kapiri Mposhi was tiny, in fact, if you blinked, you might have missed it. The importance of this 'hamlet' was that it stood at the road and rail junction from Lusaka in the south to the Copperbelt (where the Nation's wealth was) and the Great North Road going all the way to Cairo. There was also a railway goods yard where cargo was off-loaded to go on up the Great North Road. After this first visit, I have always thought of little Kapiri Mposhi as the 'other centre of the universe'!

Transport Nobody had told me in London that being able to drive is an essential requirement for a water engineer in Africa. I had not taken a driving test in the UK, so I had no licence and, therefore, no qualification to receive a Zambian driver's licence. What a dilemma. I quickly applied for a test and, one Saturday morning, presented myself for the ordeal. I drove very nicely, then came to a roundabout with a Stop sign. I said to the Instructor:

"I can see there is nothing coming. Is it alright to 'give way'?"

From the Instructor there came not a murmur. By the time I had waited for his reply, I had already 'given way'. We carried on to the end of the test.

"You failed to stop at a Stop sign" and handed me a fail card. I was the only expatriate he was aware of who had failed a driving test in Ndola. *"Come back in the afternoon and take the test again"*. I did and passed. Immediately, I bought a second-hand Vauxhall Velox and was mobile to travel across Africa.

Playtime

Theatre workshop It was the mid-1960s; the Zambian expatriate fraternity appeared to play for 80% of their time and only work for the other 20%. When I started to prepare for my first experience of Old Time Music Hall, I was conscious there should be no real difficulty in remembering the tunes, but could I learn the words? As I mulled over this in the heat of the night, I realised I was treading new territory, which was beginning to worry me as performance day approached. I decided to use a 'prop'. I had amongst my workbooks a buff-coloured London Borough of Barking Dagenham Sewer Investigation Contract Document I had produced while at JTS! It was thin, but foolscap and I pasted onto its front the words of my two ditties, line by line. Peggy Hazel (my future landlady) made up my face, stuck outsized air-force moustaches on my upper lip – and I was off. It was like being back in the boxing ring for Seconds House at Lancing. There was nothing but myself to stop me from falling into the abyss. The good news was that nobody in the 400-strong boozy audience would know who I was, and the even better news was the more I strutted across the stage, Sewer Investigation Document held high, the greater the audience's 'encouragement'. There was no stumbling over words – a star was born!

With this success under my belt, I moved on to more 'serious stuff'. My time was taken up first with playing Pooh Bah in *The Mikado* and then Hajj in *Kismet*. I enjoyed *The Mikado*; Miss Jennings, my 'maiden aunt' (and first Secretary of the Friends of St Paul's Cathedral), had taken me to a performance at London's Savoy Theatre in the early 1950s, so I vaguely remembered some of the music. Rehearsing at the Lowenthal was fun. The producer saw Pooh Bah as a bulbous individual, and I was stick thin (in those days). My torso was covered in pillows back, and front and my face spread with enough make-up on to make me feel important and evil at the same time. The performances ran for two weeks, but my main memory is of kind words sent to me in a blue coloured air-mail letter from London by Ian Aitkin FICE FIMechE FIEE, a senior Partner of BC&P who, having travelled out to Central Africa on one of his last trips for the Firm before he retired, came to see the show just before he left that night for Ndola airport and London. He was gracious enough to say:

> "...I enjoyed your performance of Pooh Bah. It was superb and right up to the standard of the best-ever Pooh Bah – Leo Sheffield. And that is going back to the 1920s. .... Clearly, should you ever decide to abandon engineering, you have an alternative field open to you."

I liked reading the first bit of his letter, but the second half – was this a hint that Leslie Hall was about to give me the sack? *Kismet* was my last show in Zambia. The Producer, Frank Knowles, believed I was the son he never had, and by some miracle, I was able to respond to his commands. He was a Yorkshireman and believed his show was the best thing that had happened to Zambia since Independence, notwithstanding there was not an African in the cast.

To act or not to act – that is the question Flushed with my success on the musical stage, I tried for a bit of straight acting. Fatal. One Sunday, I had the gall to attend an audition for Richard III. In the queue in front of me was a lady who politely asked what part I was auditioning for. In my innocence I replied, "*I only go for the leads*"! I must have had a thing about wanting to be a hunchback and talk like Lawrence Olivier. I was 'given' the part of Lord Rivers, not because of my excellent delivery; they were short of men. Shakespeare gave him about ten lines – the producer cut out six. One that remained was "*She may my Lord, for ....*" and then it was off with his head, way before any of the other courtiers. The production had great potential; some very good actors, a minimal set copied from a recent London production, first-rate costumes, and all in all, it should have been good enough to put on at Stratford. In the end, it turned out to be pitted with disasters; the producer fell in love with Lady Anne fairly early in the proceedings, which meant we were all left to our own devices. The play was put on as Ndola's contribution to the 1967 Zambia Theatre Arts Festival in Kitwe. A professional adjudicator came out from the BBC in London and criticised Queen Margaret's French accent with: "*What a pity she had an impediment in her speech.*" Rubbish. One of the young princes was sick all over the stage in the ghost scene because he was told on pain of death, he was to remain still. The producer flicked the wrong switch on the lighting console in the last Act, which put out all the stage lights. The final curtain came down on Henry Tudor's outstretched arms with him behind the curtain, but arms and crown still in full view of the audience; etc. etc.!

There was one very good thing that came out of the production. The lady in front of me at the auditions was Kay Pountney, my future wife, to date of more than fifty years. She was appalled at the criticism of her French accent but went on to 'wow' theatregoers in major roles at the Ashcroft, Yvonne Arnaud, Caterham's Miller Theatre, the world-renowned open air Minack Theatre in Cornwall, several National Trust Houses and Livery Companies in the City.

Close encounter The 40-mile stretch of road from Ndola to Kitwe was a single-carriageway, relatively straight, with many blind rises. I was driving my Volvo 122S (with chrome-plated engine) on a bright sunny day, becoming a little bored. As I reached the junction with the main road coming up from Lusaka, I saw an African by the side of the road, thumbing a lift. I had never given a hitchhiker a lift before, but a spur-of-the-moment decision made me stop and ask him where he was going.

"To Kitwe", he replied, *"to see my solicitor"*.

"Hop in" was the only response I could think of at the time.

He seemed nice enough, a bit dishevelled but none the worse for that. There was no need for me to make idle conversation because he could talk for Zambia.

"I have a meeting with my solicitor. It's necessary for me to clear my name".

"I'm glad I can be of help. Can I drop you in the centre of Kitwe?" I asked.

"I have been in Chainama Hills for the last three years, and my lawyer says my case is solid."

My heart stopped a beat. I had recently read an article in *The Times of Zambia* where two Zambians had a quarrel about a woman (inevitably) in Kitwe's Chamboli Mining Township. One drew a knife, injuring the other. Within one-month the man who drew the knife was dead – poisoned. Later, the man who had been injured was found guilty of manslaughter and given a three-year sentence in Chainama Hills Mental Hospital, Lusaka, for examination and treatment; and here he was in my car, munching a bag of sweets.

"Have a sweet," he said.

"That's kind of you, but no, thank you."

A sensible decision. Mother told me never to accept sweets from a stranger, particularly from a convicted poisoner. The man carried on jabbering away about his life, how he had been wronged but convinced the solicitor he was going to see would put all that behind him to start a new life. I never did read or hear what happened to him; and I have never picked up a hitchhiker again.

Trips away from the office

The Congo The Democratic Republic of Congo is large geographically, reflecting the southern catchment of the Congo River. In 1885, it became the private 'state' of Leopold II of Belgium. Leopold was a distant relative of Queen Victoria, who was already Empress of India and also controlled the Congo's neighbouring territory of Northern Rhodesia. As a gesture of goodwill between royal families, the UK Government was instructed to secede the lower half of Katanga to Leopold's fiefdom. This 'gift' is depicted by one of those interesting straight lines on the map, carefully drawn up by civil servants sitting in Westminster. Little did they realise that, by the mid-1900s, prospecting for minerals would identify the land 'given away' as one of the richest parcels of land on the Globe (rich in cobalt, copper, uranium, and diamonds).

King Leopold II had little daily control over what actually went on in Katanga. As a result, the land became the site of one of the most infamous international scandals at the turn of the twentieth century, with regular mass murders undertaken by 'white' officials. Roger Casement, the then British Consul, estimated that maybe as many as ten million locals had been killed. By 1908, public and diplomatic pressure led Leopold II to annex his fiefdom as the Belgian Congo colony under the control of the Belgian Government. This state of 'control' remained in place until Independence in 1960. Katanga was in total conflict on Independence because of the potential wealth of its mineral resources. Later that year, Moïse Tshombe took control of the State of Katanga.By 1963, many thousands of majestic-looking tall Congolese men and women were seen walking through the Copperbelt and on down south in search of a new life.

I had heard these stories of a mass exodus of refugees from The Congo to Zambia during the Katanga civil war. Kay and I, newly courting, decided in 1968 to make a visit over a long weekend to Elizabethville (*now called Lubumbashi*) to see for ourselves what had been a war zone involving the UN as well as mercenaries from Belgium, Britain, Rhodesia, France and South Africa and the US acting for and against different Congolese tribes. It may have appeared foolhardy, but you are only young once. Our initial journey was sedate enough across the Copperbelt, through Kitwe and Chingola, to the border post at Chililabombwe. Here, the road turned from tarmac to laterite.We passed through Zambian Customs into No Man's Land without incident and drove for about half-a-mile until we saw a large sign saying Douane (Customs). We had arrived in a foreign territory with a foreign tongue. Immigration was in a small rondavel, half of which was taken up by a desk and a Congolese official waiting to see our passports. He acknowledged our documentation was all 'in order' and then proceeded to place them in a drawer on his side of the desk. We were <u>not</u> leaving without them. He was waiting for this reaction and, with a beaming smile, opened the drawer and invited us to look inside. To our amazement, it was full of passports of various nationalities. How extraordinary that so many international travellers should succumb to immigration bush guidelines. It was apparent we could not proceed on our 'mystery tour' with our passports, so, after little thought and much debate, we left our 'lifelines' in the hands of this charming Congolese official with not a great deal of confidence they would be waiting for us on our return two days later.

Elizabethville was only 50 miles away, but what a surprise was in store for us. No colonial architecture as we had seen in Rhodesia and Zambia, but a Belgian city planted in the middle of the African bush, planned with wide thoroughfares and aesthetically appealing buildings and monuments. This was Leopold II spending his riches gained from exploiting Katanga's wealth to embellish his personal 'state' and to ensure its future economic potential. Alas, the hotel we stayed at felt unloved. The war-weary city had not been cleared up over the last five years, as was illustrated by many bullet holes through plate glass windows, by the lack of maintenance allowing rooms to decay, and by an overall feeling of malaise and no hope for the future. We were glad to see a lot of continental food. Sabena Airlines still flew from Brussels to the Congo once a day, importing European cuisine and wines. This was very different to what we were used to in Zambia, where the availability of food was what you could grow locally or imported from South Africa or Southern Rhodesia, and the only wine available was a Portuguese Mateus Rosé in those strange-shaped bottles, imported from Mozambique.

Our time was up, and we travelled back towards the Zambian border with our hearts in our mouths, not expecting to be able to cross over into Zambia. Why should we have worried? The same official was waiting for us at Congolese Immigration. He opened his drawer, handed back our passports and ushered us on our way.

Game Park If you live in Africa, you have to visit a game park. We visited South Africa over the 1967 Christmas break to stay with Brian Newenham (a school friend from Lancing who had gone to Witwatersrand University, stayed, and got married). His father-in-law had a farm adjacent to the Kruger National Park and, from a vantage point halfway up a tree, we saw some amazing sights of animals visiting a watering hole in the half-dark of dawn.

In Zambia, we had the opportunity to visit the southern Luangwa Valley; 170 miles of tarred road down to Lusaka and then 360 miles of dirt road up to Fort Jameson (re-named Chipata) – and back. The Luangwa River is a major tributary of the Zambezi and stretches right up the Eastern Province to the Tanzanian border. The

Great East Road serves the whole of the Eastern Province and runs desperately close to the Mozambique border for about 40 miles. Communications can be cut off relatively easily in this unpopulated part of the African bush, should any disenchanted outsider wish to cause a nuisance. Freedom fighters came furtively across the border from Mozambique (only two miles away) the week before we were due to travel. A military-style attack blew away the 300m-wide bridge across the Luangwa River. It was said President Kenneth Kaunda's lack of support for freedom fighters in neighbouring countries (Mozambique and Rhodesia) led to the bridge being destroyed as an act of revenge[6].

Change of plan – we flew to Fort Jameson direct from Ndola, a much better idea. We were met at the airport by rangers from Kapani private game reserve on the Luangwa's eastern bank. This reserve is situated on an oxbow lagoon between the Mwasauke and Kauluzi Rivers. The safari lodge was started in 1960 by Norman Carr after he had spoken to Paramount Chief Nsefu from the Northern Province. The Chief was mystified as to why people would want to pay to watch animals but was willing to try the experiment. Norman's first visitors shot with cameras instead of rifles and during the first year, he paid the Chief and his Council the then substantial sum of £100 for the privilege. After that, surplus income was given directly back to the local community. Eco-tourism in Africa was born.

Norman Carr with two orphaned lion cubs

Norman Carr played a pivotal role in the history of the Valley by pioneering commercial walking safaris upon which Luangwa founded its reputation. It is rich in game. Elephants, lions, and giraffes visited the camp at night, and the dawn chorus was aided by the raucous honking of hippos. Going out on safari was an exciting adventure. Norman Carr was living at Kapani safari lodge when we visited. He had passed on his vast knowledge and experience to the African game wardens, which meant they could sense in advance what was going on around them in the bush. The camouflage of animals is one of nature's mysteries. Our warden, with a rifle slung over his shoulder, could spot a lion lying in the long yellow grassland from 100 yards away; it only came into our vision when we were about 20 yards from them – and on foot, albeit downwind! One of our most vivid memories was seeing, as the sun was

---

[6] Interesting to discover later the replacement cable-stayed bridge was designed by Freeman Fox and Partners. FFP was to join forces with JTS in 1989 to form Acer Consultants, later Hyder Consulting. Unfortunately, this bridge was also sabotaged, and it took a further 20 years before Danish Aid (DANIDA) rehabilitated the structure to allow traffic to flow freely again.

beginning to set, 50 or so elephant crossing the river to secure a better feeding ground on the other side (it's not just chickens who do this, apparently); the babies, completely submerged, held their trunks aloft like snorkels.

We were encouraged to buy Norman Carr's book "Return to the Wild", in which he describes the rehabilitation back into the wild of two orphaned lion cubs called Big Boy and Little Boy. Norman kindly signed our copy, and we were off back to Ndola.

The Copperbelt Concert Society

We were very fortunate to have culture 'flying in' to keep the miners happy. The standard of performers the Copperbelt Concert Society was able to attract was remarkable, but maybe understandable, as Zambia is en route from Europe to South Africa. One international celebrity who 'fell out of the sky' on his way to Johannesburg was Hans Richter Haaser, a pianist renowned for his interpretation of Beethoven, Schubert, and Schumann. The Society Secretary, Graham Platt, went to meet him at the airport, took him to his hotel, and then on to the Lowenthal Theatre so he could acclimatise himself to the piano on which he was to perform that evening. Graham discretely left him to his rehearsing, only to return an hour later to see the maestro on all fours under the piano.

> "*Are you alright?*" was the only appropriate thing Graham could think of saying under the circumstances. Hans' response was edifying:

> "*When I play on a Steinway, I always like to know its official Steinway Number. I can't find a Number anywhere. It must be the Number One!*"

The piano is likely to have come up by 'special camel', second hand from South Africa shortly after World War II. It is not surprising the bush climate had allowed the odd note to lose control compared with that of a more conventional well-maintained Steinway in Europe or America. The concert was, inevitably, a great success, and he introduced me to Beethoven's Waldstein Piano Sonata No 21 in C major Opus 53, composed some 165 years earlier in 1803.

Mufulira - supervision of construction

Reality My university engineering degree course lasted three years, but full qualification as a Chartered Engineer and Associate Member of the Institution of Civil Engineers (AMICE) required a minimum of three years of practical experience, of which one year must be on a construction site. 1968/69 was to be that year.

Construction site I was 'banished' from the Ndola office and took up residence in Kamuchanga Township, Mufulira, near the Congo border, in charge of supervising the construction of a duplication of an existing 2,000,000-gallon reinforced concrete ground-level water tank, a pumping station, and a 250,000-gallon concrete water tower, all on the same site (*the pumping station is required to lift the water up to the adjacent water tower*). Roberts Construction was the contractor (a future colleague of mine in the 1990s, Tim Wade, was their Zambian Managing Director later in the 1970s). My technical 'training' on-site generally went without a hitch. I learned about concrete technology, slump tests, and sending concrete blocks to the lab for strength tests at 7 and 21 days: and about mechanical/electrical plant by religiously following the letter of the contract specification. An old Boer technician demonstrated to me his technique for approving an over-designed 250m long laterite access road (with the width of a motorway). He dropped his hollow bamboo stick from a height of two feet and listened to the precise pitch it made as it hit the ground. His experience then decided whether or not the road compaction was acceptable. This basic intuition and sound judgement were good training for my career ahead, so necessary for determining appropriate engineering solutions.

250,000 gallon Water Tower

Climbing a tower Halfway through construction, I cracked the scaphoid in my left wrist as I tripped, exercising someone else's dog. Not a good move. The hospital put my wrist in plaster just before I was required to climb scaffolding wrapped around my half-built water tower. I had to inspect reinforcing steel 100 feet up in the air. The site foreman generously set up a bosons' chair to lift me up. I felt important until I was about 10 feet off the ground. I looked down and, to my considerable disquiet, saw my safety relied on five Africans pulling at the end of a rope. The other end was secured around a pulley at the top of the already half-built concrete structure. The famous five hard-working Africans looked up at me with loveable beady-eyed smiling faces.

"*Alright Bwana?*" they asked.

I probably was, unless they decided to walk away when I was 80 feet up because they bore a grudge related to past colonial days (about which I knew nothing). Had my education taught me anything about diplomacy and about being good-natured to <u>all</u> my fellow humans? I certainly hoped so, but Gerard Hoffnung's 1958

61

address to the Oxford Union (*the Bricklayer's Lament*) immediately came to mind, which wasn't funny. As I reached the 100-foot threshold, I jumped out of the chair to safety with more speed than was really necessary. I was now in safe mode and in a position to approve the reinforcing steel configuration or not, ready for a concrete pour. I don't think my judgement was impaired, but I was conscious I had the boson's chair trip all over again to get down onto terra firma. This first trip was 'memorable', but it became my daily routine during the next four weeks, each time carefully priming my newly found African friends with modest bribes to keep them at peace with their conscience.

Enjoying culture on the Copperbelt My girlfriend, Kay, came to Mufulira one day in her red left-hand drive VW beetle. We were going to the cinema, some 120 miles away in Luanshya, to see *Doctor Zhivago*. It was a great film, but we returned only to discover the house had been burgled. Thieves had obviously watched us as we drove off. A pickinin (young child) had been put through a window, and everything below three feet was gone, including a judge's wig I had borrowed for a production of Gilbert and Sullivan's *Trial by Jury*. All the coca cola and other drinks in the fridge had been consumed, and bottles were scattered over the floor. A cold chill must have gone down the adult thieves' spines when the child handed out the judge's wig! The police found it later, dumped on the ground not far from the house. I was 'house-warming' for some friends who had gone to South Africa on holiday, so nothing too serious of mine was lost. The young lad had missed one 'gem.' Kay had just sold her car for K400 (£200 at 1968 exchange rates) in cash and hidden the money in my bedside table amongst my socks and underpants. Who would want to look there when there was a free drink in the fridge?

Local fauna

Spiders It is only to be expected that I would have run-ins with creepy crawlies. There were huge flat black spiders on most internal house walls in Zambia. They were impossible to catch and looked evil, but they were good friends as they preyed on mosquitos. I was sitting one evening in an armchair at Peggy Hazel's (my landlady). Just before I went to bed, I felt my lower left arm begin to throb and become quite hot. I spent an uncomfortable night because I could not avoid the growing pain. In the morning, my whole left arm was swollen from elbow to wrist. I took myself to Ndola Hospital Outpatients Department. They took one look at it and decided to operate. I was given a local anaesthetic and a scar that I have to this day. The surgeon ended up with a large cup-full of poison and, having observed two neat puncture holes, suggested they were probably that of a spider bite.

Snakes I am not too keen on snakes, either. Kay loves them. She fondled the most venomous of snakes when we visited Johannesburg Snake Park. One day, she came with me into the bush near Mufulira to survey a pipeline route. I was at the theodolite when out of the corner of my eye, I noticed a spitting cobra about ten feet away, uncoiled, erect and ready to strike. I was off like a shot, faster than when I got my School Colours for the 100 yards. Kay, on the other hand, stood motionless by the surveying equipment knowing the snake's eyesight was far from perfect. She stayed absolutely still. The snake could not 'sense' her and slowly backed down and slithered off into the undergrowth.

Kay had a friend, born in Northern Rhodesia, who told the story of how her nine-month-old baby was resting in the garden. When she came out of the house, to her horror, she saw the baby playing with a black mamba (the deadliest of snakes). The baby had no fear, and the snake enjoyed the warmth of the child. The mother knew if she rushed in to beat off the snake it would strike and, most probably, that strike would be fatal. She had the sense of mind to back off into the house and watch through the window for what seemed hours. Eventually, the black mamba had tired of its fun and slid silently across the grass into a garden border.

I have heard it said that when humans become frightened, we emit an 'odour' from every pore of our skin. It is at that moment an animal or insect is encouraged, out of self-preservation, to bite or strike. This theory is certainly true with Matabele ants. It is only when you first notice 50 or so have crawled up your leg that they all strike at precisely the same moment – as I have experienced, dancing at speed, ripping off my trousers and scraping off the blighters.

Bulldozer demolishing an ant hill

Termites The bottom of each hardcover to my textbooks, lodged on a shelf in my site office, was 'haute cuisine' to local termites. While I was supervising the water tower contract in Mufulira, BC&P instructed me to supervise the bush clearance for explosives bunkers and associated road infrastructure for the local mine. It is extraordinary how termites, being the size they are, have created 'ant hills' across the bush. Some can be 30 feet high and 120 feet in circumference at the base. These hills are like concrete, which can only be explained as being the result of the chemical reaction when you mix laterite soil and formic acid (provided by the termites). The contractor tried using explosives to demolish them, but this was not very effective; a bulldozer could be written-off after trying to demolish two or three of the larger ones. What was also amazing was that, as you uncovered the indigenous undergrowth across the African bush, it became apparent the ant hills were all positioned in a grid formation. I know the Egyptians and ancient Britons could line things up without the help of modern precision instrumentation – but termites? Clever things, these termites. Today, the 'ant hills' are devoid of their makers. Where have they all gone? The hills today are covered in local flora and fauna, disguising the fact they play host to pythons. When we came to site in the morning, there were always python tracks in the dust. One or two of the Europeans working for the contractor used to get very excited and followed their tracks with enormous enthusiasm until they vanished into a hole in the 'ant hill'. The Africans and I had a different approach and often walked fast in the opposite direction.

My marriage

Pre-nuptial happenings As I write this paragraph, my wife and I have been married for over 50 years. I can't remember whether I proposed to Kay or she proposed to me but no matter, we were engaged. Father had flippantly said Mother chased him all around Europe. In practice, it was probably just one brief trip. So it was with me, but this time my call was all around Africa! My parish priest in Ndola, Father John Brooks, took Kay under his wing because, although she had been brought up a strict Baptist and recited reams of scripture at me, she was not confirmed into the Church of England. Father John was an interesting character who had become ordained relatively late in life, having been a submarine commander in the Second World War. What he was doing in Central Africa, I don't know (so far from the sea!). We knew he had been Vice Principal of Cuddesdon Theological College, Oxford, before coming to Ndola; but it wasn't until we went to his funeral in 2002 that we realised how influential he had been to his young charges because seven bishops and many other high serving clergy were also present there to remember him.

Wedding Ceremony at the Boma, Ndola

Kay and Jessop with Father John Brooks

You could not plan a normal family wedding in the middle of Africa in those days. Travelling from Europe was prohibitive, so we knew our close relations were going to be denied being present. We both assumed a few friends could bear witness to our marriage. Zambian law required us to have a civil ceremony. Kay called in at the Ndola Boma (the Town Hall) the week before just to confirm all was ready for Saturday, 15th February. A sheepish official met her:

"I have to go off to the bush for a political meeting that day, could you manage Friday instead?"

And that is how we got married on St Valentine's Day, 1969.

Our Wedding Day Twelve seemed a good religious number to witness our wedding. The Ndola Theatre Club was well represented, with Campbell Hastie and Roger Hulley (who later was for many years Production Manager of the Lyttleton at London's National Theatre and became Godfather of our daughter, Eleanor and was present at our Golden Wedding Anniversary held at Lewtrenchard Manor in West Devon), the 'mad' Carol Greene and her husband Chris, Alice and Ian MacKay, Kay's cousin Pam Adams who was also living in Ndola, and Carol Knowles as well as my best man Graham Platt and his wife, Mandy. The ceremony at the Boma went without a hitch, and after a few photo shoots, we walked on to the Parish Church, where Father John presided over a blessing for the future of our marriage. Then all returned to our flat in President Avenue for a few drinks and the odd speech before setting off in my Volvo 122S on our honeymoon.

The honeymoon Our destination was the Eastern Highlands of Rhodesia. To get there, we had to motor south through Lusaka, across the border at Kariba, where we not only had to pass through two customs and immigration but also had the added benefit of looking at the wonderful concrete gravity Kariba Dam, designed by the highly respected Sir Alexander Gibb & Partners (a firm I was to come to know well a few years later)[7].

---

[7] Today, the Kariba Dam is in a serious state. The original turbines had reached the end of their useful life. Management had changed them like for like but of Chinese manufacture. Unfortunately, the new machines could not meet the same power output without passing more water through the new turbines. The increased water released from the dam and the excess fast-flowing water eroded the river bedrock in the plunge pool downstream of the dam wall. Over time, this carved a vast crater downstream of the dam wall which threatens to erode the very foundations of the dam itself. Maintenance engineers report 7 cont. that, when they are in the corridors within the dam, they can hear the concrete structure creak, which certainly would worry any dam engineer. Engineers warned that, without urgent repairs, the whole dam might collapse. If that happened, a tsunami-like wall of water would rip through the Zambezi valley, reaching the Mozambique border within eight hours. The torrent would overwhelm Mozambique's Cahora Bassa Dam and knock out 40% of southern Africa's hydroelectric capacity. Along with the devastation of wildlife in the valley, the Zambezi River Authority estimated the lives of 3.5 million people are at risk. In practice, the power output from Kariba has been reduced, causing power cuts and blackouts throughout Zambia, both to the industrial and domestic sectors.

Escape surrounded by Cambell Hastie and other guests

I called the Salisbury Office for a quick meeting which lasted four hours, apparently. When I came out, I met a tearful wife who not only gave me my first wigging for being so long but also confessed to having crashed the car – someone had driven into the passenger side as she passed over a crossroad junction. Why should all that spoil our holiday?

We motored towards the Eastern Highlands. The countryside got more magnificent the further east we travelled. Our initial destination was an old homestead at Troutbeck called the Rhodes Nyanga Hotel. This was built as a holiday cottage in the 1800s by Cecil Rhodes and converted into a hotel just before the Second World War. We certainly had an 'Out of Africa' experience. The hotel was furnished in true colonial fashion and had breathtaking views from the veranda overlooking a lake. There was a lot to see, including World's End, which had an amazing view of the plains and hills in the foreground as they rolled away from the Inyanga National Park mountain range towards Salisbury. The Mtarazi Falls has a 761m high majestic two-tiered granite waterfall that spills over into the imposing Honde Valley with the most amazing display of water sprays.

Kay in Rhodesia (now Zimbabwe)

Nothing could have prepared us for our next venue, the Leopard Rock Hotel. Set in the Vumba Mountains, the hotel architecture reflected that of a French Chateau, with turrets and large expanses of lawn. The Queen Mother visited in 1953 and described this resort as the most beautiful place in Africa. I doubt if anything had changed much and, as a honeymoon couple, we were put in the 'Queen Mother's' Room, which was tastefully decorated in a pale Cambridge blue. From the window, you looked out onto a 'Scottish' Africa. The monsoons had brought mists to these highlands, and the lawns were a vibrant green, something we had not seen since leaving England. A golf course stretched to infinity across the landscape. A swimming pool in Africa was a real luxury. When I went in for a dip, the Swiss wristwatch given to me by Miss Jennings when I left the Choir School fell to the bottom of the pool. I did eventually rescue it, but only after causing much amusement for my new wife, who was a far better swimmer than I was (or am). We were treated like royalty, but after a few relaxing days of walking in the mountains, we motored south to Melsetter, on the border with Mozambique.

The Melsetter settlement is in the Chimanimani mountains at the southern end of the Eastern Highlands and was named by a Scottish trekker from the Transvaal after his home in the Orkneys. We visited the Bridal Veil Falls and climbed a mountain, beyond which was Mozambique. As we climbed, the temperature seemed to rise, and a little bubbling stream looked very inviting. We stripped off and rested a while in the really freezing waters. We thought we were about to reach the summit, only to find the land flattened out and then rose again. This exasperating scenario happened three or four times before we were able to sit down and look down towards the Indian Ocean to the east and back across the Rhodesian velt to the west. The climb down was easy by comparison. When we reached the bottom, there was a herd of cows surrounding our treasured Volvo 112S. I saw, to my total embarrassment, that I had a flat tyre on the rear offside. On further inspection, I noticed the little valve to which you connect the compressor had gone. My immediate reaction was that the cows had thought it was a teat and had chewed the thing right off! Kay laughed at me, but this was serious as we were miles from any rescue. I changed the wheel and drove gently back to a garage near our hotel. The mechanic also laughed at me. No cow damage, just the rubber tube had slipped inside the tyre, causing the valve to rotate out of view. We were now set to return 700 miles or so up to the Copperbelt.

Professional interview

Shortly after I finished my time on site, I was called down to Lusaka for my ICE Interview. I was the last candidate to be seen by the invigilator before lunch. He appeared to have lived in the 'colonies' since before the Boer War. The Professional Interview is supposed to be a deep interrogation to ascertain whether or not you are worthy to become responsible for building the most complicated of structures to serve the universe for the good of mankind. However, he didn't give me confidence he was interested in anything other than his imminent lunch.

"*How are you enjoying Zambia?*" That was, I think, the most technical question he asked me.

I was able to show him a photograph of the 'as built' structures of the formal designs for Bristol's Avonmouth Sewage Works I had prepared when I was with JTS. I was also fortunate to present to my invigilator an ICE Proceedings article written by the Bristol City Engineer describing the philosophical raison d'être of the design, namely providing secondary effluent as a water resource to serve the Avonmouth Aluminium Smelter (closed down 45 years later in 2003). The article had an aerial photograph of the completed works of my design. The invigilator gave me no indication as to whether it impressed him or not,

In the afternoon, he set me an essay – on what, I can't remember. I returned to the Copperbelt and soon afterwards to the UK as an Associate Member of the Institution of Civil Engineers – thanks to the kind old man of Lusaka.

Chapter 5: United Kingdom

"Where the waters do agree, it is quite wonderful the relief they give."
Jane Austen, novelist (1775-1817)

Return to the UK

The return My three-year contract in Zambia came to an end in August 1969. Kay and I returned to the UK, first via Nairobi to visit a thriving conurbation focussed on tourism and then to Athens, staying with my brother Martin's in-laws and seeing the ancient sites. Kay suffered from the searing heat of Athens in August, even though we had come from Africa, but she was pregnant with our first child Anna Megan Jessop. We cut short our visit and arrived in London early in September with the knowledge I had been paid by BC&P for the next two months. We hired a car and motored down to Benenden to visit my parents. We got to Goudhurst when Kay suggested we phone up to let them know we were coming. I looked at my watch. It was one minute to nine in the evening.

> *"No,"* I said. *"Father will be listening to the Nine O'clock News on the Home Service ....!"*

Search for new employment I was officially unemployed. I had said to myself, "I have worked for John Taylor & Sons and Brian Colquhoun & Partners, so let me see who else I can work for at this early stage of my career". Most consulting engineers operated from Victoria Street in London because of the need to be close to Parliament to provide the Government with expert opinion.

I made appointments with Westminster-based JD & DM Watson (wastewater) and Rofe, Kennard, and Lapworth (water supply), both of whom had good reputations. I then thought it would be a good idea to combine a series of interviews with Consultants outside London and, with Kay, enjoy a holiday around the UK at the same time. Interviews were arranged with AHS Waters & Partners in Birmingham, Ward Ashcroft and Parkman in Liverpool and another Consultant in Newcastle. We had a good time. I did my interviews and saw parts of the country neither of us had visited before. On return to Benenden, there were several letters waiting for me. Some were rejections, including one from JD & DM Watson (which I think they might have secretly regretted down the line); others were conditional offers. However, there was one letter with familiar handwriting from John Haseldine:

> *"I am fed up writing references for you to all our competitors. If you are genuinely 'on the market' why not come back and work for JTS".*

How could I refuse such an invitation? I abandoned my principle of working for a Consultant with whom I had no experience and homed in on Artillery House once again.

I was given my own office and began to work on a variety of different projects, including sewerage for the London Borough of Hillingdon, which took me out to Heathrow to the south of the borough, and Northolt Airport in the north, lugging a heavy theodolite to measure levels across the borough. I was encouraged by the Partners to look at the future workload for JTS. They asked me to make a long trip to Africa, visiting several countries, including Uganda (where I visited Jerry Karugonjo, who I had worked alongside in JTS five years previously - he was now Chief Engineer, Ministry of Works), Kenya, Zambia, South Africa (where I met David Hall, son of my boss in Zambia) and Botswana. I then prepared the winning proposals for the Tehran Wastewater Master Plan (for WHO), where Nick Paul went to be Project Manager, and the Mauritius Water Resources Study (for the UK Overseas Development Agency), where I was appointed Project Manager and where I spent a couple of years. The work was varied and interesting, and I kept alive my interest in visiting overseas, although ongoing engineering projects tended to be UK-based.

Plymouth Water – Swincombe Dam

Existing Burrator Dam

Government funding for water engineering projects prior to 1970 UK municipal water undertakings were obliged to seek funding from Central Government whenever they wanted to implement a capital works project. The first part of this process required their project to be debated in the Houses of Parliament in front of a Select Committee. Barristers would put the case for and against the project (supported as required by expert witnesses to argue the technicalities on which the particular project was based). The Committee would consist of three 'non-interested party' MPs, who would listen to the arguments and then dismiss the legal teams and debate amongst themselves whether or not the project should be put forward to Government for funding. If the Select Committee supported the project, then the second part of the process was for the parliamentary legal team to prepare a detailed Bill. This Bill would then be put before the House of Commons and the House of Lords for Members' consideration in the usual way. If the House of Commons secured a majority after a full debate, then an Act of Parliament was passed requiring Government to fund the project. After this, the

70

project would enter the implementation stage until the works were complete and commissioned.

City of Plymouth Water undertaking The City is, and was, fortunate to rely on upland catchments for all its potable water requirements. Run-off from Dartmoor is captured in the Burrator Reservoir, completed in 1898. The dam was raised in 1928 to the height it is today. To supplement the city's raw water resources, surplus water on the River Tavy is abstracted at Lopwell and pumped to Burrator. Water drawn from the dam is good quality and feeds the City by gravity.

Proposal to augment the City of Plymouth's water resources In the 1960s, the city's Water Management Department decided it was necessary to promote a scheme to augment their water resources to meet requirements up to the end of the millennium. They retained Binnie and Partners as their consulting engineer who proposed the Swincombe Dam Project. The River Swincombe is a tributary of the West Dart, which has its headwaters right in the centre of Dartmoor, south of Princetown. Although there is no ideal dam site, impoundment would catch run-off in a highly wet part of Dartmoor (annual average rainfall at Princetown is 1,970mm). The principle of the scheme was to store run-off from this rainfall in a new reservoir on the River Swincombe. The proposed structures would capture the flows and prevent them from passing on down the Dart. The area to be flooded was Fox Tor Mires which, as the name suggests, is mainly bog land. Stored water would then be diverted over the watershed by enlarging the conveyance capacity of the existing Devonport and Prison leats for eventual discharge into Burrator Reservoir[8]. Binnies developed this scheme and documented it in a detailed 3-volume report. The City Fathers studied their recommendations, voted in favour of the Swincombe Dam Project, and instructed their legal department to liaise with Westminster to promote a 1970 Plymouth Water Bill to provide funding for the necessary capital investment. Government had decided in the late 1960s to review funding for water projects in a more pragmatic way, so it turned out that this Plymouth Water Bill was to be the very last water bill put through Parliament.

Public reaction Dartmoor is a place of great mystique, a National Park that lobbyists believe should be 'protected at all costs.' When the decision of Plymouth Council to build a dam on Dartmoor was made public, every protector of the status quo, conservationists, and environmental campaigners laid battle plans to oppose this scheme as it went through due process in Parliament. Local County politicians were persuaded to fight the Bill, including the Devon River Authority (salmon fishing lower down the River Dart was 'big business'). Devon County

---

[8] Leats are a feature of the Dartmoor landscape and are man-made channels that follow the natural contours to reduce the gravitational force sufficiently to permit gentle and manageable flow of water across catchments

Council approached John Haseldine (JTS Partner) to represent their interests. John retained me to carry out a detailed review of all available documentation. The Dartmoor Preservation Association also was a vociferous objector led by its chairman, Lady Sylvia Sayers, who had referred to the proposed reservoir site as:

> "a great natural amphitheatre ... a place of immense spaciousness and wildness: it has nothing to do with "prettiness"; its character is one of austere beauty, challenge, and inspiration – Dartmoor itself".

Detailed review My first port of call was to go up three floors in Artillery House to meet Christopher Hetherington, a Binnie engineer of about my age, who had been instructed to make all plans and reports available for me to study. My analysis produced a few interesting phenomena:

- The Rivers Tamar and Tavy both had serious arsenic contamination (due to 19th-century mining activity)
- Argument with the Devon River Authority – impounding headwaters of the River Dart could have a serious effect on fish stocks (salmon) unless a substantial residual flow was released down the West Dart from the proposed dam. Plymouth compromised by increasing the volume impounded in the dam, which had the effect of both satisfying fish stocks in the Dart and storing enough water to meet projected demands in Plymouth over the next fifty years to 2020.
- Input into supply during 1969 was equivalent to 50 gallons per person per day (gpd), well above the national average
- Binnie's 3-volume report was comprehensive and a good example of how a detailed proposal should be written

My briefing to John Haseldine was focused on the disadvantages of the Swincombe Scheme. At first glance, the political dimension appeared not to be a weakness; after all, if you want adequate volumes of water discharged down the River Dart to satisfy salmon breeding habits, then store more water in the reservoir by raising the dam wall. The corollary of such action made more water available for Plymouth. Was that a problem? Plymouth City's historical development has been totally navy-orientated (i.e., a one-industry conurbation). Binnie had originally developed a 30-year water demand curve for the city, after which time future development assumptions would become unreliable. Conceding a reservoir enlargement to satisfy salmon had the effect, therefore, of obliging the City Fathers to meet a spurious 50-year water demand for Plymouth until 2020. This 'weakness' needed further examination.

Plymouth put into supply 50 gallons per person per day (gpd). John recognised this as a very high figure. We quickly established a correlation between cities and towns relying on upland catchments for their resource and those with high consumption per capita (which included Cardiff, Sheffield, and Liverpool). An argument for this phenomenon was they would all have low operating and maintenance costs for both treatments (because of good quality raw water) and pumping (because of gravity feed). There would, therefore, be no management culture in these utilities to minimise wastage and leakage, resulting in a higher than necessary usage of raw water.

Consultation with our Barrister Armed with this information, we went for our first consultation with the Barrister chosen by Devon County Council to represent their objection to the Plymouth Water Bill. Magdalen College Oxford was renowned for training lawyers. However, this was my first encounter with a real practicing lawyer in his own Chambers in the Temple. John and I were wheeled into what appeared to be someone's drawing room with bookcases floor to ceiling on every wall. The Barrister was seated at a 'Partners' desk piled high with files tied with pink ribbon and with his back to the window. He was not the Horace Rumpole look-a-like I was expecting; in fact, he appeared like quite a normal professional and beckoned us to sit down on the other side of his table while he reached for his pink-ribboned file.

I was ready to disseminate all the technical details of the Swincombe Scheme. He seemed not to be too interested in such matters but rather wanted to focus on what we perceived to be the main weaknesses of the case. There was another dimension to Plymouth's 50 gpd input to supply. John reminded him the City had been heavily bombed during the war, so much of the underground water distribution pipe systems in the City could well be 'disturbed'. Hitler could have caused considerable treated water leakage before it reached the consumer. Our barrister asked:

"Why haven't the City done something about it?"

John responded that they rely on a cheap resource, so there is no incentive to carry out good housekeeping practice, unlike other water undertakings in the UK which might be obliged to pump river water or groundwater from a deep aquifer. There is a strong argument, therefore, for Plymouth's distribution system to be 'leaking like a sieve', which the City may have difficulty denying.

The Barrister made a note that the whole scheme depended on Plymouth providing a resource large enough to meet a projected water demand over the next 50 years. Had we been in Victorian times, this might have proved acceptable, but in the new Elizabethan age, cost-benefit analysis and other accounting phenomena would not support future demands over such a long period.

73

Four other Barristers had been retained to oppose the Bill, one on instruction from the Devon River Authority, two from environmental bodies (including Lady Sayer, who was a passionate conservationist and environmentalist, particularly in opposing any sort of development on Dartmoor - even a road kerb) and one from the Ramblers' Association. Although our Barrister would be interested in what aspects of the Bill they would try to undermine, he felt it best to ignore their specific interests and concentrate on harpooning the Bill on engineering arguments.

Site Visit We made one visit to Devon, taking the train first class from Paddington to Exeter. We were met by a County Council chauffeur and driven to the Judges' Lodgings, a former stately home still with butler and servants. The evening was spent with other 'residents' in an environment reminiscent of dining at Magdalen. We were driven to Princeton in the morning, left the car at HM Prison and walked south to view the saucer-shaped marshy catchment that surrounds the headwaters of the West Dart. Not a lot to see, not a lot to learn, except that it is not a classic site for a dam and no doubt the environmentalists would have a field day.

Select Committee hearing The day arrived when we should visit the Houses of Parliament to participate in the case for and against the proposed Swincombe Dam Bill. The Select Committee was made up of four MPs. The chairman was John Hunt (*Conservative, Bromley*), who was supported by Michael Cocks (*Labour, Bristol South*), John Cordle (*Conservative, Bournemouth East, and Christchurch*) and George Wallace (*Labour, Norwich North*). They introduced themselves as uninterested parties, and John Hunt spelt out how they would like the proceedings to progress. First, it was Plymouth City who would present its case as to why an increase in water resources was needed now, and the Swincombe Dam Scheme was the best technical solution to meet the City's requirements. The City opted for allowing their internal solicitor to present their case rather than retaining a charismatic Barrister to persuade these four MPs the scheme was good for the citizens (and therefore for the voters) of Plymouth. Big mistake! This solicitor lacked presentation skills and, as a consequence, allowed the four MPs to fidget with their pencils and glare out of the window more than they should. He spent 21 days laying out the City's case for Swincombe. Plenty of expert witnesses were introduced one by one who were then cross-examined by the opposing Barristers. Roger Hetherington, a Binnie Partner, who was a very distinguished dam engineer and a good friend of the JTS Partners, was the engineering expert witness. His turn to sit in 'the chair' came on day 20. The Plymouth solicitor enabled Roger to give the Select Committee all the detailed technical information about the dam, the catchment area, and the ability to transfer raw water from the Dart across the watershed into the Burrator catchment. As we were breaking for lunch, our barrister asked us to come back with the per capita water requirements for Bristol, Bournemouth, and Norwich (the constituencies of three of the MPs adjudicating the case). This information was all published in the 1969 Water

Yearbook, so not an arduous task - but not one I would have immediately thought appropriate here. Armed with these three figures, we returned to Parliament and gave them to our Barrister. He absorbed the facts and did a quick double-take back in our direction. With a certain degree of relief, he gave us an enthusiastic smirk and a wink and prepared for his turn to cross-examine the Binnie Partner. The four MPs ambled back into the room, having had a good lunch at the Members' Restaurant; they nodded to the Parliamentary Clerk for the afternoon session proceedings to commence, and our Barrister was off:

> "Mr Hetherington, can you tell me the consumption per capita in Bristol?"

You could see Roger wince and then put his head on one side as though to say, 'why have you bowled me a googly when you know I am very unlikely to know the answer?'. On the dais, the head of the MP for Bristol South jerked up suddenly. You could visibly understand what he was saying to himself - 'Bristol, that's in my constituency, I thought we were supposed to be discussing Plymouth.'

> "Mr Hetherington, if I was to tell you the consumption in Bristol last year was 35 gpd, would you agree with me?"

Poor Roger's face went white and completely blank. He then lifted his head with a quizzical look in our direction as if to say, 'can you help me out here?' In response, John's head bobbed up and down in support of our Barrister's suggestion. Roger Hetherington responded

> "If you are telling me that Bristol's consumption is 35 gpd then, yes, I will accept that".

Our Barrister was off again, with more enthusiasm than before:

> "Mr Hetherington, can you tell me the consumption per capita in Bournemouth?"

By now, Mr Hetherington was well aware of the legal game our Barrister was playing. This time it was the head of the MP for Bournemouth East and Christchurch's turn to be raised from his slumbers after a good lunch.

> "Mr Hetherington, if I was to tell you the consumption in Bournemouth last year was 42 gpd, would you agree with me?"

Again, Roger looked in our direction only to see nodding heads agreeing with our Barrister.

"If you tell me the consumption in Bournemouth is 42 gpd, then I will accept that"

"Mr Hetherington ..."

"Yes, I will accept the consumption in Norwich is 38 gpd!"

These three MPs suddenly realised that, when compared with their own constituencies, Plymouth's per capita consumption of 50 gpd seemed unacceptable. Within twenty-four hours, the four MPs had made their recommendation not only to reject the Swincombe Dam project but also to recommend Plymouth should concentrate on reducing the basic consumption rate through a strategy of leakage and waste control. This approach was put in place, but it took a decade to resolve. In the meantime, Plymouth had a water constraint that, alas, deterred new development in the City.

John Haseldine never did have to present his proof of evidence to the Swincombe Dam Select Committee. This whole experience began my great respect for Barristers. Like Rumpole, they seek out the unexpected and are not necessarily interested in the minutiae of technical detail - unlike the Engineer.

Subsequent development 1974 saw the formation of the Regional Water Authorities, which meant all the Plymouth Water Undertaking team and apparatus became part of a new regional South West Water. The new Authority engineers had a more global remit and developed two regional reservoirs along the A30 trunk road corridor, one at Colliford on the River Fowey (volume 28,500Ml, commissioned in 1983, near Bodmin) and the other at Roadford on the River Wolf (volume 34,500Ml, commissioned in 1989, near Launceston). Today, Plymouth continues to benefit from drawing water from Burrator (volume 4,200Ml) and resources are supplemented by water drawn from the Roadford supply zone as the need arises.

Expert witness

John Calvert, Professional Advocate John Calvert was the JTS Senior Partner and an internationally respected public health engineer. He was often retained as an expert witness for some of the large building firms in the South East. I used to accompany him to Barrister's chambers in the Temple and learnt how democracy works in the interests of nobody except those who promote the project. If such meetings were in the afternoon, John asked me to give him a nudge if he started to snore, which he did on several occasions.

Goldsworth Park Estate in Woking, Surrey I cut my teeth on one such scheme with John Calvert taking the lead. It provided me with a good understanding of how the legal mind operates. Looking at the map of Woking Borough in 1970, the northeast quadrant had yet to be developed. It was wholly taken up by a specialist rhododendron nursery owned by the Slocock family, who had been winning gold medals at the Chelsea Flower Show since the 19th century. The family had decided this 100-acre site had potential value as real estate and wished to turn it into a major housing development to build 4,500 homes for 15,000 residents. New Ideal Homes Ltd (the developer) and Oliver Slocock (the landowner) retained John to advise on necessary water engineering matters. Other technical advisers were engaged in transportation, landscape architecture, and town planning.

The first principle of an expert witness is to identify those organisations with responsibility for the operation and maintenance of your discipline and then negotiate to secure an agreement on how to deal with any technical issue that may arise due to the proposed development. Once such agreements have been achieved, Barristers (for and against the proposed development) can divert their argumentative 'mud-slinging' to other less technical issues. They then rely on the engineer's proof of evidence to demonstrate, in front of an independent Inspector hearing the case, that there is no engineering issue that cannot be resolved by means of an acceptable technical solution. Water supply was not a problem as JTS was the Consultant to the Woking and District Water Company. Sewerage was also not a problem because, again, JTS was Woking Borough Council's Consultant and had designed all the sewers in Woking over the previous seventy years and been responsible for the design and implementation of what is called the Old Woking sewage treatment plant, and similar ones at Chertsey and at Walton and Weybridge.

Surface water run-off, however, presented a challenge. The existing estate subsoil was full of nutrients and porous, so rainfall run-off soaked into the ground (for the rhododendron's benefit). The topography of the land was shallow saucer-shaped with only one surface water outlet, the Parley Brook, a polite name for what is no more than a ditch. In turn, this drains into the Bourne (a name derived from the Anglo-Saxon, meaning "from a spring," which suggests it is not conveying water regularly and hence will have carrying capacity constraints), which in turn discharges into the River Thames at Weybridge.

We went to have discussions with the Thames Conservancy (forerunner of the National Resources Authority and the Environment Agency), who understood the proposed development would substantially increase rates of surface water run-off by putting the catchment under tarmac and housing. They would only agree to the proposed development at Slococks if future run-off was restricted to that calculated as the 'maximum' rate of run-off before any development commenced. With this principle as our 'constraint,' we devised a scheme to pump surface water run-off into Parley Brook, limiting the pumping station output to be no greater than the agreed pre-development rate of run-off from Slocock's Nursery.

Our proposal required an artificial lake to be constructed, which needed to be surrounded by playing fields, all adjacent to this proposed pumping station. When run-off was in excess of pre-development flows, the pumps would perform at full design capacity (lifting the agreed amount into the Parley Brook) while the surplus run-off would overflow into the lake. In the event of significant downpours, the diverted flows would further overflow from the lake onto the playing fields (thus creating an artificial flood plain) and ensure the new housing development remained 'in the dry'. This engineering design could also act as a significant landscape architectural feature for the whole of the proposed development, creating a kind of 'lungs of Woking' – if you should need such an anatomical attribute. The logic appealed to the Thames Conservancy, and our Barrister enjoyed the luxury of not having to defend the indefensible. Development went ahead, and as of 2020, the Goldsworth Park Estate in Woking has been fully protected against all rainfall events thrown at it over the last forty years and more.

Wates Built Homes I was the preferred expert witness for Wates Built Homes (and Countryside Properties). Both were family firms and highly respected developers. My job was to persuade the various water authorities that proposed housing developments were an 'acceptable' fact of life and engineering solutions were achievable. There was always the reminder that the Council would benefit in the long term with increased water rates. By coincidence, our first house in Croydon, purchased in 1970, was a Wates Built Home – 28 Tipton Drive, a development that was previously a market garden.

Beckenham, Kent This project was to try and develop housing on a nine-hole golf course near Beckenham Railway Station. I had done my negotiations with the National Rivers Authority and got their agreement on how to handle the '30-year storm'. The 'opposition' employed a weather expert from the Meteorological Office, designed to cause chaos in court. He produced a graph of 'recorded' rainfall events going back to the year 1080 (no, that is not a misprint) to demonstrate that weather patterns of intense rainfall were cyclic (the term 'climate change' had yet to evolve). The purpose of this graph was to persuade the independent Inspector that a '30-year storm' today may not necessarily continue to be defined as a '30-year storm' in a few years' time. This may be true in principle, but the concept had not been aired in Her Majesty's Inspectorate before. My Barrister used a technique of asking the witness to explain all sorts of side issues which he was not expecting, all designed to throw doubt in the Inspector's mind as to the integrity of the witness. This ensured that the Inspector failed to take serious note of rainfall behaviour in the reign of King William I as being in any way relevant to the planning enquiry in hand. There were other planning issues, alas, which caused the Inspector to reject the Wates development proposal.

Langshott Development, Horley, Surrey The largest development proposal I was involved in for Wates was a 5,000 homes proposal between the M23 and the main London to Brighton railway north of Horley to service potential housing needs surrounding an extended Gatwick Airport. The Burstow Stream flows through the Site and drains into the River Mole, both of which have very flat catchments. When entering the proposed development area, the first property you came to was called Great Lake Farm. This was a Grade 2 timber-framed house, which should have told the developer the land had flooded regularly over the years. I became an expert on the behaviour of the River Mole and got an agreement with Thames Water on solutions for dealing with increased run-off by flood storage on site so that flows downstream would not be affected by the Wates development. The developer had three attempts to secure planning permission by public inquiry over a fifteen-year period. On each occasion, they withdrew because local politics weren't secure enough for them to be confident of victory. A small development adjacent to the main railway embankment did go ahead, but the main area still remains agricultural land.

Partner of John Taylor & Sons

One day in September 1974, John Calvert invited me to his office and told me to sit down. John Haseldene and Gwilym Roberts were also there. Quite out of the blue, John told me that Oliver Taylor was retiring and that he also intended to retire in a couple of years. The Partners wished to invite me and Nick Paul, two years my senior, to join the Partnership to secure a plausible succession. There would be huge responsibility and liability to 'feed the mouths' of 400 staff and their families, but the rewards should create great professional satisfaction. He recommended I should discuss this with Kay. The Partners would appreciate a quick response so that staff could be informed. I consulted with Kay when I got home that evening to secure a decision; and spoke with John first thing the next morning. A note was sent to all staff and clients on the formal embossed JTS letterhead.

National Committees

When I first left University, the only tools available to calculate mathematical equations and work out angles for engineering applications were a slide rule and log tables. The slide rule was invented back in the 17th century by the Rev William Oughtred, an Englishman. It was about the size of a ruler and had a moving part enabling you to set one number against another to work out whatever answer you were looking for. In effect, it was a mechanical analogue computer and could be accurate to two decimal places. The book of log tables was more accurate, either to four or seven decimal places. Both of these became obsolete by the early 1970s when the handheld electronic calculator came onto the market for scientific and engineering purposes.

There were a lot of clever mathematicians/scientists in the 18th and 19th centuries who played around with developing formulae for partial flows in channels. First, there was Bernoulli, then came Manning and Chézy, whose formula for establishing the velocity in a channel $v = c\sqrt{rs}$ was in constant use by the engineering profession by the end of the 1890s; where v = the velocity of the flow in a channel, r = the hydraulic mean depth of that flow and s = the gradient of the channel. This equation was adopted by most engineers in the 19th century.

When I first became a Partner, I occupied Oliver Taylor's office. Inside one of his Partner's desk drawers was a copy of Crimp and Bruges Hydraulic Flow Tables for Sewers and Water Mains. These tables were introduced in 1895 in an attempt to simplify for the engineer the choice of diameter for a partially filled pipe with a range of diameters, slopes, and quantity of flow. The engineer made his decision on pipe size knowing the quantity to be conveyed and knowing that the velocity of the fluid in the pipe should not fall below 2 ft/sec (to ensure solids don't settle out) or exceed 12 ft/sec (to prevent scouring of the pipe invert). The Crimp & Bruges Tables were a magnum opus and a significant improvement in accuracy on the Chézy formula by adopting figures derived from the more complex equations of Darcy & Bazin and Ganguillet & Kutter. Every drawing office in JTS had a copy of the Tables. The interesting thing about this particular copy in Olly's desk was it had handwritten alterations in red over many printed numbers, presumably made by Santo Crimp (a former Partner of JTS) in an attempt to improve the accuracy of his published calculations.

Early in the 1970s, the Department of Environment (DoE) noted they spent a lot of money on sewer pipes. Questions had been made in the House as to why this expense on the public purse relied on nineteenth-century calculations. Believing computer design was just around the corner, the DoE decided to set up a Working Party for the Hydraulic Design of Storm Water Sewers. The subject is complex, involving meteorology, hydrology as the rainfall passes over the land (depending on different soakage rates for agricultural land, woodland, roads, and gardens), and sewer pipe hydraulics, all to determine the realistic pipe size and, therefore, the eventual cost to be borne by Government. The civil servants thought a more detailed analysis of these three specific scientific studies would reduce the annual burden on the Exchequer. About twenty UK scientists, meteorologists, academics, and engineers (of which I was one of four) were drawn together and met every other month for ten years (1974-84). We looked at what other countries were doing, which seemed to be very little, and then spent time arguing about accuracy and practicality. The scientists and academics believed the important issue was to provide a pipe to take the exact flow as determined by their complex equations and procedures. The engineers argued that a small increase in pipe diameter would enable a significant increase in flow capacity without incurring much extra cost. The argument fell on deaf ears and went around and around for years. Eventually, a storm drainage computer-aided design programme evolved, and I chose to have it verified in JTS Plymouth Office by Roger Howard, who analysed the total design proposals for Torbay. The programme was adopted by the UK water industry and used for the next thirty years and may be more.

While this exercise was going on, the British Standards Institution suggested they should update their code for best working practice on the detailed design and laying of sewers. I became a member of the much smaller Technical Committee for the Revision of the Sewerage Code of Practice (1978-88).

Chapter 6: Marketing

"Thou visitest the earth, and waterest it:
thou greatly enrichest it with the river of God, full of water."
Psalm 65 v9

Lack of training in the art of marketing

Membership of the Association of Consulting Engineers My formative education sourced technical treatise and equations to solve stresses and strains in all sorts of media but taught me nothing about how to resolve the global theorem that man is not owed a job. John Taylor & Sons had been a stalwart of the Association of Consulting Engineers (ACE) – Midgley Taylor (son of John Taylor) was its first chairman in 1913, and the firm produced several subsequent chairmen, Godfrey Taylor in 1941, John Calvert in 1958 and Midgley's grandson, John Haseldine, in 1982. It is no wonder, therefore, that JTS abided by every rule in the ACE's constitution.

Competition or the lack of it One of these rules was that *"No member should compete for work against a fellow member"*. Government had agreed to a 'sliding scale of fees' (based on eventual construction cost), and time-based work was always charged out at twice an engineer's salary (compared with today's bankers who charge up to ten times salary). Consulting engineers tended to be individual specialists in either water, transportation, ports and harbours, irrigation, structures, or power. When firms were offered a job not in their own speciality, they would either contact the ACE, who would 'distribute' the work to a member firm with the appropriate experience, believing that in so doing, they were upholding the reputation of all ACE members, or contact a particular fellow Consultant directly.

This is what happened in 1947. Rendle Palmer and Tritton were the designers of the King Feisal Bridge across the Tigris in Iraq and had been asked by Baghdad's Lord Mayor if they could recommend a drainage Consultant. Godfrey Taylor (a drinking partner at St Stephen's Club) had his name put forward, and JTS was invited to prepare a report on the main drainage for the complete city of Baghdad. The firm's fee was 1,000 Guineas. The City paid only £1,000, and the early letters on the Project file related to explaining the difference between Guineas and Pounds and requesting payment of the £50 shortfall. Following acceptance of the report, JTS was offered the design work by the Baghdad Main Drainage Board and proposed to do it at half ACE fees (2%) because of the enormity of the project, and Godfrey didn't want to be making unnecessary and unseemly profit! That was how honourable consulting engineers were in those days; professionalism came first, followed by commercialism, tempered with prudence.

By the time I joined the Firm in 1963, 'offers' were usually made on two pages of foolscap, which identified the 'agreed' fee and not much else. Senior engineers managing a job were never told what fees had been secured and were instructed to engineer the job to the standard required by the Partner concerned; some projects were undertaken at a loss, therefore, but JTS usually made a modest profit in any financial year, influenced by whatever the firm's external accountant would allow as 'work in progress'. The Partners believed that if the drawing offices were full, the firm must be doing well. I think that was how most engineering Consultant firms operated up and down Victoria Street in Westminster.

The Firm's first real tenders for new work

Tehran City In 1971, the 'ACE' rules relating to competition were about to change. I was told to prepare a joint 'bid' with Sir Alexander Gibb and Partners for a UNDP/WHO-financed 'Pre-investment Survey of Sewerage Needs and Facilities' for the whole of Tehran. Gibb was the Tehran Regional Water Board's in-house Consultant on water supply and had complained to the Board that they had not been invited, apparently, to bid for this Tehran Sewerage study. After some heated discussions, they were eventually invited to present a detailed offer in association with JTS (because of our Baghdad experience), along with six other international Consultants. JTS had never before put together a detailed bid for a major international project. I worked with John Hennessy, a young engineer from Gibb (who, many years later, became a Partner of Sir AGP). He knew AGP's track record in Tehran but had little experience in drafting proposals and no knowledge of sewerage. It was an interesting experiment for us both, a good example of the blind leading the blind. We produced a hard cover 'book' to describe our understanding of the Project, how we would carry out the work, the two firms' previous experience of similar or associated work, a manpower structure accompanied by 'everybody's' CV – and the proposed fee. The proposal had to be approved by the Partners of both firms and then duly signed and posted to WHO Headquarters in Geneva. I rather enjoyed the experience of how international consulting firms behaved to secure new business in the 'real' world. We won the bid, too, which was good news. My JTS colleague, Nick Paul, became resident in Tehran for two years with the team John Hennessy and I had identified. The Survey produced a seven-volume leather-bound 40-year Master Plan to implement a sewerage scheme for Tehran. The principal recommendation was to replace the small open channels (known as "jubes") that were the only existing wastewater facility to serve the city's 7 million population. If the Shah's regime had not been overthrown in 1978, the two firms might still be working there, providing a 'first-time' sewerage scheme for the city.

Mauritius The UK Government's Overseas Development Administration (ODA) used to offer work to consultancies as part of the Government's aid programme. JTS had never been invited until 1972, when we were asked to bid for a Master Plan of the Mauritius Water Resources – with particular emphasis on meeting future potable water demands on the Island. (*This was to complement an ODA irrigation study just completed by Sir Murdoch MacDonald and Partners*). Binnie and Partners and Howard Humphreys were also invited to bid. Both these firms had considerable overseas experience; Howard Humphreys was in Kenya, Tanzania, and other former colonial territories, while Binnie was seen as <u>the</u> UK water supply Consultant, particularly in the UK, Hong Kong and elsewhere in Asia. The JTS recent overseas experience was mainly in wastewater engineering, and almost exclusively working in the Middle East; so, I saw us as 'making up numbers' for the bid rather than as a serious competitor. Our bid identified John Haseldine as the Partner–in–charge (who had considerable UK water supply experience); I put myself forward as Project Manager (with virtually no clean water experience, except that of a young graduate in Zambia); we engaged Economic Consultants Limited to give us credibility on cost analysis, demography and the review of existing industrial and commercial potential on the island, and Dr John Knill (later Professor Sir John Knill) as our dam/geology Consultant. Whatever we submitted seemed to please the adjudicators in Whitehall. We won the contest using ACE rates, and that was how I got to spend years visiting Mauritius.

MRT Consulting Engineers Limited

The collaboration Working at JTS was stimulating in the early 1970s. On the one hand, Partners would never take on a project they could not engineer themselves – and you can't get more complicated chemical and biological issues than those of dealing with high temperature wastewater in arid zones such as those the Firm had experienced in the Middle East. On the other hand, they all subscribed to global intentions, as did previous generations of JTS Partners who worked as far afield as St Petersburg, Bombay, and Shanghai. The Partners always lunched at St Stephen's Club in Queen Anne's Gate on the pretext of being too busy during the rest of the day to meet and discuss the firm's day-to-day problems. (*Binnie and Partners, the other consulting firm in Artillery House, overcame this by sitting around the table every morning to open the firm's post.*). Inevitably, when lunching at the 'Club', they met Partners from other consulting firms still based in Victoria Street. Gwilym Roberts found himself one day sitting with Partners of Sir Murdoch MacDonald and Partners (dams/agriculture), Mott Hay and Andersen (tunnels/roads/bridges) and Rendel Palmer and Tritton (roads/ railways/ bridges/ harbours); together, they were the world's experts across the full spectrum of civil engineering. The concept of a worldwide collaboration between the four firms was discussed, and a seed was sown. This developed a few months later into a formal collaboration, which they called MRT (the initials representing the four firms).

The MRT Committee I was the JTS representative on the MRT Committee. The committee met once a month with John Fleming of MMP, John Bartlett of MHA and Peter Cox of RPT (all Partners of their respective firms, with the latter two having been Presidents of the Institution of Civil Engineers). We talked mainly about South America and the Far East, where MHA and RPT had a presence. The intention was to identify mega-projects that would involve the expertise of all four firms. No such projects materialised at the time, and MRT soon became a listening post for MRT members in territories where only one of the four firms was present. We came to understand how the other firms behaved commercially, which was a real benefit to JTS.

Nigeria We had one or two forays into Nigeria. Before visiting for the first time, I met with Matthew Mbu, an 'international lawyer' whose daughter was a pupil to Barbara Calvert (John's barrister wife) at the Temple. Matthew was highly intelligent and rich, with five children, all costing him money at UK and US universities. I felt encouraged that I had found at least one friend in West Africa and headed for the BOAC terminal in Victoria to get the bus to Heathrow.

On arrival in Nigeria, Matthew invited me to lunch at his home on Lagos Island. I was to study two possible opportunities; first, a storm drainage solution for Lagos Island itself; and secondly, a trip out east to Biafra, where there had been a three-year bloody insurrection which only ended a few years before in 1970, with over one million dead. I stayed with an MHA ex-army surveyor in his bungalow close to Lagos Airport within a largely expat environment. I don't remember much about Lagos storm drainage, but I was fascinated by the one record he had that I thought I could listen to – Mahler's 1st Symphony. My musical education had yet to reach Mahler, and I really enjoyed this piece, which I played over and over again.

My trip to Biafra is also a deeply distant memory. I was accompanied to Enugu by a young local African engineer who insisted on introducing me to the local cuisine. I have always eaten what has been put in front of me, but this meal was a lamb stew where all the sheep's bones were included. I believe the concoction was allowed to ferment over time to give it that extra richness; the end result was a taste of unwashed dog that revolts me to this day; however, all was (and had to be) consumed. The trip concluded with my trying to 'check in' for a return flight to Lagos. There was no departure hall as we know it today. Instead, everybody was obliged to join the scrum in the African heat, surging three abreast in a totally un-British 'queue'. Bulk and a long arm were essential to progress towards a row

85

of booths in which 'check-in officials' were well protected from the herd by vertical iron bars. A passport and a ticket were insufficient to get you on the flight as the clerks were clearly waiting for something more than the regulated documentation.

Eventually, a local took pity on me and offered help. If I gave him my passport and ticket plus ten Naira, he could get me a seat reservation. I don't recommend this process at all. But it worked. We did win one contract in Nigeria - Paul Johnson designed a river intake at Ajaokuta (for a 30m differential in flood levels); we never got paid and learned some hard truths from this experience. There were one or two British Consultants who got sucked into Nigeria, including MMP and Ward Ashcroft and Parkman from Liverpool; but when I returned to Artillery House, my recommendation was to stay well clear of such countries.

Opportunities in Brazil MRT set up MASTER, a joint venture with a local Brazilian firm; John Hounslow from MHA became our resident representative. Both MHA and RPT had contracts in-country, and the potential looked encouraging. We were asked to submit a tender for designing a 250 MGD pumping station in Rio de Janeiro. This was within our competence because we had recently designed a similarly massive pumping station in Cairo. I had the bid documents translated from Portuguese, flew to Rio, and was met by a young Brazilian MASTER engineer who introduced me to the government department handling this international tender. My colleague was in awe of anything to do with Government. This opportunity was important for him, and, if we were to impress his potential client, it would secure brownie points for his future. In the taxi on our way to our first meeting, he showed real concern when I pulled my small strapless wristwatch out of my trouser pocket, the strap having long since perished (even though it was Swiss). Because I had been a serious violinist, I had a thing about wearing a strap around my left wrist (it weighed my arm down when holding the violin!). I was loath to replace the strap and found it comforting to have time in my pocket. My new friend considered this was definitely non-professional and not to be expected of an international Consultant.

> "Mr Price, when we are with the Government Engineer, can you please not take out your watch from your trouser pocket."

How weird, I thought and went back to reflect on the forthcoming meeting and how we might impress our prospective Latin American client.

I knew the consultancy fee was to be awarded as a lump sum. What I didn't have translated in the UK was the small print relating to the rules for awarding the contract. These were now explained to me. To my amazement, these 'rules' involved several rounds of mathematical decisions and were bizarre. The Brazilian Government had decided the consultancy fee would be 200 million Cruzeiro

Novo (about £150,000) - no consideration was allowed for rampant inflation nor for the firm's experience. This figure was not disclosed to the bidders, but for those locals with access to government officials, it was 'understood'. The small print I uncovered was this:

> "Round One - successful bidders will be those whose fixed price comes within 10% of Government's secret estimate. Round Two - Government will add together the prices of the successful bidders from Round One, add the Government's secret estimate, and divide the summation by the number of successful bidders from Round One (plus one) to reach a new mean for the 'contest'. Successful bidders of Round Two will be those whose fixed price comes within 10% of this new mean. This process will continue with more Rounds until a single Bidder is identified. In the event of a tie, the successful Bidder will be chosen at the toss of a coin".

No mathematical formula could determine a winning bid; we were engaging in a lottery, and the concept of tossing a coin was like some French farce. Why had we become involved in such a process? We sensibly declined to bid and headed for the airport.

Appointment in Brazil John Hounslow had spent two years in Rio and wanted to move to Hong Kong, where he had relatives in high places and with influence. The other three firms thought I would be a good replacement. Kay and I prepared to move out of Croydon again to live in Brazil; we even started to learn Portuguese. Two months later, the MRT committee decided to close MASTER down, and I was relieved not to have the responsibility of visiting Brazil again or learning their language. It was also the beginning of the end of any real effort in marketing the full capacity of the MRT team.

The momentum for growth among UK consulting engineers continued. Fifteen years later, there were different pressures, and JTS led the way by merging with Freeman Fox and Partners, who had different disciplines and geographies. MHA and MMP followed five years later to form Mott MacDonald. RPT had a less attractive future. Caught with business exposure in Libya (and the Libyan Government reneging on fees), they became an acquisition target, which was taken up by a previous employee who changed their name to High Point. Table 6.1 lists those Consultants in the water sector in the 1960s who were obliged to move with the times and merge or be bought out by other British or foreign Consultants.

Submissions as a business

The need to market Gwilym Roberts had been the main force for winning new JTS business in the Middle East and almost single-handedly secured long-term contracts in Abu Dhabi, Oman, and Cairo. After I was made a Partner in 1974, apart from several project duties, I was put in charge of bids for new work. We were heavily committed in the Middle East with profitable contracts, but this exposure could be dangerous in the event of an oil crisis or some other event, which might close business down in the region. The Partners decided to look for work elsewhere across the world. This meant I had to make regular trips to the World Bank (Washington), EEC/EU (Brussels), Asian Development Bank (Manila) and Eland House, Bressingham Place in Victoria (HQ of the UK's Overseas Development arm). Once or twice, I visited JICA (Tokyo) and DANIDA (Stockholm). The purpose of these visits was to make sure the firm's name was considered for a Consultant's short-list when financial institutions tendered a development project. It was a soul-destroying job because, although I was able to develop good relationships with technical officers concerned within each institution, in reality, unless you were visiting when the short-list was being prepared, the competition was eventually held between those who had just visited and those who had become regular 'pet' Consultants.

Athens Wastewater Treatment Plant, Pystallia Island

European Union We were sometimes invited to bid for EEC-funded projects and were fortunate to win two, Bahar Dar & Gondar Rural Water Supplies in Ethiopia (which lasted 8 years) and the project management for Athens' first wastewater treatment plant, the largest such works in Europe, which would take over the whole of Pystallia Island. This latter project was to be judged purely on man-months rates for four individuals of varying seniority, each with assumed durations determined by the EU. We played an 'intelligent' game, relying first on our experience of designing large-scale wastewater treatment plants and secondly on what levels of input we thought necessary for each category of staff for a project of this scope and size. We submitted high rates for the 'defined' shorter inputs and 'as low as we dare' rates for the longer inputs. Our four basic rates won us the job, but Brussels got considerable complaints from our European competitors citing 'unfair process'.

As it turned out, we were right in our assumptions and made a reasonable profit, but not before much argument with the Greek Government. (They were determined not to have outside Consultants supervising any project in Greece, where the standard practice of civil servants was to squirrel away monies to their own advantage, whatever the source of funding). It took 6-months of prevarication in Brussels between Eurocrats and Greek government ministers before common sense prevailed, and we were allowed to commence our assignment.

As more of our business came from overseas, the workload of preparing submissions increased. Damodar Shirwaiker joined the submissions team early on, followed by Peter Beattie, Eric Combes, and Chris Bosker. Writing proposals had become a business in its own right.

Preparing a mega bid

Map of Egypt

Egypt's National Water Plan In 1976, JTS was successful in winning an international competition to prepare a Master Plan for Cairo Wastewater in a joint venture with Binnie and Partners. The two firms believed it appropriate to form a new consultancy for this work, Taylor Binnie & Partners (TBP). A World Bank-funded assignment emerged in 1978 to develop a potable water supply National Plan for the whole of Egypt (outside of Cairo, Alexandria, and the Suez Canal, towns which had recently had studies undertaken by USAID). The UN had decreed the 1980s would be the Water Decade, after which time the whole of the world would have access to potable water. Egypt's National Plan would ensure the country's politicians were in a position to act throughout the coming decade to respond to this UN Directive. TBP decided to make every effort in Washington to ensure we won the 'British' ticket to bid for this Project with an estimated fee of US$2 million, which in 1970s terms was huge and was indeed the largest fee by far that either firm had ever secured for a 'study.'

We won the British ticket and knuckled down to put together a bid that would outmanoeuvre our US, European and Japanese competitors. Bob Arah of Binnies would be the Project Director, and I nominated myself as his Deputy, being fifteen years his junior! We joined forces with Dr Ahmed Abdul Warith. The 'Doctor' had been a professor of Public Health Engineering at Cairo University. We believed he was well thought of at the Ministry of Works because he had been appointed by President Nasser to design the rehabilitation of the water and sewerage systems for Alexandria and the Suez Canal towns after the Israeli onslaught of the 1967 Six Day War. We all put forward candidates with appropriate experience in major studies, practical water engineering and Middle East experience and pruned them down to present a strong relevant team that comprised the great and the good of the three firms. Our competitors lacked in-country experience because Egypt had been off-limits to the West since Nasser exerted his authority on the world stage in 1956, so our presence in Cairo since 1976 was important.

Negotiation and the sweet sweat of success The Ministry concluded that our proposal was the most attractive, and we were called to Cairo to see if they could negotiate a contract with us. Bob Arah was in charge of Binnie's Chester office, so I went to meet him in the comfort of his own environment. He was a King's College Cambridge graduate and had earned his spurs as Resident Engineer on the Cameron Highlands Dam in Malaysia, which 'qualified' him to become a Binnie Partner. He was an intelligent man of about 50 who was always reading Aeschylus, Byron, or some such tome. This was in stark contrast to my reading matter of Wilbur Smith and John Grisham, which made me feel inferior.

Bob and I went to Cairo in August 1978, which happened to coincide with Ramadan that year. This did not augur well to be interrogated by Ministry officials who were fasting during the day and 'gorging' after sundown until the early hours. Cairo was hot and dusty in the summer months, and air conditioning in the Ministry building was limited to leaving windows open, and then only if they could be prised open. Ministry staff wore sleeveless shirts that had never seen an iron. Sensible. Bob insisted that our attire would be a suit and tie. Ridiculous. I was sure our interrogators thought it was not surprising Nasser threw the British out if it was a national characteristic to behave in this way. The exercise turned out to be detailed and tedious. We were obliged to explain our methodology, and then they went through everybody's CV. There was always some criticism related to inexperience or irrelevance to Egypt. Several times they scoffed at the age of an individual and how could he be described as an 'expert' with not a grey hair on his body. Bob was a good negotiator and poker player. He did not allow the inquisitors to divert our mission to secure this assignment with staff intact and at the rates submitted. I must have registered a modicum of self-consciousness that some of our engineers being criticised were older than I was, to which their reply was

"Ah, but you are a Principal."

It put me in my place, but I still felt a certain injustice at some of the staff being downgraded by the Ministry when we knew their excellence was exceptional.

90

After four sweltering days of going through our proposal line-by-line, from cover to cover, we were invited to sign the contract and commence mobilisation.

Bob and I retired to the Hilton Hotel for a celebratory 'je ne sais quoi'. The trouble with Bob was he didn't know either. Having spent four concentrated days negotiating ourselves out of holes that appeared inescapable, Bob spent a good twenty minutes not being able to decide whether to have tea, a cool drink, beer, or a whisky. I believe there may be a syndrome that relates to his predicament – dependent personality disorder, aboulia, or may be Hamlet syndrome? We had secured the contract and so to bed, Bob with Aeschylus and me with Wilbur Smith.

The next day, we spoke with Hugh Ellingham, the Binnie Taylor HR man on the Cairo wastewater team. He was about six foot three or four and broad with it; and extremely knowledgeable about how to administer a team in Cairo. He gave us several pointers as to what to do and what not to do with a team of engineers in this very busy city ("*don't have salad in the Hilton, because lettuce is washed in the adjacent canal close to a raw sewage outfall*" was one such advice). We then headed home to London to invite about twenty staff to spend a couple of years in a foreign land. Their work would require them to visit the whole of Egypt along the River Nile, from Aswan in the South to the highly cultivated Nile Delta in the North (and the Governorates of Beheira and Kafr el Sheikh, in particular).

Liverpool

The Merseyside Development Corporation MDC was formed in 1981 to renovate the Albert Dock for the 1984 Tall Ships race and the adjacent site at Otterspool for the 1984 International Garden Festival. In 1982, our Liverpool office bid and won a contract with MDC to deal with Liverpool's principal wastewater outfall installed in the 1700s. This passed under the Albert Dock in a wooden inverted syphon and discharged its flow untreated into the River Mersey. MDC 'owned' this outfall because North West Water had refused to take over the works (in 1974) on the grounds they had no knowledge of the structural integrity of 1700s engineering! The public did not see the untreated discharge because Liverpool's docklands lay between the city and the river. (*Out of Sight, Out of Mind,* was the title of a UK Government 1980s white paper on pollution in the environment.) Once the Albert Dock was renovated, however, the public would have access to the riverside and see and smell untreated wastewater being discharged into the River Mersey from Liverpool's 500,000 population. This was going to become a serious environmental health problem.

Liverpool's lack of treatment facilities Not all marketing initiatives lead to success. The city continued to have no wastewater treatment facilities in the mid-1980s. Michael Heseltine MP (who had been responsible for Liverpool's rebirth) was asked to chair a conference at which North West Water and the public were to debate options for solving Liverpool's unacceptable wastewater disposal situation. JTS had had a Liverpool Office for over 20 years, led by Alan Verncombe (Father of Colin Verncombe, pop star of *Black* fame). Gwilym Roberts (who was soon to become President of The Institution of Civil Engineers) decided he would make a presentation at this conference. In the early 1970s, he had been the engineer for the North Wirral 5km long sea outfall that had been deemed a great success. Could we come up with a solution to collect Liverpool's wastewater and, after pre-treatment, discharge it way out into Liverpool Bay? The firm's marine experience was in our Plymouth office. Roger Howard was instructed to undertake a desk study of the wind, tide, and other hydrographic behaviour to see how far offshore that discharge point should be for the effluent not to return into the tidal estuary. We developed a plausible project; Gwilym prepared visual aids and a basic text, and we were off by train to the Liverpool conference. We sat down in the front row with Alan Verncombe, presenting a solid national/local team. Michael Heseltine opened the proceedings and welcomed proposals from the floor that might shed light on how to resolve Liverpool's wastewater problem. He gave us confidence that our proposal would get a fair hearing.

The North West Water's proposal Brian Staples, Engineering Director for North West Water, was the first speaker to present his water company's point of view. In a monotonous voice, he spent over half an hour describing their solution to build a wastewater treatment plant in the disused Sandon Dock and discharge the treated effluent into the River Mersey:

> *"We have been given permission to do this by the Mersey Docks and Harbour Board so long as it is deemed to be 'port orientated activity. The Company has bought a vessel, therefore, to convey all sludge generated at the new plant and drop it into the Irish Sea."*

We had discounted sea disposal of sludge, believing the EU would ban such activity within the next ten years – which they did. Having made his technical presentation, Brian turned to Michael Heseltine and said in a derogatory tone:

> *"You see, we have a plan. Just give us the money, and we will show those buggers from the South we are quite capable of managing our own affairs. Thank you,"* ......

.... and sat down.

The delegates were awestruck by this display of ostentatious bravado. Gwilym thought for a moment and then reached the wise decision that now was not the time to debate with a hostile NW Water Director in his own territory and in public. The carefully prepared JTS proposal to use the aggression of the sea to treat

Liverpool's wastewater well out of sight and mind (maybe as far as 15km offshore) remains unsaid and tucked away in the firm's archives. Local politics have to be understood, but sometimes they can be overpowering.

Later, NW Water spent £200m to develop their treatment plant at the former Sandon Dock. By the time it was commissioned, the EU had ruled dumping sludge at sea inadmissible. NW Water was obliged to sell the sludge vessel – and thus, any 'port-orientated activity' was terminated.

Malaysia

Resident representation In the late 1970s and early 80s, David Yaw was based first in Hong Kong and then in Kuala Lumpur with a remit to win JTS new business in the Far East. He was an entrepreneur *par excellence*. We put many a bid together for Indonesia, Malaysia, and Thailand. He 'held my hand' when visiting the Asian Development Bank (ADB) in Manila. As a quid pro quo, I allowed my shoulder to be cried on by Arlette, his lovely French wife, who had to manage with David away for far too many days and weeks elsewhere in the Far East chasing business.

Nationwide water project The best bid we put together was for the UK's Overseas Development Ministry (ODM) in 1987 to provide advice and technical assistance to the Federal JKR (Ministry of Public Works) during the implementation of a US$350m rural water supplies turnkey project, involving many individual schemes across Peninsula Malaysia, North Borneo, and Sarawak. The history of this project dates back to 1981. Maggie Thatcher cancelled free education in the UK for rich foreign diplomats and politicians. Whereas most former recipients understood her motive, the Malaysian Prime Minister (Mahathir Mohamad) objected strongly and decreed a 'buy British last' policy for all government contracts. This ruling held fast for 5-years, after which time diplomats from both countries began to argue that enough was enough. This rural water supply project was conceived by one of Maggie's bright captains of industry, Adrian White of Biwaters, and had become a highly political initiative. The UK Government wanted to see their UK contribution (£50 million) was well spent and value for money, so we were determined to win this assignment. We had the advantage of being the only UK Consultant working on water projects in Malaysia at the time (Petaling Jaya Non-revenue Water Project for Selangor JKR and Kluang Water Supply Scheme in Johor financed by World Bank). We knew the details of the project and the JKR technocrats involved. None of our competitors had the opportunity to visit Malaysia, let alone understand local politics, which were a vital component of our proposal. We were bold to offer Bob Owens, a JTS Associate Partner, as our proposed resident representative, who was a highly experienced engineer and had just finished being our Project Manager in Santiago, Chile. We worked hard on the submission content, using visual aids on local knowledge, detail of which our competitors would not know about, to conceive an 'unbeatable' bid. Our offer turned out to be unbeatable.

Privatisation of the UK Water Industry 1989

Opportunities for Consultants Margaret Thatcher had signed an all-embracing agricultural agreement with the EU in Brussels, which included small print requiring member countries to significantly improve treated water quality distributed to consumers, and effluent discharged to rivers and coastal waters. She returned to London and asked UK water industry leaders what implications the small print represented for the UK Government. She was horrified to be told that the improved standards required an injection of £10bn of capital for which consumers would perceive very little benefit. This bombshell resulted in Maggie privatising the whole industry in 1989 to relieve Government of both future capital investment and liability for water quality, as these would be picked up by the private sector.

All ten regional water and sewerage companies were instructed to prepare five- and ten-year plans to meet the new EU quality targets. The investment had to be supported financially, assuming a maximum increase in water tariff of 4.5% per annum. Their detailed plans had to be approved by Ian Byatt, the Director General of OFWAT, who was able to impose fines, both for late delivery of capital investment and for any contravention of the new quality standards. Preparation of such plans was a major task, and implementation posed significant opportunities for UK Consultants in detailed design and construction supervision, particularly with Ian Byatt's sword of Damocles of fines for non-performance hanging over the private water and sewerage companies. In 1987, JTS merged with Freeman Fox & Partners to form Acer Consultants Ltd. The privatisation of the water industry, therefore, presented an opportunity for this new larger organisation, with its increased marketing power and influence within the infrastructure industries.

Severn Trent Water ST Water had identified in their "Offer for Sale on behalf of the Secretary of State for the Environment" dated October 1989, that their future capital works programme:

> "...represents a major expansion of Severn Trent Water's capital and infrastructure expenditure and a major commitment in terms of management and engineering resources. The Directors have confidence in their programme. They believe that the programme can be managed effectively and will be seeking improvements in capital productivity."

In practice, ST Water was predicting an annual spend of more than double their historical cost. We learnt that Watson Hawksley, one of our main UK competitors, was in the process of clinching a deal with ST Water to undertake a large slice of their capital works programme. Acer Consultants had no recent work with this particular utility. The ST Water Prospectus looked 'inviting', so we decided to make a serious proposal to out-manoeuvre Watson Hawksley. I went to Birmingham with our Chief Executive, Eric Bridgen, and briefed him on the train as to the detail of ST Water's situation. Eric was not an engineer. His background had been in chemical industry marketing for BP and BOC; and (before joining Freeman Fox as a non-executive director in 1986) he had been Managing Director of IMS, the UK Government's 'gun-running' business. We met with Frank Earnshaw, ST Water's Director of Operations, whom I had never met before. I was about to witness a class act on how to win business without knowing what on earth you were talking about. My role was to shield Eric from technical questions that might compromise our integrity:

> "We have read your Company Plans for capital spend" started Eric "and notice that whereas your budget is to spend £150m in the current year, you have agreed with OFWAT to spend £2,300m by 1995 and a further £1,700m between 1995 and 2000. That is a huge expansion for the Company. I see also Severn Trent employs 80 firms of Consultants to carry out individual components of your capital investment. Because they are separate entities, you have no control over any of them in how they perform, either in terms of quality or in delivering the final product on time."

Frank did not deny any of these facts.

> "Let me make you a proposal", Eric continued, "Acer does not work for you today, but we are the largest UK player in water and wastewater engineering both at home and overseas. Acer and Severn Trent should form a Birmingham-based joint-venture company, who would be given a pre-determined amount of Severn Trent's capital works programme to design year by year. Acer would manage the whole operation and bring non-water engineering projects into the JV Company; and at some stage in the future, the JV company would seek work overseas in its own right, in line with Severn Trent policy. We would offer Severn Trent 35% of this JV Company's shares and allow you two non-executive board members. If the JV company ever appeared to be failing in performance, Severn Trent would have the right to take over the running of the JV company until such time as performance was back on track, at which time management of the JV Company would return to Acer. This would mean Severn Trent achieves control over whatever component of its capital investment programme is entrusted to the JV

95

company. With 35% of profits returning to Severn Trent, such work would, in effect, be undertaken at 'cut-price."

Frank was clearly not expecting this diatribe from us and was impressed but lost for words. He recommended we put a proposal in writing to his CEO, Roderick Paul, who would give it serious consideration and then discuss it with his Chairman, John Bellack and the Director of Business Planning & Marketing, Victor Cocker (whose brother is Jarvis Cocker, the pop star of *Pulp* fame).

We wrote the proposal letter on the train as we returned to London and had it hand-delivered within 24 hours of our meeting. The concept was alien to the UK water industry, but the Severn Trent management was at the birth of a new era where they had the ability to approve our proposal, as they were masters of their own destiny. The ST Water Board accepted the principle, and Acer Engineering Ltd was formed. The two ST Water Board members of the JV Company were John Banyard and Richard Satchell (who had joined JTS in 1964 and with whom I had shared a drawing office in Artillery House. He left JTS ten years later to work for the National Rivers Authority and later joined ST Water when the NRA was disbanded in 1989).

The new Joint Venture Company was a huge success with a turnover of £10 million per annum after three years of operation (which was the same level of revenue JTS had as a whole in 1987, prior to the merger with Freeman Fox). The Birmingham-based Manager of Acer Engineering was Dick Taylor, a 'Freeman Fox' highways engineer, so it was appropriate for the M4 motorway widening between Junctions 4 and 10 to be 'injected' into the JV as promised and designed in the Acer Engineering Birmingham Office – after engaging contractors, the Government of the day pulled the plug on this and many other highway projects, only to be re-enacted 30 years later in 2020.

Northumbrian Water With the success of Acer Engineering Ltd under our belt, we looked to see which other water utility companies might be interested in our joint venture model. Northumbrian Water was small but a potential target. Nick Paul and I visited Newcastle and put forward such a proposal, which was accepted rather too quickly. This might have been because their aspirations were to become a significant overseas operator. A handful of such assignments would double the size of their UK operation and hence become a real benefit to shareholders. A deal was struck with Northumbrian Water to allow all their in-house design staff to transfer to the Acer Group. All issues were resolved except how to make the attractive Northumbrian staff pension arrangements (civil service-based) compatible with that of the more modest Acer pension scheme. Our Acer Group HR Director Kate Price (no relation) spent ages on the phone and flying up to Newcastle to discuss the issue with her opposite HR director. Six months passed, and then the Northumbrian Water CEO was fired. His successor was not a supporter of the JV, and so the initiative fell by the wayside.

Southern Water A few years prior to privatisation, Southern Water purchased McDowell Consulting Engineers to bolster their in-house design team. We made approaches to Southern Water in 1990 to bring their in-house design unit within the Acer Group. Nick Paul and I made several visits to their Head Office in Worthing. Negotiations were with Southern Water's Managing Director, Bruce Hewett. We proposed the same principles for operation, management, and ownership as we had put forward to Northumbria Water. Eventually, our proposal was agreed upon, put to the Southern Water Board, and accepted. During the final stages of bringing the two teams together, Acer acquired the US firm PSC Engineers & Consultants Inc. from their parent group, the Philadelphia Suburban Water Corporation. As soon as the news that Acer had moved into the US market was in the public domain, the Chairman of Southern Water, Sir William Courtney (who was big in Anglian windows), was incensed. Anything American was anathema to him, apparently, and he wanted to renege on the Agreement, even though his Board had approved the deal. He made a telephone call to Eric Bridgen:

"The deal is off ...."

... he said and put the phone down.

That was a shame because we were likely to have an annual fee turnover in this subsidiary of £2 to £3 million. In practice, Southern Water continued for the next ten years or so to design virtually all their capital works programme in-house, and eventually, Nick Paul (*fellow Partner in JTS*) went to head up this unit.

Shortly after Courtney's outburst, Acer was successful in bidding for two of the few projects Southern Water was to outsource. The first was for Brighton's Wastewater Disposal Project. We proposed a large, combined stormwater storage facility to be located under Brighton's famous esplanade, releasing flows eastwards for full treatment at the existing works below Rottingdean cliffs, once the storm had passed. The second project was to collect all stormwater generated at the new Eurotunnel rail terminal at Folkestone and divert it underneath the riverless Folkestone out to sea.

The Rest We were already the 'Consultant of choice' for dealing with wastewater from coastal towns for South West Water and Wessex Water. Thames Water was too big and unapproachable, whereas we thought Anglian Water and Yorkshire Water were too small. The Welsh had acquired the small Welsh consultancy, Wallace Evans. North West Water was arrogant and believed they needed no outside help (particularly from a southern firm). They decided later to form a relationship with Bechtel, the US engineering giant, to manage their in-house design team. We did bid through our Liverpool Office for a rare out-sourced tender and became NW's advisory engineer for the Blackpool wastewater disposal project as mentioned above, which had similarities to that which we had proposed for Brighton. Later, we engineered their outfalls for the coastal towns of Whitehaven, Workington and Maryport.

The United States

An opportunity in a foreign land Our newly found friends at Severn Trent were keen to enter the US market and had identified a potential acquisition of a small operations and maintenance (O&M) business, which was part of the Philadelphia Suburban Corporation (PSC). This business was owned by a subsidiary called PSC Engineers & Consultants Inc., based in Lancaster, Pennsylvania. Roderick Paul asked us if we wanted to buy this US consulting firm. If so, they would enter into an agreement to purchase the O&M business from us immediately after we had acquired the US consultancy. The consulting firm had about 140 staff and operated principally in Pennsylvania and Maryland, with a focus on water and wastewater. Acer's business plan was silent on the question of operating in the US. However, after a 'modest' discussion between Eric Bridgen, Terry Baughan, our finance director, Nick Paul, and myself, we decided it was an opportunity worth looking at if only to curry favour with Severn Trent, our now largest UK water client.

Philadelphia Suburban Corporation The origins of PSC go back to 1886. By 1990, it was supplying water to a population of 240,000 around the outskirts of Philadelphia in Chester and Delaware Counties. It was an old-fashioned water supply-only company very similar to the not-for-profit model we had in the UK before 1989 (like Essex Water, Colne Valley Water and the Folkestone and District Water). I flew with Eric Bridgen to Philadelphia and visited the company's Head Office in Bryn Mawr (you can't get more Welsh than that!). We met with PSC's chief finance officer, who appeared keen to be 'rid' of this subsidiary. At the meeting, Eric and I were at our diplomatic best and secured the necessary information for us to perform a 'due diligence'. We met with Chairman John W. Boyer Jr, who waved the PSC flag and was encouraged to do an 'entente cordial' with the Brits. We then said our goodbyes and headed for the airport and home. By the time we landed at Heathrow, we had established this US consulting firm was not profitable and, in recent years, had annual losses of around US$300,000. Eric met with Roderick Paul to keep ST Water sweet and told him his invitation was not without 'a challenge'.

John W Boyer Jr

How to negotiate a purchase. There are many ways to purchase and transform a company into profitability and long-term health, lots of people have done it; but we had not. This consultancy company was a million miles away across The Pond in a culture we thought we might know (in reality, we didn't – just passing through immigration at Philadelphia airport should have told us that). Eric persuaded himself we could turn the company around. He then received a telephone call from the States to say John W. Boyer Jr was coming to London on holiday with his wife, and could we entertain him? Eric saw this as an opportunity. He discovered John Boyer's wife was a keen gardener. Kay, my wife, is a hugely talented and creative gardener. She was given instruction to take John Boyer's wife to the RHS at Wisley for the whole afternoon, which should give us enough time to 'interview' John at our Head Office on the Surrey Research Park in Guildford. I am embarrassed to say I was party to an immaculate charade which obliged a company chairman to part with his subsidiary. Eric sat John in our conference room and persuaded him to tell us what a financial burden PSC Engineers & Consultants Inc. was to his whole Group operation. This put Eric in a strong negotiating position. He put an offer on the table, which was not for negotiation:

> *"We would have an uphill struggle to turn PSC Engineers & Consultants Inc. around because today's losses are consistent and large. We lack any understanding of US culture, but we do perceive this may be a building block for us to expand in the US outside Pennsylvania."*

You could see John W. Boyer Jr was encouraged and warming to Eric's suave British approach:

> *"We think there is an opportunity for us to share the profits of the consultancy with you once we have turned the company around."*

The Chairman began to beam with enthusiasm at what Eric was saying.

> *"But in order for us to do so, we cannot afford to pay more than US$1 for the consultancy."*

John W Boyer Jr nearly fell off his chair as he shifted uncomfortably to counteract the blow to his self-esteem, as though it had been landed by Cassius Clay. That was all. Eric had delivered his message, and the Chairman was left to digest it in a foreign land on his own, in a room full of insurgents whom George Washington had repelled; was he strong enough to do the same and maintain his dignity? He asked to use the phone and backed off into a small side room while he had a conversation with his Chief Finance Officer in Bryn Mawr. It was not a happy telephone conversation, and we could hear the expletives from where we sat. John W. had been given instruction and returned to suggest we had a deal if we could raise our offer to US$100,000. We stayed our ground and were adamant that, for us to participate in the US market, we could not risk any capital at all. Our generosity in sharing profits was the only carrot the Acer Board would entertain. John W. looked unwell. He was here on holiday; the thought of phoning Bryn Mawr again was the last thing he wanted to do; and he was wondering how his wife was getting on with Kay. Eventually, he got up and asked to phone his Head Office again. There was more irate talk, but it became clear that, whatever happens, PSC Engineers & Consultants Inc. was no longer a business the PSC Group wished to be in. John W. reappeared and beamed as much as he could to say we had a deal – so long Acer no longer has the right to use the name PSC. We suggested a name change to Acer Engineers & Consultants Inc., shook hands, followed by smiles all round. He then produced two volumes of Reflections on Water – a centennial history of Philadelphia Suburban Water Company 1886 - 1986 and handed one to each of us. In mine, he wrote

"To Jessop Price. May our first meeting be the beginning of a continuing relationship in water"
and signed it
John W. Boyer Jr.

I visited Bryn Mawr again, but this time with powers to purchase PSC Engineers & Consultants Inc., which transaction was undertaken successfully. I then met immediately in an adjacent room with a Severn Trent official who purchased the O&M subsidiary, as previously agreed. Our deals were complete. We did have a continuing relationship with PSC for the rest of my days with Acer/Hyder, but I think our annual financial figures were perhaps massaged to keep profitability teasingly out of reach.

Success in the water and wastewater sector

Basic principles Our approach to winning new work was based on two principles; first, undertake all assignments to the very best of your ability (and thus have happy clients to continue engaging us) and secondly, be aggressive in the search for new work by broadening our geographical base and becoming a prospective client's 'consultant of choice'.

Increases in revenue Before we merged with Freeman Fox in 1987, the JTS annual revenue in water and wastewater was about £10m. After the merger, we called ourselves Acer Consultants, and I had two roles in the business: Head of marketing across the enlarged firm and Head of the Group's water and wastewater sector. Revenues began to increase with our success in the UK water and wastewater market, as well as widening our base in the Middle East, entering the US market and winning work in Europe and the Far East. In 1989, we were acquired by Welsh Water and became known as Hyder Consulting. This had some positive marketing points, but it meant an end to our lucrative Acer Engineering Ltd joint venture with Severn Trent. When I was 'retired' in 1997, our annual revenue in the water and wastewater sector was £63m (*up from £57m in 1996*). In the ten years I was in charge of the Acer/Hyder water & wastewater sector, revenue increased six-fold. This turnover was massive compared with our competitors' and, from evidence in the New Civil Engineer Consultants File of 1998, we were, without doubt, the principal UK water and wastewater Consultant. The equivalent 1997 revenue of our nearest competitors were:

Table 6.1	1997 Revenue - UK Water & Wastewater consultancy market
Hyder Consulting	£63m (*£57m in 1996*)
Montgomery Watson	£38m (*£29m*)
Binnie Black and Veatch	£33m (*£23m*)
Mott MacDonald	£30m (*£29m*)
Halcrow	£23m (*£21m*)
WS Atkins	£16m (*£12m*)
Gibb	£14m (*£14m*)
Babtie Group	£10m (*£ 9m*)

Sadly, after I left Hyder, the firm's annual revenue stream in the sector began to decline and was only £55m at the millennium, but by 2013, it had grown back to circa £70m.

The Group was acquired by Arcardis NV in 2014, which has 27,000 employees worldwide. Today, Hyder Consulting has a more diverse business focus engaging in such sectors as energy, mining, and space, but it still continues with those of its parent companies in transportation, infrastructure, and the environment.

Dubai Twin Towers

Dubai became my fiefdom During my time at Hyder, I was responsible to the Board for the whole of its Middle East business from 1992 to 1997. Dubai had been a merchant's enclave since biblical times. With the introduction of Islam in the 7th century, trading and religion went hand in hand with the Indian subcontinent and East Africa. The British signed an exclusive business deal with the Maktoums in 1892, and Dubai became one of the Protectorates shortly thereafter. That is why today, Dubai is so pro-British, and once oil was produced in 1969, Freeman Fox benefited by designing half of the Emirate's road infrastructure.

Model of the Dubai Twin Towers

Negotiations commence Harvey Binnie was our local representative in Dubai. In 1995, he identified a private initiative of Sheikh Mohammed bin Rashid Al Maktoum (*third son of the Emir, Râshid bin Sa`îd Âl Maktûm*) to design and project manage a US$350m construction project to build twin towers, both triangular in plan (*one 355m high, to be the 10th tallest building in the world, the other only 309m*) produced by a Canadian architect. One of the towers would house the staff of Emirates Airlines, while the other was to be designed as a hotel; the whole project represented a birthday present from Sheikh Mohammed to his brother, apparently. I was called to Dubai to meet Brigadier Michael Lovat Barclay, Sheikh Mohamed's financial adviser and confidant, who was trusted to implement his most significant decisions. Brigadier Barclay had been a soldier in the British army until 1979 and ended up in command of the Dubai Defence Force. He clearly had an enviable rapport with Sheikh Mohamed and was asked to stay on as his professional mentor. The Brigadier was a larger-than-life character whose negotiation strategy to lower the other side's guard was to engage in a wealth of amusing anecdotes with no constraint on the topic. I would not have liked to get on the wrong side of him. He was a Korean War veteran and known to have acted for the Sheikh to remove those who took advantage of the Maktoum trust. I liked him, we had no other agenda, so it didn't matter if our 'guard' was down; we just enjoyed each other's company.

Requirement to provide a guarantee The Brigadier informed us we were one of two Consultants Sheikh Mohammed wished to invite to design his Project, the other being Ove Arup. We both had skyscraper design capabilities, although it must be said Ove Arup was by far the more experienced, our skill being based in Melbourne, Australia, through the acquisition of Wargon Chapman. The Brigadier was not a technical man and assumed we were both equal to the job. There were a number of contractual issues which were his responsibility to resolve. The most critical negotiation for the Consultant was the requirement to provide a financial guarantee for the full value of the Project (in the event the towers fell down, he said!). The Brigadier let it be known Ove Arup was having difficulty in providing this surety. I spoke with Stuart Doughty, Hyder's CEO in London. By this time, Hyder was part of the Welsh Water Group, and Stuart was a Group Board member. He agreed to try to gain the support of Graham Hawker, the Welsh

Water Group CEO and then take it to the Welsh Water Board for approval. To our considerable surprise, Welsh Water eventually agreed to meet this commitment, not as a formal Banker's Bond, but as a Letter of Surety for US$350m, signed off by the Board. Such action meant we had seen off Ove Arup.

The Sheikh also wanted to have the complete design team based in Dubai for the duration of the project. We were not happy with this. Our expertise was spread across the world; architects in Canada, structural engineers in Australia, mechanical & electrical engineers in London and civil engineers who could be based anywhere. If all these disciplines were permanently resident in Dubai, they would inevitably be working part-time. We argued this would not be the best use of their time. To counter the Sheikh's wishes, we proposed providing a dedicated office in Dubai divided in two, one to house our civil engineers and the other to be a specialist 'war cabinet' comprising our four discipline leaders in architecture, structures, the clever electrical/mechanical engineering (for lifts, air conditioning, etc.) and civil engineering. 'Chinese walls' would be religiously upheld between the 'war cabinet' and the rest of the Hyder team, wherever they were located, be it Vancouver, Melbourne, London, or Dubai. To make this a practical solution, we would develop an 'electronic drawing chest' where all our teams could make changes to their own drawings but only comment on each other's drawings. This would allow individual team members to be aware of the thought processes of every other team member as the project evolved, creating much more efficiency, and reducing the costs of our contract. The team would be working a 24-hour day across the world, which was an issue that seemed to impress. The Brigadier was convinced and accepted our proposal.

Trouble at mill All looked good for our appointment. The Brigadier held me back after the meeting and said, in a confidential sort of way:

"*We have a problem*". I politely asked him to be specific.

"*Your agent in Dubai is Mahdi Al Tajir.*"

"Yes," I replied, "*but he has never brought us any work in Dubai so far, not even this initiative. Is there a conflict of interest?*"

"*No. But we are not surprised he has failed to win you any Government business. He is very well connected, very rich, too rich. In fact, the Sheikh thought he was richer than their family, so they packed him off to London to be the Nation's Ambassador at the Court of St James in 1971 (where he stayed until 1987) in the belief it would restrain his money-making activities. It didn't. The problem for the Sheikh is not so much that he is rich, but he makes no investment at all in Dubai's development. Sheikh Maktoum does not want any part of your fee ending up with Al Tajir. That is the nub of our problem."*

I understood the predicament. Somehow, we had to relieve Al Tajir of his Agency commitment to Hyder Consulting. I went back to the Dubai Office and shared the news with Harvey, whom I found to be already celebrating our victory over Ove Arup. He recognised his celebrations were premature, so we diverted our attention to looking at our options. Eric Bridgen and Jim Robinson were responsible for proposing Mahdi Al Tajir as our Agent throughout the UAE as a result of pressure from the Abu Dhabi Sewerage Committee, our most favoured client in the Gulf. The due diligence had been flawed because, although Al Tajir's credentials looked immaculate, we had failed to uncover the fact that he lacked credibility to secure Dubai Government work. Much to my relief, I discovered there was a Termination Clause in the Agency Agreement and clutching this close to my chest, I headed for Al Tajir's office.

"Good luck" was all I heard from Harvey as his office door closed behind me.

Negotiations with your agent Mahdi Al Tajir has a gentle manner, but to be so rich he must have a ruthless business streak, which should not be tampered with lightly. I had met his soft side, drunk many cups of Arabian coffee in his office, which was festooned with antique silver artefacts and silk carpets. He owns 15,000 acres of Perthshire near Gleneagles as well as Highland Water, the Sheraton Park Hotel in Knightsbridge, and Mereworth Castle, and it was believed he had the world's largest collections of antique silver and Persian rugs. Two years before this meeting, he had paid £2.27m at Christie's for a 1736 silver chandelier made by Balthasar Friedrich Behrens. This is the man whose office I was about to enter to relieve him of being our Sponsor, for which we were under contract to pay him an annual retainer of £10,000 plus 10% of all fees we earn in the UAE. My task appeared brief. Lay the Agency Agreement on his pristine table, draw his attention to the Termination Clause, and head for the door. All this I did, and Al Tajir's reaction was expected but not quite to the severity that emanated from this 'gentle' man.

"Who has told you I am not accepted as a genuine Agent in Dubai?"

I calmly and as diplomatically as I could, replied it was Sheikh Maktoum via Brigadier Barclay. I thought World War III had broken out. There was a lot of Arabic, none of which I understood, but I was left with an explicit impression he was not pleased with what I had just said. He then went on to tell me Brigadier Barclay was a snake and a conniving irritable has-been, and as for the Sheikh, he said:

"We are like family, my children have grown up with his children, how can he suggest an honest Dubai citizen and businessman cannot be a

genuine Agent for an internationally renowned company" – or that was the gist of what he was saying.

"I will not let you break our Contract"

"But we have a Termination Clause drafted specifically for such a situation as this"

Al Tajir smiled at me (more of a smirk). *"Mr Price, how long have you been doing business in the Middle East? When two parties enter into a Contract, we shake hands, and this becomes a binding contract between us - for life! No, I will not release you from your obligation, and you can go and tell the Brigadier that I am disgusted; with all his experience of working in Dubai, he should know better than to recommend you abandon your obligations to me."*

I felt like replying, "Do I take that is a 'no', then?" but I thought it might bring on another tirade. Diplomacy must be my best course of action - limit the debate and withdraw gracefully without too much further damage either to his self-esteem or to my understanding of the human race. I stood up and politely thanked him for his frank and unambiguous point of view. We shook hands, and I left by giving him the confidence I understood his position completely and would consider (in the calm of our Dubai office) how to move forward to win this Contract for the Twin Towers, in full knowledge of the predicament in which we both find ourselves.

"I shan't release you from your obligations" he repeated as the door shut behind me with a bang.

I should have loved to stay on as a fly on the wall and hear how his side of the story unfurled, but this was not the time to dilly dally as we had some decisions to make. I returned to London the next day, but before leaving Dubai, I took advantage of going to see the Brigadier on my own and report back regarding the content of my meeting with Mahdi Al Tajir. He was not surprised at Al Tajir's harsh words, but I think he was genuinely sorry for my having been put through the experience. He advised me to let things lie low for a while to see if any attitudes might change once the dust had settled. He did let on that Mahdi Al Tajir had been to see Sheikh Mohammed, but he was not able to persuade the Sheikh to change his point of view.

Sweet Mediterranean Two weeks later, I received a telephone call from Mahdi Al Tajir's Personal Assistant inviting me to an audience with 'our Agent' at his villa in Nice. I had never been to the South of France, let alone to a 'rich man's' villa. He paid for my flight, and his chauffeur, of Middle Eastern origin, was waiting for me at Aérport Nice Côte d'Azur, together with his larger-than-life Mercedes. I was shown all the interior hospitality features and driven luxuriously eastwards along the Promenade des Anglais with panoramic views of the Mediterranean reaching all the way to the horizon until we reached Saint-Jean-Cap-Ferrat. Here, property density reduced somewhat. The car slowed as the distance between villas increased. When we reached the end of the road, we turned into a magnificent driveway among tall Mediterranean pine trees; and there was this jewel of a building with a double-height portico and the largest front door I had seen since my chorister days at St Paul's Cathedral, all set against an azure blue sky and the sea.

I was ushered into a large hallway and obliged to walk delicately over Persian silk rugs. The villa seemed devoid of inhabitants but was immaculately furnished with Middle Eastern artefacts. The chauffeur seemed to be Mahdi Al Tajir's general factotum. He made me comfortable in an armchair positioned in the middle of an airy sitting room overlooking the sea. I was served the proverbial Arabian coffee and waited a little nervously for my 'assailant' to appear. After a few minutes on my own, Mahdi Al Tajir swept into the room in his flowing white dish-dash. I was welcomed like a long-lost friend. He said all the right things to make me feel comfortable, which had quite the opposite effect. Eventually, he came to the point. He had thought long and hard about the debacle in Dubai and had decided the only honourable solution was to release Hyder from their obligations to him as an Agent. We would then be able to accept the award of the Twin Tower Contract from Mohammed bin Rashid Al Maktoum, and he would make peace with his conscience. There was a sting in the tail of the conversation. He looked me straight in the eye and said,

"But I will charge you 10% of all the fees you earn from the Project!"

I was enormously relieved my trip had not been in vain; a little concerned we might have to pay the penalty for the pleasure of being released by Mahdi Al Tajir from our predicament, but we could manage that as the project proceeded. Mahdi Al Tajir never did bill us – an honourable gentleman.

Table 6.2	British Consultants in the Water & Wastewater Sector Change of Ownership
Babtie Shaw & Morton	Babtie (qv), then Jacobs Babtie (2004), Jacobs (2006)
Binnie & Partners	Binnie Black & Veatch (1995), then Black & Veatch (2003)
BMMK Cotterell	Merged with Bingham Blades to form Bingham Cotterell (1988), acquired by Mott MacDonald (1998)
Bullen	Faber Maunsell (2005) now Aecom
Burrow, John	Burrow Crocker, then DHV Consulting (c. 1991-2), then Aspen Burrow Crocker, then Waterman Burrow Crocker
Colquhoun, Brian	Thorburn Colquhoun (c. 1993-4, with Thorburn), URS (1999)
Cooper Macdonald	Practice dissolved (1993)
Crocker, Trevor	Burrow Crocker, then DHV Consulting (c. 1991-2)
Cuthbertson, R H	Cuthbertson Maunsell (1999), part of Balfour Maunsell, then FaberMaunsell, now Aecom
Dobbie, C H	Dobbie & Partners (mid 1980s), then Babtie Dobbie (1987), then Babtie in 1990
Ferguson McIlveen	Scott Wilson (2006), retains name
Gibb, Sir Alexander	Law Group (US), Jacobs Gibb (2001), Jacobs (2002), then Jacobs Babtie (2004)
Haiste Group	Carl Bro (1988), subsequently Grontmij

Halcrow	Purchased by CH2M Hill (2011)
Harris & Sutherland	Babtie Harris & Sutherland (1997), then Babtie, Jacobs Babtie (2004), Jacobs (2006)
Haswell, Charles	Haswell Consulting, then (2005) taken in-house by Severn Trent
Hawksley, T and C	Amalgamated with J D and D M Watson to form Watson Hawksley (1978), now MWH
Hill, G H	Closed down following 1984 Carsington Dam failure
Howard Humphreys	Brown & Root, Halliburton, Kellogg Brown & Root (KBR)
Kershaw and Kaufman	Practice dissolved in the 1970s (they had undertaken the Master Plan for Tel Aviv, which put them on the Arab Boycott list held in Damascus)
Lewis and Duvivier	Merged with Posford Pavry to form Posford Duvivier (1987), incorporated T F Burns and Partners (1992) and was acquired by Royal Haskoning (1994), becoming Posford Haskoning (2001) then Royal Haskoning (2005)
Livesey & Henderson	Binnie, now Black & Veatch (2003)
Sir Murdoch MacDonald & Partners	Mott MacDonald (1989, with Mott, Hay & Anderson)
Mander, Raikes & Marshall	MRM, then Rust (a subsidiary of Rust International), then Rust Environmental, now Parsons Brinckerhoff

McDowells	Taken in-house by Southern Water. Closed down (1996)
Mouchel, L G	Mouchel Parkman (2003), now Mouchel Group
Pencol	Penspen Group
Rofe Kennard & Lapworth	Arup
Taylor, John	Merged with Freeman Fox to form Acer Group (1987), then Hyder Consulting (1996) and Arcadis (2014)
Wallace Evans	Acer, then Hyder Consulting (1996) and Arcadis (2014)
Ward Ashcroft Parkman	Bought by Welsh Water (1990), merged with Acer as Acer Wallace Evans (1993), then Hyder (1996) and Arcadis (2014)
Waters, A H S and Partners	Acquired by Mott, Hay & Anderson (1985)
Watson, J D and D M	Amalgamated with T and C Hawksley to form Watson Hawksley (1978), merged with James M. Montgomery to form Montgomery Watson (1990), merged with Harza Engineering Company to form Montgomery Watson Harza (2001), shortened to MWH (2003)

Of these 35 Consultants, 13 are now under American ownership and 8 under Dutch ownership.

Chapter 7: Yugoslavia

"Let yourself be open and life will be easier. A spoon of salt in a glass of water makes the water undrinkable. A spoon of salt in a lake is almost unnoticed."
Buddha (563BC-483BC)

Introduction

Connections with the UN John Calvert *(my Senior Partner)* was highly qualified, very distinguished, and well-respected in the profession. His first degree was in Chemistry from Christ Church, Oxford, after which he went to Freiburg to read Public Health Engineering and to the Massachusetts Institute of Technology (MIT), where he held a Commonwealth Fellowship. His father had been Chief Chemist at the Ministry of Health and then became the first Director of the Water Pollution Control Laboratory (WPRL) at Stevenage. John's training meant he was destined to follow in his father's footsteps, but he joined John Taylor & Sons instead. He was frequently approached by the World Health Organisation (WHO) to give expert advice on wastewater problems, including those for the cities of Auckland, Athens, and Istanbul. In 1975, he was approached by Gregg Watters of WHO to spend six months in Yugoslavia. *(Gregg had been the last JTS Resident Engineer based in Baghdad.)* John was about to retire and did not relish the thought of being cooped up in Croatia at his time of life. I drew the short straw.

Brief history of Yugoslavia The Kingdom of Yugoslavia was formed after World War I in an attempt to allow the Serbs, Croats, and Slovaks to live in peace with one another. There was continuous insurrection, assassination, and invasion until Josip Broz Tito emerged as a national hero at the end of World War II. He threw out King Peter and ruled with an iron fist as President for Life over the individual States of Slovenia, Croatia, Bosnia and Herzegovina, Vojvodina, Serbia, Montenegro, and Kosovo. Tito was able to contain this conglomerate of States from internal strife. By the time I arrived in Rijeka, clutching my UN Blue Passport, he had ruled for nearly 30 years in apparent peace[9].

---

[9] *The death of Tito in 1980 resulted in political instability across the Region. Civil war broke out in Croatia in 1991 and continued until 1995, after which Croatia secured peace and became an independent State. Further troubles, ethnic cleansing and all sorts of atrocities occurred in Serbia and in the rest of former President Tito's Yugoslavia. By that time, I had been out of the territory for nigh on twenty years.*

The Protection of the Human Environment in the Yugoslav Adriatic Region

The Project WHO created a Project to look at all the potential effects of man's intrusion into the coastal belt along the Adriatic, from the Istrian peninsula in the north, down past Split and Dubrovnik, and on to Montenegro in the south. Apart from Istria, the coastal belt is divorced from the rest of the country by the Velebit and the Dinaric Alps. This barrier of karstic limestone is massive, with little vegetation on the Adriatic Coast side and with very few passes into the hinterland. Once you pass through this barrier, you are into subsistence agriculture and what appears to be a developing country. The bulk of the Project Area is characterised by fishing villages joined together by a tortuous road (funded by World Bank) and by a plethora of offshore islands, the most famous of these being Krk, Cres, Brač, Hvar and Korčula. The Project was managed for WHO and the Jugoslav Government by Shankland Cox, Town Planning Consultants from the UK. Individual experts were seconded to the team as and when required. Their purpose was to provide the necessary technical expertise for the production of a Master Plan for environmental protection against man-made development along this remarkable coastline. The individual inputs were short, and once given, the experts retreated back to their home territory and were 'lost' to the Project. Study work was virtually complete by the time I became involved. All potential development projections had been made, particularly on tourism. All that was left to appraise was how to manage wastewater generated from the existing and projected development in the Project Area, so the citizens of Europe could have holiday heaven right on their doorstep.

JTS involvement I spent four extended visits in the Adriatic Region over a three-year period; the first two were in Rijeka, one in Split and the fourth in Titograd (now called Podgorica). My role was to listen to those that had produced designs for dealing with wastewater from many existing and potential touristic developments along the coast, as well as the big cities like Rijeka with its 200,000 population and shipbuilding industry. John Calvert was the world's expert on the disposal of wastewater from coastal towns. My own personal experience was not focussed on this topic at all. I had to rely, therefore, on appearing to be his right-hand man without John being there to extend it. All discussions were undertaken in Serbo-Croat. This whole scenario had the potential of developing into a mega nightmare.

I was supported by a young graduate engineer called Borut Čičin Šain, who was keener on sailing than engineering (understandably, as he represented Yugoslavia for one class or another), and by Jaro Gasparovitch, a forthright middle-aged economist who had been a mainstay of the Shankland Cox resident team and was now my official interpreter. Later, I learnt Borut wanted to work in the UK, so he spent a year or two in our Plymouth Office where he could sail to his heart's content.

Initial appraisal There was no wastewater treatment anywhere along the Jugoslav Adriatic Coast. The locals didn't seem too embarrassed about it; it became clear they believed all this public health 'protection' was deemed necessary, but something for the future, not the present. They liked to talk about it. International conferences were held regularly in Rijeka and the other centres, mainly supported by Italian academics with little practical technical expertise. The Italians were not known in the international wastewater market as having much home-grown expertise of their own. I was obliged to attend these conferences when I was in the country as a UN Adviser in coastal wastewater treatment and disposal (I was 34 years old, why not. We have had Prime Ministers in England younger than that).

During the first of these, I sat in the front row with Gasparovitch. He volunteered to interpret from Italian and Serbo-Croat into English to let me know what was going on and put on headphones to do so. The session started well, and the interpretation flowed with the ease of someone who was used to listening to technical arguments. His voice was understandably loud because, with headphones on, you do speak louder than your natural delivery. The flow of translation was drying up. I became anxious not to miss out on some vital new theory for treating wastewater. Then, all of a sudden, after about three or four minutes of silence (which had felt like an eternity), Gasparovitch blurted out at full pelt, "the man is talking rubbish". This didn't seem to worry Gasparovich, who was now concentrating on the next topic. For me, however, on the front row and knowing that everybody on the platform could not have misinterpreted the 'expletive', including the Speaker, this was a real embarrassment. Not only was I mortified because my neighbour Gasparovitch thought the Speaker was talking "rubbish", but also, I had no knowledge about what "rubbish" he might have been talking. I was none the wiser, therefore, to agree or disagree with the debate! The conference dragged on as they always do. No solutions here, and every speaker was pleased with themselves as they munched their way through biscuits and 'prosciutto' washed down by copious shots of Slivovitz during the inevitable post-conference 'bash'.

A UN Adviser is an important person I found most of my time was spent with Borut visiting towns and villages along the Jugoslav Adriatic Coast. We always had an appointment with the local Mayor and his technical advisers. They would spread out their master plan proposals in front of us for that particular conurbation. The Mayor would be pleased to have a plan but frustrated that implementation was prohibited because of the meagre funds available. Wastewater master plans were being shelved all along the Croatian coastline, and the design engineers (who were usually from Belgrade, a million miles away as far as the Mayors were concerned) discredited.

I believed this particular UN Adviser could come to their rescue with a 'cunning plan' by latching onto an issue I felt comfortable to deal with. None of the Mayors' plans allowed for phased implementation. Why not develop plans to secure a gradual enhancement of health standards for the town? With a little ingenuity, local politicians could promote a three-pronged attack to secure votes for the foreseeable future. First, demonstrate to the public that a significant improvement to their existing environment could be achieved by the implementation of Phase I of their Wastewater Master Plan. Secondly, boost local public confidence by heralding that subsequent phases of their Wastewater Master Plan would provide an acceptable waterborne sewerage system and a safe treatment and disposal method for increased flows from future touristic developments – eventually. Thirdly, local politicians would be able to say it was their initiative that was responsible for allowing tourism to flourish in their particular stretch of the Adriatic coastline. Once a Mayor adopted this strategy, practical solutions could be implemented to raise the immediate funding requirement to secure the start of his project.

The Mayor would (most probably) be politically astute, and the local developer would be ecstatic at my suggestions. I would then be subjected to the predictable bear hug, taking wind out of my lungs. The net result was an invitation to lunch, even though it would most likely be only 11.30 am. We would then be escorted into a back room of what would appear to be the shabbiest restaurant in town, and, in his politest Serbo Croat, the Mayor would 'instruct' me to sit down. I would then experience some of the best food I have ever tasted, together with excellent wines and, of course, the inevitable slivovitz, which accompanied absolutely everything put on the table; all this in the company of the Mayor, his entourage, Borut and the adoring restauranteur. We would emerge way after 3.30 pm. Is this typical of a UN expert's working environment? It certainly was in Yugoslavia, and it was repeated day after day up and down the Adriatic Coast

I topped and tailed the proposed wastewater disposal scheme for each conurbation to match good coastal wastewater engineering; then submitted them to the relevant authorities for approval to start off the whole process. Over the coming years, tourist developments evolved along the whole of the Dalmatian coast, which became a haven for Europeans at play; each development considering the ground rules set by a certain UN Adviser who, at the time, knew very little about discharging purified effluent into the crystalline waters of the Adriatic.

Rijeka

First stop Opatija My first stay in Yugoslavia was at a small tourist hotel in Opatija, just outside Rijeka. The room was 'confined' but with a view that stretched out over the Gulf of Kvarner towards the Adriatic. I learnt the hard way that living in a communist state was going to be different from that of my London upbringing. From an early age, I had walked across busy London streets, dodging on-coming traffic with considerable expertise. You might have thought there was a universal technique to walk across a road. Not so. I heard a shrill whistle in Opatija, which stopped me in my tracks halfway across the highway. As I turned my head towards the noise, I saw a very angry policeman who had already stopped traffic in both directions. His gesture needed no interpretation, for he ordered me to get back to where I had come from. You don't argue with an armed policeman when he has no intention of speaking in your language or of backing down from his committed instruction. I meekly returned to my original position, hoping that nobody in this crowded street would have noticed that he was referring to me. I used to travel to Rijeka on one of those bendy buses, but soon thought it more appropriate if I was based in Rijeka; Borut could then pick me up from my hotel.

Lodgings The Grand Hotel Bonavia has been supporting the rich and famous since 1876. Could they refuse a mere UN official for a two-month stay? One of the problems guests face when staying at the best hotels for an extended period is the eating department. What can restaurants do to make meals appear fresh and appealing with a limited menu? You start at the top and work your way down until you strike up a choice you feel you can endure having four times a week. In my case, the dessert section troubled me. I have a sweet tooth, and I like pancakes. They are best presented in the English way, crispy thin with lots of sugar and lemon juice oozing out of the rolled-up ends. However, the Grand Hotel Bonavia offers 'chocolate' pancakes. I am a chocoholic, nearly. I found myself engaged in a masochistic psychological analysis of what a 34-year-old UN expert was doing in Rijeka when he could be warmly tucked up in bed with his good wife in Croydon. So, I had chocolate pancakes every night in the hope of a Freudian damascene revelation before the coffee. The revelation never came, so it was chocolate pancakes for dessert the next day.

The family visit There is no airport at Rijeka. When my wife, Kay, and two children, Anna and Eleanor, visited, I had to rent a car and pick them up from Zagreb, over 100 miles away. Driving on the wrong side of the road is difficult when you are not a very experienced driver. However, returning from the airport, we had to travel over a forested escarpment through the darkest of nights in the swirling mists. As we twisted and turned around hairpin bends, I could not help but think a Transylvanian apparition was about to come galloping towards us with Boris Carlos at the helm to have his way with my whole family. In the end, we arrived safely at the Grand Hotel Bonavia, but at a late hour. We played in Rijeka for a few days and then took the night ferry to Split. Eleanor fell from her top bunk, but apparently with no permanent damage, as she later became a demon hockey player with a reputation that nobody messed with her on the pitch. There is much for the tourist to see in Split, with its evolution based on Greek and Roman occupations; and the history of revolutions and overthrows by outside powers which occurred right up to the 20th century. It was good my family was able to visit where I 'worked' from time to time, but I have no particular yearnings to revisit this territory.

Montenegro

The State Montenegrins are, as their name suggests, mountainous people. They are very friendly to outsiders like me and are generally of the Eastern Orthodox persuasion of Christianity rather than Roman Catholic, as in Croatia. Their average height seemed to be well over six foot and the men folk were heavily moustached. Forgive me for suggesting that their appearance reflected that of the archetype 'brigand', but they have been very protective of their corner of the Earth, and most appeared frustrated that they had seen peace for far too long under the dictatorship of arch-communist President Tito. The dictator was clearly fearful of these people and insisted on calling the main city Titograd.

Presidents take precedence In March 1976, I was 'billeted' at the Hotel Montenegro (now Crna Gora), the best hotel in town; that's the advantage of being a UN official. The icy wind blew cold across the plain to freeze everything in its path. I have never been so cold. The warmth and special service I was given at the hotel were essential to counteract the vagaries of the local weather.

The task in hand was two-fold, looking at wastewater proposals for Titograd itself and for the coastal town of Bar. I was three years into the Project and three years as a JTS Partner, and I was becoming more confident, therefore, in pronouncing solutions to satisfy my position of trust with the locals. My 'minder' in Montenegro was Gregor. He was a young engineer from Titograd University who giggled throughout my stay, seemed not to take the project too seriously; and insisted we went hand in hand wherever we went.

Kay was due to come and visit me on her own, leaving our two daughters to attend school in Croydon. The hotel manager handed me an envelope on the day Kay was to arrive. Inside, the letter was formal and urgent.

> "*You are to leave the Hotel immediately*", it said; "*arrangements have been made for you to be housed at a hotel down the road.*" The reason for this unacceptable action was left until last – "*President Tito is arriving,*

and I have been instructed to commandeer the whole Hotel for him and his entourage".

Quelle dommage! There was no hope for an argument. I had no alternative but to up and leave. The President was coming to Titograd to officially open the new World Bank funded railway line Belgrade – Titograd. (*This was a modern civil engineering wonder of the world as the railway passed through tunnel followed by high valley embankment, followed by tunnel, and so on.*) As I was finding my new 'lodgings', Kay arrived at the Hotel Montenegro, very concerned not to find me waiting dutifully for her. The Commissar put her in a taxi and ordered the driver to go to a second-rate hotel a few blocks around the corner. Kay was pregnant and not particularly enthralled by being pushed around by a communist.

Ostrog Monastery

Blessed Basil One of our trips out of Titograd took us up into the Prekornica Mountains, where we visited the Ostrog Monastery. We were allowed in to see the monks at prayer. It is the most amazing place perched precariously halfway up what can only be described as a vertical cliff face. One of the monks, whose habit was much in need of mending, entered into conversation with us in broken English but with a decipherable deep base voice that emanated from within his bushy, unkempt beard.

He noticed Kay was 'with child'. In those days, scanning in the UK was not the norm, so we knew nothing of the embryo's gender or health. The Monk blessed Kay and informed us with authority our unborn child was to be a boy. In September of that year, Kay gave birth to a son in May Day Hospital, Croydon. We thought about naming him Basil, but after a little thought, christened him Nicholas after St Nicholas of Myra, patron saint of Lancing College – apart from other things.

My brother Richard's resting place My Brother died in 1957. I knew he was buried in a Zagreb cemetery, but I had no knowledge of where the grave might be. I phoned John Wilde, the British Consulate General in Zagreb and was pleasantly surprised to learn it is their tradition on All Soul's Day (2nd November) to lay flowers on the graves of all known British nationals.

He sent me a note to say:

> "Richard's grave is in the new Miroševac at Dubrava on the outskirts of Zagreb. The hotel should be able to direct you there. The precise details of the grave are No. 94 (Klasa I) in Polje (Field) 221. You are advised to tip one of the gardeners to show you to the grave; 10-15 dinars (YUDS) should be enough."

I was obliged to visit Zagreb from time to time to report on the progress of my work. I planned time off in June 1975 to find the cemetery. I took the bus and found the senior attendant in charge of Miroševac. He spoke no English, but with sign language, my English, and his Serbo-Croat, he directed me to my brother's grave. It was a sorry sight and one that I would not have photographed, even if I had a camera. My parents had arranged for a stone cross to be positioned at the head of the grave and for a bush to be planted on the grave. Richard had rested in peace for 18 years when I visited. The bush had outgrown the grave, and its roots had persuaded the cross to tilt at about 10° to the vertical (I was going to report nothing of this to my mother on return to the UK). I stayed a moment in quiet stillness. There was an inscription in Greek. He was a Greek scholar, so it was appropriate even if it was not to me, as I had never studied classics at school. The rest of the writing was in English and reflected what you might expect to see in English graveyards. The attendant, who had been so respectful to me on my arrival, was waiting to catch me as I left the cemetery. He handed me a scrap of paper with words written in Serbo-Croat and various numerals, which I could read. Their meaning was not clear to me until I got Borut to translate them for me. The explanation was very specific. My brother was in a 'family grave'. (I was not thinking of joining him anytime soon). My parents had paid for the original burial but had failed to make any annual payments since 1957, and the 'plot' was 18 years in arrears. If payments were not received soon, my brother would be exhumed and placed in a pauper's grave. Well, here's a 'how do you do'. I learnt from John Wilde two things; first, the annual maintenance fee is YUD 11.50 but is about to increase to YUD 33.70; secondly, the Authorities allow you to pay for ten years in advance (1976-85) which all amounted to YUD 622.20.

> *"This should be paid by bank transfer into the foreign exchange account of Gradska groblja, with Jugobank, Zagreb, Jurišićeva."*

Borut was well amused when I asked him to help me plan to pay money to a cemetery.

My other brother Martin visited shortly after 1985 and made further payments. I have no knowledge of the present situation except to say that, as I write, there must be arrears of many YUDS that have accrued over 30 years or so.

Chapter 8: Saudi Arabia

"Fire, water and Government know nothing of mercy"
Latin Proverb

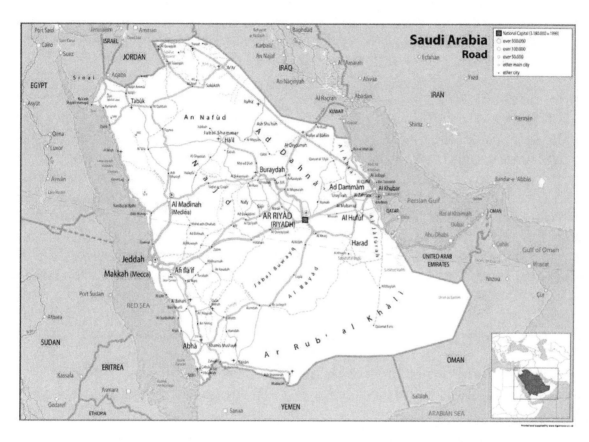

First time sewerage schemes in the Kingdom

Introduction While I was working in Zambia with Brian Colquhoun & Partners, the Saudi Government decided to install first-time sewerage schemes in all their big cities. JD & DM Watson was awarded contracts for Riyadh and Jeddah, while JTS accepted the 'second division' cities of Buraidah, Hofuf, Alehsah and Makkah. When I re-joined JTS in 1969, the Artillery House offices were full, and a specific Saudi design team was housed at the back of the old Army & Navy Stores. I had nothing to do with this team and only visited that office in the late 1970s when it accommodated the Mauritius design team.

Staff rates re-negotiation

Three-yearly negotiations The Saudi sewerage schemes progressed from design to construction supervision. By the mid-1970s, JTS had over 50 engineers and inspectors in-country, all being charged out on a time basis. Every three years, the

Saudi Government would re-negotiate our man-month rates to take account of inflation and how the Saudi negotiators were feeling at the time. Peter Banks (Project Partner) had experience with this re-negotiation process. He used to pre-empt events, therefore and started negotiations six months in advance. In 1978, these negotiations were sluggish. The pre-six months came and went, and a further six months also saw no resolution to our contractual method of payment. JTS continued to pay their staff while the contractors remained on site. Ministry clerks refused to pay the Firm a single riyal after our previous rates had 'expired'.

Called to account Time stops for no man. Soon, JTS was 'owed' more than £1,000,000 by the Saudi Government. We had a good day-to-day relationship with our Westminster Regional Bank Manager at the Midland Bank (*now part of HSBC*), but when overdrafts crept over a particular threshold, decisions were beyond his control. Eventually, the Firm was obliged to attend Midland's Head Office in Threadneedle Street to explain our predicament. As Gwilym Roberts (Senior Partner) and Peter Banks were ready to leave for the City, they put their heads around my office door and 'instructed' me to join them for a visit to the City. I don't know why I got involved because Saudi Arabian projects were not my daily concern; and I had no knowledge of the minutiae of Peter Bank's negotiations with the Saudis. One reason could have been that presenting three Partners might give us a psychological advantage. On the other hand, including a younger face in the 'team' might convince the bank that our Partnership was serious about continuity of ownership for the Firm's very survival. This might just give us an edge if arguments became 'difficult'. Whatever the reason, the three of us marched into the lion's den at Midland Bank HQ, knowing we had a six-figure overdraft - and growing.

Interview with a Banker We were ushered into an 'expensive' conference room with thick-piled carpet on the floor, old Italian masters hanging on the walls (paid for by all our bank charges) and a conference table large enough to house a Government Cabinet. Three managers from Head Office were waiting for us, most probably all with mathematics degrees from Oxbridge. Our 'friendly' Regional Bank Manager from Westminster completed their team; he was the only one to give us any modicum of a welcome. A very senior Midland Bank manager was leading our interrogation, and I felt that he probably had most of the aces on his side of the argument.

The JTS approach Gwilym and Peter had done their homework to prepare for this difficult meeting. Documents were presented to the four bankers. This initial strike from our side demonstrated we had a signed contract with the Saudi Arabian Government, and there was a liability on JTS to have staff in-country representing the client; their purpose being to supervise contractors and ensure the works were constructed in accordance with the contractors' tender documentation (which JTS had prepared). Our second salvo demonstrated we had contracts with the

Kuwait Government for the use of all the State's purified sewage effluent for agriculture, the Bahrain Government for Manama's water supplies, the Qatari Government (with Pencol) for Doha's sewerage and sewage treatment, the Abu Dhabi Government for Abu Dhabi's sewerage and sewage treatment, the Wali of Dhofar for Salalah's water supplies in Oman, the Government of the People's Democratic Republic of Yemen for Aden's water supplies and sewerage, the Government of Libya for the sewerage and sewage treatment for Yeffren and Sabha and the Government of Egypt for the Cairo wastewater master plan; all of whom were paying us regular fees in accordance with the signed agreements. We felt justice was on our side and thought our banker (with whom we had probably banked for over 100 years) would sympathise with our Saudi predicament.

The Midland Bank approach The senior Midland Manager made his opening gambit:

"The reality, Mr Roberts, is that you have incurred payroll costs associated with over 600 man-months for which your Saudi 'client' has no obligation to make any reimbursement, either in whole or in part."

Let battle commence Gwilym was put on the back foot and replied:

"We have worked with this client for over ten years. The Saudi Government is well aware of our reputation in the Gulf and elsewhere in the region. He has never suggested our professional performance has been negligent."

This was a strong retort to the bank's initial approach, and he went on to say,

"The question in front of us today is this; when can we realistically expect our fee re-negotiation to be complete? This would then allow monies from outstanding invoices to flow into our bank account. The principle of submitting these invoices over the last 12 months is not in dispute, it is only the quantum of the man-month rates (last year's rates plus an uplift, which remains to be negotiated)."

"You are right, Mr Roberts."

At last, the Bank has understood our position.

"But" (always a but) *"what if the Saudi Government reach a conclusion that is not acceptable to your Firm?"*

This was an alien thought as far as Gwilym was concerned, for which there was no logical argument until negotiations were complete.

> *"The Saudi Government needs these engineering works, and they are paying contractors ten times our supervision fees, based on formal 'payment certificates' prepared and signed-off by our engineers. The delay in renegotiating our fee structure is purely a bureaucratic hiccup, for which we had prepared ourselves and are now the cash-flow loser. This whole issue is a normal occurrence in the Middle East. Rest assured, it will soon be sorted out and our back-fees paid, which will result in our Midland account being restored into the black."*

> *"We have a problem, Mr Roberts,"* said this banking 'fat controller'. *"Banking is our business, to lend funds to clients like John Taylor & Sons. We lack confidence you have the business acumen to recover these monies from a foreign government, particularly the Saudi Government, with whom we also have considerable experience. Can we discuss how you manage your financial affairs? First, what is the calibre of staff in your finance department?"*

There was a pause for a moment while Gwilym thought about whether or not we had a finance department.

> *"The individual Partners have their finger on the financial pulse of projects for which they are responsible. This knowledge is shared with Freda Salter, who then has a full understanding of all financial matters relating to John Taylor & Sons. She has been in this position of responsibility for over 15 years and produces all invoices for presentation to clients based on information provided by the senior engineer concerned. The Partner-in-Charge is then responsible for chasing clients for payment until fees are in the bank, your bank. That is our system of financial management; it works well now, just as it has worked well for the last 100 years."*

> *"But not so well in Saudi Arabia at the moment."*

> *"Well, no, but this situation is exceptional, and it will all be resolved in a matter of days, or at worst, weeks."*

> *"Do you not employ an accountant?"* enquired one of the other senior Bank employees.

> *"Oh, no"* said Gwilym, *"an accountant would not understand our business."*

There was a long pause while the four bankers on the other side of the table (who probably employ over 1,000 qualified accountants) digested this informative statement. Their eyebrows then moved in unison, ever-so-slightly in an upward movement.

"Mr Roberts, we are delighted to see the Firm's annual revenues display growth. We are very pleased for you that John Taylor & Sons received the Queen's Award for Export Achievement. All this is very positive. But I believe I speak for my colleagues when I say we are concerned that your 'finance department' is under-staffed now you have become a significant player in the overseas market, especially that of the Middle East. The Bank's experience has persuaded our senior management that these markets are fraught with difficulties and pitfalls – like the one you are currently experiencing in Saudi Arabia.

"We wish to make a deal. The Bank needs to regain confidence in John Taylor & Sons. Are you a viable unit; can your present predicament be resolved (and quickly); and is your management structure strong enough in all departments to grow the business for John Taylor & Sons to weather the financial bullets and other firepower that may be thrown at it over the next 100 years? We are prepared in the short-term to allow your overdraft to slide further upwards. In return, we insist you accept a qualified accountant into your management team for a period of six months at the Bank's expense. You will provide him with unfettered access to your accounting system and to all Partners and senior managers. He will report to us on a weekly basis to describe his understanding of each and every contract entered into by John Taylor & Sons. At the end of the six-month period, he will present a report both to the Bank and to the Partners of John Taylor & Sons to define whether your Firm is a viable ongoing business or not. If he decides you are not, we will have no option but to call in your loan and commence proceedings to secure outstanding monies from the Partners in any way that is legally appropriate."

Immediate reaction Strong stuff. What could any of us say to that? There was no Plan B. No other high street bank would accept our account in its current state. We thanked the four bankers for their kind offer and made an exit for the door, feeling we should move backwards as though they were royalty (in reality, we didn't want to be shot in the back as we left). We took a taxi and headed for Westminster and St Stephens Club to lick our wounds and down a gin and tonic – or two.

Result We were 'sent' Terry Baughan, a freelance accountant with experience of looking into firms' accounts and offering advice that owners may or may not like to hear.

The corollary to this story is the Saudi's paid up within a couple of weeks. All the Partners got on well with this Baughan fellow, who concluded we were an on-going business. We offered him a consultancy role which he held until we merged with Freeman Fox and Partners in 1987, at which time he became Finance Director, first of Acer Consultants and then of Hyder Consulting.

Jeddah sewerage

Influence in high places Eric Bridgen, CEO of Acer Consultants, employed Geoffrey McMorragh Kavanagh in the late 1980s, whose background was in architecture of grade-listed buildings. His expertise did not fit easily with our line of business; however, his real benefit to the Firm was his ability to 'engineer' a meeting with anyone in high places, be it the chairman of a FT100 company or politicians of any political persuasion. One such contact was Dimitri Dondos, who worked for Yannis Latsis, the Greek shipping magnate and bank owner. In 1993, Geoffrey invited me to attend a meeting in Bridgewater House (the Latsis London HQ) to discuss an issue that came straight from King Saud himself. The Saudi Government had paid millions of Saudi rials to a well-connected Saudi contractor to lay sewerage in modern Jeddah (*the old Jeddah had been sorted out by JD & DM Watson in the 1970s*) to alleviate an odour nuisance that pervaded the city, not least in those areas adjacent to King Saud's principal Palace. The funding went to place manhole covers all around the city. Underneath the covers, the soil was undisturbed, and no pipework had been laid between 'covers' – in essence, this was a fraud of enormous proportion, but, being amongst friends, the scandal had been hushed up. All this 'theatre' was taking place in one of the richest countries in the world, with a GDP per capita of US$20,000. Saudi Arabia was an energy superpower, and the largest petroleum supplier in the world. Yannis Latsis had been asked by King Saud to resolve the sewerage problem in Jeddah once and for all and overcome this personal embarrassment caused by one or more of his cronies, known or unknown.

Yannis Latsis Yannis (or John) had been a 'barrow boy' who, through his own initiative, had become one of the richest men in the world. He bought an oil tanker when tankers were going for a dollar, then bought another and so on until by the time of the oil crisis of the 1970s, he owned a whole fleet of tankers which were able to convey oil to 'difficult' parts of the world at very encouraging rates. During the 1960s, he was able to gain access to the Saudi royal family. The royal court revered King Saud as though he was a god. John Latsis took a different approach. He had no hesitation in recounting risqué stories to the King that would be banned in St James' gentlemen's clubs. His approach to curry favour was successful because nobody else had ever dared to treat King Saud like an ordinary human being. This was an unconventional approach for a businessman, but it secured the King's friendship for life. Contracts with the royals kept rolling in, and by the 1980s, included the management of all royal estates in the kingdom, whether these were palaces or yachts lying offshore. When I visited Jeddah later in 1995, Latsis had an office compound close to Jeddah airport with over 150 expatriate 'experts' all being charged out to the royal household on a time basis.

Developing a sewerage project for a Royal Geoffrey McMorragh Kavanagh's contact with Dimitri Dondos was 'solid'. If we were able to secure an odourless Jeddah, then we would make a truly royal business friendship. We had at our fingertips a potential project that would lead Hyder Consulting directly to the King. The potential project looked worth following up! Geoffrey did not trust me. He enjoyed Dimitri's company and insisted on accompanying me to my meetings. However, a side reason for his attendance was that Berry Bros and Rudd's shop was just around the corner from Bridgwater House at 3 St James' Street. After our meetings, he would persuade me to enter their hallowed quarters, the interior of which had not changed one iota since they opened in 1698. The purpose of this diversion was to discuss the latest Chateau Lafite with one of their eight Masters of Wine and to see how many 'tastings' we could get through before wending our way back to our Regent's Park office (or before I was then persuaded to join him for lunch at the Royal Yacht Club, 60 Knightsbridge, one of his haunts to get close to men of wealth and influence). I enjoyed the friendship of a Greek because it reminded me of my brother Martin. Bridgewater House, next door to St James' Palace, is not the ideal 'office' because it was a Grade 1 listed mini palace. The original house was built around 1625 and redesigned in the Palazzo style by Sir Charles Barry in 1840. It got a direct hit during World War 2 and was then bought by John Latsis in 1980 and renovated to its present state. Its claim to recent fame is that it hosted a G8 London summit in the early 1990s.

I was given various maps of Jeddah City. New Jeddah was developing on land recovered from the sea that was basically a coral reef; totally impervious. Every new property was drained into a septic tank, none of which could work satisfactorily if the effluent was not allowed to infiltrate into the sub-soil. There were no public sewers, and the septic tanks were never maintained or emptied, with the result that New Jeddah was a significant public health disaster. Wealthy Jeddah businessmen came home from work every day and had to wade through pools of raw sewage to get to their front door. Evaporation was the only natural process to whisk away domestic sewage in the Saudi heat. The King was right, the stench was totally unacceptable for a modern city in one of the world's richest countries. The odour nuisance indicated the magnitude of the problem.

Site visit I travelled to Jeddah with Dimitri Dandos to meet government officials responsible for the city's sewerage. Dimitri told me that when the king first visited Geneva, he was really impressed with the huge vertical fountain spout. John Latsis said he would install one for the King in Jeddah. That is how the world's largest fountain got built in Saudi Arabia and is now known as the King Fahd Fountain - and it didn't cost the King a rial. Such stories gave me the assurance the Latsis relationship with the King was solid.

Spiro Latsis was an academic economist. He was persuaded to join his father's business in 1989 when he was 43. He was also visiting Jeddah at the time of our trip and told us he was keen to progress thoughts on how to solve this odour nuisance, as the King was much displeased. It was not easy to secure a meeting with government officials as they did not like to meet foreigners on this sewerage issue, where funds had previously been 'misappropriated'. They recognised Dimitri's credentials, without which we would never have had an audience. We spent many hours developing the draft of an outline master plan. Once completed, we put it to their government and headed for a meeting with the officials concerned for discussion. Our proposals were never going to be accepted, and we were summarily dismissed. Dimitri was not amused, and we looked for an immediate discussion with the Latsis' contacts in the royal household for guidance on the way forward.

No one could avoid the significant odour nuisance in Jeddah, particularly in the vicinity of the King's main palace. There was no doubt the business community was embarrassed every morning and evening when they left/returned to their home. No one can argue that New Jeddah has been built on impervious coral. Unfortunately for us, the ministry officials were in no mood to agree on a solution unless there was a Royal Decree to solve the problem, and this was not going to happen in 1996. This time, Hyder Consultants were not allowed to help, even though the request came (discreetly) from the King himself. I waited to fight another battle at some other later date.

Chapter 9: The People's Democratic Republic of Yemen Aden and the Wadi Hadramaut

"We never know the worth of water until the well is dry"
Thomas Fuller, 1732

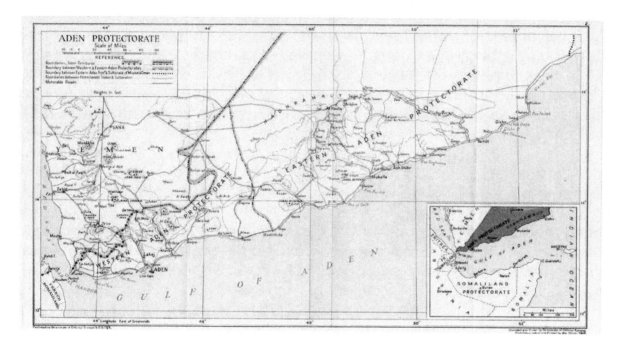

Introduction

Early history of Aden The Bay of Aden represents the largest natural 'port' in the world. The first Europeans to occupy Aden were the Portuguese in the 16th century. They were ousted by the Ottoman Empire, which ruled Aden for nearly 100 years until 1645. Aden had only a population of 600 Arabs, Somalis, Jews, and Indians and was then administered by the Sultanate of Lahej under the feudal control of the Zaidi Imams of Yemen. It was a strategic trading port between Arabia, East Africa, and India, as well as a gateway for pilgrims visiting Mecca.

Early British influence The first English trading ship to visit Aden was East India Company's *The Ascension* in 1609, before sailing on to Mocha. For the next 200 years, the Company sailed across the Indian Ocean but became tired of their ships being attacked by pirates. They decided to 'acquire' Aden in 1839, purely for anti-piracy reasons. The population in Aden at that time was 4,600. (*It is not surprising that even today, the Gulf of Aden remains an area known for its acts of piracy; this time caused by a lack of any viable government across the water in Somalia.*) British influence soon spread inland both north and east as far as the Wadi Hadramaut. Once the French built the Suez Canal in 1869, Aden grew in importance as a staging post between Europe and the East. Ships could pick up water and coal before venturing out across the Indian Ocean. Nine tribes in the immediate hinterland of Aden signed informal protection arrangements with the British Government, and by 1875, 'Aden and its Protectorates' was formed (with a population of about 20,000). The new territory was administered from the British power base in Bombay, and by 1890, Aden's population had grown to 46,000.

Early involvement of John Taylor & Sons JTS was retained by the Bombay Waterworks Company in the late 19th century. The Firm first became involved in Aden in 1904 (the year Father was born). Midgley Taylor was a regular visitor to the Indian sub-continent and was the Consultant of choice, therefore, to go and install the first wells at Sheikh O'thman to serve Aden with an abundance of fresh water.

World War II The Second World War was an important time for Aden's development. The RAF built a runway as a hub for aircraft controlling the Middle East and flying on to the Far East. (*They also constructed another runway up the coast in the Salalah Plain, now in Oman – see Chapter11*). The British navy took advantage of Aden's natural harbour to develop the port facilities. Aden was of strategic importance, therefore to the Allied Forces. It is understandable that they chose to house the atomic bombs that fell on Hiroshima and Nagasaki in a safe environment on the hillside above Aden, waiting for their deployment.

John Taylor & Sons Involvement Post-World War II

First-time sewerage system for Aden After the Second World War, Aden had a total population of 85,000 and became a major British naval and air base. Staff housing was built, and associated trades and facilities were provided, all requiring infrastructure. JTS was retained by the Ministry of Public Works to design sewerage systems for the enlarged town. John Calvert CBE, who later became JTS' Senior Partner, often reminisced about his first trip to the Middle East in 1947. It took him seven days – by air from Poole to Cairo, with overnight stops at Marseilles and Rhodes, then three days in Cairo until a DC3 was available to fly him down the Red Sea to Aden. He booked in at the Crescent Hotel, which was renowned as the best hotel in the whole of the Middle East[10]. Once John Calvert had met with the Chief Engineer and established the Ministry's requirements, the design was left to new Partner Oliver Taylor (great-grandson of the founder of the Firm) and Tony Harris, his assistant. Individual sewerage and pumping systems were required for each of Aden's commercial areas and suburbs, including Crater, Al Ma'alla, Al Tawahi (Steamer Point) and Khormaksar, giving them their own disposal system

---

[10] *Opened in 1932, the Crescent Hotel's spacious colonial style with deep verandas and high ceilings was appropriate for the hot, humid climate of Aden. Later, HM Queen Elizabeth II stayed there.*

through a series of short sea outfalls – an innovative proposal in the 1950s - to make the best use of the sea as a huge natural 'treatment plant' (a technique that today's environmentalists would consider having passed its sell-by-date). The construction phase was carried out directly by the Ministry of Public Works. JTS' involvement was restricted to the occasional visit from London by Oliver Taylor and Tony Harris to ensure the works were carried out in accordance with the Firm's designs and specifications. In the 1950s, JTS was instructed by Wimpey, on behalf of BP, to design a sewerage system for the new township at Little Aden across the bay, where the Middle East's first oil refinery was being built.

Asbestos cement pipes An innovation adopted by the Ministry during the implementation stage in Aden was laying sewer pipes in asbestos cement (AC) instead of conventional glaze ware or concrete. This became a *cause célèbre* in the wastewater industry. Once the AC pipes were in operation, it became apparent pumping sewage at high ambient temperatures is a catalyst for hydrogen sulphide to come out of solution and attack the cement in the sewer fabric. As a result, cement was being eaten away at pipe soffits. In less than ten years, only a few strands of asbestos remained at the top of many AC pipes, causing several sewer collapses across town. The good news was that JTS became a recognised 'expert' in sewer corrosion in arid climates, and by the 1970s, their services were being sought not only across Arabia but also for the three capital cities of Cairo, Baghdad, and Tehran.

1967 evacuation JTS was asked by the Ministry in 1965 to extend their brief to design a new sewage disposal system for the residential areas of Sheikh O'thman and Al Mansura, both on the mainland adjacent to Aden town. Surveys were completed, and designs commenced back in Artillery House early in 1967. In November of that year, the British Armed Forces were forced to leave Aden because of continued insurrection by the Egyptian-backed communist National Liberation Party. Design work in London was put on hold, therefore, and further site visits were neither practical nor possible. By the end of the year, Aden had become the capital of the People's Democratic Republic of Yemen (PDRY). A communist government was installed with allegiances first to Russia, then to China and finally to North Korea.

The start of new workload in PDRY

New instructions A cable was received in April 1976 at Artillery House, London:

> *"For the attention of Mr John Calvert. Good sir. All is forgiven. Please come back and finish off what you started."*

Signed
Abdul Wahad, General Manager, Aden Public Water Corporation.

John was about to retire, and because I had just spent six months with WHO on The Protection for the Human Environment in the Yugoslav Adriatic Region, they thought I might know something about communist countries and how they operate. A reply cable was sent to say how honoured we were to continue our work in Aden and asked if they would please expect Jessop Price and Tony Harris on the next flight!

First impressions We were dispatched, but it was not easy to travel to Aden. First, we had to fly Middle East Airlines from Heathrow to Beirut. There was a civil war going on in Lebanon, with regular fighting activity around Beirut airport. Flights never took off from Heathrow until there was confirmation that all was quiet around Beirut airport. Secondly, the London flight arrived in Beirut at eta 8.00 pm. We had to transfer onto an old Alyemda Airlines (AA) Boeing 707 to fly us to Aden, which was not scheduled to leave Beirut until midnight. We were obliged to wait in 'no man's land' in Beirut's special departure lounge for four hours. When eventually we were called to leave, we discovered the aircraft was doctored inside, with passengers in the front half and 'cargo' behind a thick rope curtain at the back of the plane.

Arrival in Aden was at 4.00 am, with the outside temperature 27°C and rising. We were aware of being the only Western Europeans as we walked across the tarmac, not towards an arrivals hall but to a tin shack with an official notice outside announcing People's Democratic Republic of Yemen Immigration and Customs. Inside, the temperature still felt as though it was at the previous day's high of 38°C with a humidity of over 70%. Perspiration flowed off our cheeks and elsewhere as we waited for Immigration to sanction our visas.

We were met by Jim Mistry on the landside of Immigration and Customs. Jim had been the senior engineer at the Ministry in Aden, liaising with Tony in the 1950s and 60s. He was an Indian Yemini and had been locked in the PDRY for the last nine years with only communist colleagues, his family, and the small Indian community in Aden for friends. To say he knew Tony was an understatement, for he was welcomed as a long-lost brother. Jim and Tony had a lot to talk about, although, at 4.30 am, the conversation was a bit stilted.

Once we collected our suitcases, we walked across the airport forecourt to the Government courtesy vehicle to take us to the hotel. We clambered into the back of a 1950s Land Rover that had seen better days and winged our way into Aden. Jim lent over to me amid the shambolic noise of the vehicle's engine outmanoeuvring the potholes and shouted

"Any friend of John Calvert is a friend of mine."

I realised I had arrived in the right country, although I had yet to come to terms with the shock of having landed in some sort of Turkish bath without walls. Once in town, we were obliged to stop at a red traffic light even though, at this early hour in the morning, we were the only 'traffic' on the road. Tony remarked

"The first traffic lights in the Middle East"

Jim replied, *"And still the only traffic lights in Aden."*

Hotel accommodation We reached the Rock Hotel at about 5.00 am. Jim Mistry approached the front desk clutching an official letter on Government headed notepaper, instructing the hotel manager to provide two rooms for these 'important' guests. There was a frantic crossfire of Arabic between the two men. Eventually, Jim came over to where Tony and I were sitting, looking pleased with the result of his 'friendly' discussion with the night manager. It had been a long journey, and all I wanted was to go to bed for an hour or two before freshening up to attend our first meeting with the Government.

The hotel was built in 1956 and was Aden's tallest building. Most rooms had fine views over the harbour, with each floor having a balcony. The restaurant was located on the top floor. It all sounded very nice.

We waited patiently for 45 minutes when suddenly a European man (French, I thought) came out of the lift, through the lobby and out into the hot dark morning air. To our great relief, we were told

"Your rooms are ready, sir".

We said goodbye to Jim, made our final small talk to say we looked forward to seeing him at the morning meetings and went up in the lift to our rooms. I chose one and said goodnight to Tony and clambered into bed. To my slight horror, I had climbed into warm sheets, presumably at the same body temperature as the man who had come down in the lift and 'evicted' from the hotel ten minutes beforehand.

I met Tony for breakfast in the restaurant upstairs. There was nothing unusual on a fairly European menu, but I noticed a movement out of the corner of my eye. There, nestling against the skirting board, was the largest rat I had ever seen – on the ninth floor! Either it was very fussy over its food or scavenging at ground level in Aden was not too productive.

Meeting the Public Water Corporation (PWC) Our meeting with Abdul Wahad, PWC General Manager, was very formal. My experience in Yugoslavia taught me that, as a senior manager, he would have to be a member of the communist party. He was the politico the communist Government had put in place to provide excellent water and sewerage services for Aden. His head would fall if the gamble to re-appoint the British failed. I learnt later he was a geologist and not a political man at all. He was naturally nervous about meeting us, and friendly, but only interested in our technical capabilities to solve the problems now facing the PWC.

The meeting went in our favour, not only because Tony was knowledgeable in all the minutiae of our assignment as he had done the surveys in Aden and the design work back in Artillery House in 1966/67 but also because the confidence Jim Mistry displayed regarding our employment was beginning to rub off on Abdul Wahad. We adjourned for lunch. The PWC canteen showed no favouritism to guests or management. We were all workers together. Eating fish curry with our fingers was certainly a new experience – one that was not unpleasant. We were certainly viewed with suspicion, particularly by the Communist Workers Committee within the PWC, to whom the General Manager had to report. This Committee regularly gave him a hard time, particularly when anything controversial arose from his dealings with us 'westerners'.

Jews in Aden We were travelling back to the Rock Hotel when I noticed the Jewish Cemetery. I thought it strange to see such a 'memorial' amongst such a strong Arab culture. But then I thought that, as Moses took forty years to wander around Sinai and the Empty Quarter before finding the Promised Land, maybe two families might have strayed and dossed down in Aden. I also was aware that, just up the coast in Salalah, it is rumoured Moses came down from the Jebel (*Exodus 31.v18*) carrying his tablets and found the Israelites worshipping the golden calf in the very plain where JTS was soon to develop a wellfield in the late 1970s.

There is evidence of a Jewish merchant 850 years ago who sent a letter to Cairo for the supply of his groceries and other household goods. This location for a Jewish Community is understandable as they are natural merchants and would have relished being involved in international trade and spreading their influence throughout the Arabian Peninsula and as far afield as Persia and India. They built seven synagogues in Aden, the largest of which housed 2,000 worshippers. Over the centuries, the Jewish Community lived in relative tranquillity with their Arab neighbours. By 1838, their numbers had grown to 7,000.

The Jews fared considerably better under British than under Muslim rule. The Jewish Agency established an office in Aden in 1928, but in the years that followed, there were antisemitic attacks, with many Jews stoned and stabbed by Arab rioters. These outbreaks of violence were disconcerting but of minor significance when compared to the terror unleashed three days after the 1947 UN vote on the partition of Palestine. Protests in Aden erupted into unrestrained bloody violence. An organised massacre of the 8,550-strong Jewish community started on 2nd December 1947 (82 Jews were murdered and 76 wounded; 106 out of the 170 existing Jewish shops in Aden were robbed bare). There was murder, four synagogues were burnt to the ground, and 220 Jewish houses were damaged and looted. With the help of the British in 1967, the Jewish evacuation was final when it was discovered the Arabs intended to massacre what remained of the Jewish Community in Aden once the British were flushed out of the territory. An unattended Jewish cemetery is all that remains of a community that had been in Aden for over a millennium.

Greater Aden Water Supply Project

World Bank funded project The average annual rainfall in Aden is 2.4 inches, which tends to fall over about 10 days. Often, the rain falls only every other year. The water supply for the town relies on mining groundwater that flows below the Arabian Peninsula. Wells became saline near the coast, and the salinity of the Sheikh O'thman wells installed by JTS in 1904 was rising close to WHO maximum acceptable limits. PWC had access to a countrywide groundwater resource macro-model developed by French Consultants Sogreah (under French Aid). PWC and World Bank accepted Sogreah's recommendation there were substantial groundwater resources in the Wadi Bana within the Abyan Delta, some 80 km to the northeast of Aden. This sophisticated groundwater model had persuaded the authorities there was an abundance of water below ground, even though this 'recommendation' was determined by using just one reading from the edge of the macro-model. A 'project' was developed to bring that water to Aden to meet the growing demands of the urban areas.

Greater Aden Water Phase 1 PWC produced designs for the scheme based on five components: a wellfield in the Wadi Bana; 80 km of transfer pipeline; a storage complex about 10 km north of Aden; various reinforcements in the existing distribution system to improve water pressure throughout the town; and a modern telemetry system to control the project's operation. International Consultants were sought to take those designs to tender and then supervise construction. JTS were persuasive in our bid and were appointed to undertake this work. With Tony Harris in charge, we analysed tenders received and recommended the main contract be awarded to British contractor Bovis International. The development of the well field was to be awarded as a separate contract and turned out to be more problematic. The cheapest bid by some margin was from a Romanian State Department called Geomin from Bucharest. They had never operated outside their own country, and their experience related to general mining rather than water exploration. We recommended their rates were too low for the work to be undertaken but were overruled by both PWC and World Bank, who took comfort in the knowledge that the Romanian Government would not renege on their contractual obligations.

Wellfield development Geomin soon turned into a nightmare contractor. Their equipment was 'ancient', and they couldn't even order a screw without first obtaining confirmation from their head office in Bucharest. Our team surveyed the wellfield site and located the individual wells at coordinates identified in the Sogreah Plan. All that was required of our contractor was to drill for it, and volumes of water would gush out. After much argument and delay tactics by Geomin, drilling eventually started, but there was no initial comfort when drilling started because the first two holes were dry. The contractor did not appear competent. We were frustrated in 40°C heat and in the middle of a dry wadi bed.

Concern over the lack of groundwater was reported back to Artillery House in London. Drilling didn't stop, and the next three wells also proved to be dry. This was serious. Bovis had already laid 10 km of their 800mm pipe, starting from the Aden end, and heading to a yet unproven wellfield. We were familiar with how an Arab client might view these events but dared not contemplate for too long how an Arab client with North Korean tendencies might analyse our apparent collective incompetence.

I immediately talked the problem over with Dr Sally Letts, our senior hydrogeologist. She supported my original view that it was unrealistic to base a new major wellfield for a capital city on only one specific control point in a macro-model of a country's groundwater resource. We both agreed it was necessary for us to visit Aden immediately. JTS got Sally a visa[11]. She had considerable hands-on experience of groundwater behaviour in the Arabian Peninsula and had lived in the rural areas of Oman for two years as part of a Durham University initiative, both investigating groundwater resources and learning Arabic out of necessity as nobody there spoke English. When we discussed the matter with Abdul Wahad (a qualified geologist), we were grateful to recognise we had a client who understood the problem a 'dry hole' represents. He was only too keen to arrive at a solution, and quickly.

Sally went to the Wadi Bana to investigate the wellfield area. The Wadi surface was dry, but it could be green some of the year. When it rains, the run-off is very considerable because the surface of the catchment area can be like concrete, 95% of rainfall runs off immediately, causing considerable havoc in its wake. We were shown where the 'Chinese' bridge had been to cross the Wadi. The concrete bridge deck was now lying silently 100 metres downstream. The

---

[11] Securing the visa was difficult because she was a lady and we wanted it in a hurry; fortunately, by now JTS had friends in the PDRY Cromwell Road Embassy who were able to overcome bureaucracy.

alignment of the Wadi bed had totally changed as a result of the erosive nature of the flood flow a few years earlier. However, resources below ground are not necessarily connected to those above ground. Sally knew groundwater is generated over a much larger catchment area stretching out under the Empty Quarter of Saudi Arabia. Only 5% of precipitation recharges the aquifer, which has accumulated in the karstic limestone and not been tapped, ever; Aden would most likely be mining the water resource that had been there for millennia. There were none of the tell-tale signs of vegetation or other surface marks to suggest that this particular location could become a major wellfield site. After two days of site investigation, Sally felt Sogreah should be consulted to justify why they believed their chosen site might yield any groundwater at all. Sogreah was immediately defensive of their model results and accused both JTS and Geomin of incompetence. We decided to leave PWC to deal with the politics and focus on the Wadi Bana.

After walking over the area and using a hydrogeologist's intuition, Sally recommended we carry out some investigative drilling 2 km to the east of the 'Sogreah' site. Geomin's drilling rig trundled over the sand dunes and set up for action. The first well found water, but not a lot. The second proved more productive, and the third was positively gushing. Sally set out new locations for each well in a new wellfield, all some 2 km further away from Aden than those predicted in the Sogreah plan. The groundwater resources required for the Project were secure. Abdul Wahad gave a big sigh of relief and a huge thanks to Sally for ensuring they still <u>had</u> a Project. The JTS reputation in Yemen went up a notch. We could all fly back to London to let the Project progress and feel comfortable that a major political, technical, and even international crisis had been averted.

The Bovis £25 million contract Civil engineering work in a hot, humid climate requires careful planning and ensuring the equipment provided is reliable. We were slightly alarmed when we first met the project manager at Bovis' head office in London. Our fears were realised when a load of 'new' trucks arrived in Aden, which, when inspected by our foremen, were found to be ex-British Army surplus. Construction equipment for the contract all seemed to be 'second hand' and was generally not man enough for the job.

The contractor's compound was based at Bir Nasir, 10 km north of Aden, where they would also construct a new terminal reservoir. Bovis provided both office and housing accommodation for all our supervisory staff at the same site. It was acceptable, just, and gave us good access to the main elements of the Project, including the 14,000 cu.m storage on the compound and the 10,000 cu.m storage 82 km away at the Wadi Bana wellfield site.

Surveying the pipelines We asked the PWC for whatever mapping they might have between Aden and Wadi Bana to help us survey the 82 km pipeline route.

We were met with a stony silence, and their faces displayed utter amazement that we should have the gall to ask for such 'top secret' information. Apparently, there are military installations in the area; we were told it would be quite impossible for Government to release any mapping to us, particularly as we were not only foreign but also from the former 'colonial power'. However, we knew the British had undertaken mapping outside Aden in both the 1950s and 1960s. We insisted on pressing our request, saying we could not do our job without proper survey maps. Eventually, Government relented. We laid out the maps on our site office table and were amused to see little pockets of 'blank' paper at various points across the region where 'something' had been scratched out on the negative. Although we didn't need to know, we had inadvertently identified the secrete locations of PDRY Government military camps between Aden and the Wadi Bana!

Local accommodation I stayed at the Crescent Hotel on one of my visits, which was definitely no longer the 'best hotel in the Middle East' because its clientele had vanished in 1967. Very 'shabby chic' would be the best way to describe this tired building which had had little maintenance since the mid-1960s, even though it had been ravaged by the hostile environment. The hotel was operational, but only just, and to my amusement, the restaurant had a Bechstein grand piano but had not seen a professional musician for many a year.

Tony Harris, JTS representative We were all proud of Tony Harris when we learnt he had been awarded the OBE in the Queen's Birthday Honours in 1985 'for services to Civil Engineering in the People's Democratic Republic of Yemen'. Very well deserved. It was a real endurance test to live and work in Aden for so long. I learnt first-hand how much respect Tony was viewed within PDRY. I had been attending a meeting with Abdul Wahad, Jim Mistry, and Tony. PWC was giving Tony a hard time over some failing or other of the contractors. Tony continued to spell out the pragmatic, sensible view for the client's consideration. I can't remember precisely what was said, but suddenly Tony got up and silently walked out of the room with a face like thunder. Now, normally, this would be considered totally unacceptable, and you would expect Government insistence on immediate repatriation to the UK. To my surprise Abdul, instead of going off into a spout of machine-gun Arabic to show his utter annoyance that a Consultant had the audacity to walk out of his meeting, just raised one eyebrow in my direction and with a smile spreading all over his face said:

> "I think I pushed Tony too hard. We can't do without him. Please go and bring him back."

Reviewing the project Later that visit, I inspected an old pumping station in town, which was due for complete refurbishment/upgrade and for the installation of modern telemetry equipment to monitor data and control day-to-day operations. I noticed a pair of binoculars on the windowsill and commented to Jim Mistry it was good the pumping station operative was an ornithologist. Aden has plenty of resident pelicans and flamingos, as well as migratory birds who drop down onto the shallow waters surrounding the town. These birds come in all shapes and sizes, they know there is food available for them there to feed while escaping the cold winters further north, so the variety is awesome for anyone interested in birds. Jim smiled. He pointed out of the window.

> "You see that hillock over there with the reservoir on top? On the hour every hour, the reservoir keeper comes out of his hut, looks down towards this pumping station and prepares for an important act. With arms straight, he moves his left arm in a vertical movement away from his side up to his shoulder several times. He then does the same exercise with his right. Four movements with the left arm and seven with the right signify the water depth in his tank is 4 foot 7 inches. The pumping station operative would see this 'performance' and then religiously record 4 foot 7 inches in his daily logbook. See here ......"

He showed me that day's page in the logbook – there were six entries already recorded. What a wonderful and unique system of 'telemetry' which would only fail if the reservoir keeper had malaria, a good night the day before; or had inadvertently expired without telling anybody. I immediately thought 'Have we bungled our recommendation for project control? Have we proposed an element of inappropriate sophistication for local operatives? What will happen to the reservoir keeper once the project is commissioned?'

Government decisions Tony and I were walking down to PWC one day and happened to see a few trucks rush by in the middle of the road. It reminded me of a story I had heard told at the British Embassy Club the previous week. Before 1967, all transport in Aden drove on the left. The new politicians in charge wanted to do away with the British and all their wicked 'colonial' ways. Those Yemini politicos invited to Moscow had observed everybody there drove differently and with a certain military precision. Come 1968, the new PDRY Government passed an edict that all vehicles in Aden should henceforth drive on the right. In order to ease the transition from driving on the left, they qualified this order by instructing all domestic vehicles to drive on the right from 1st March 1968, followed one week later by all commercial vehicles (including buses). Six months later, Government pronounced with a great flourish the results of the National Politburo's magnificent decision, which had proven to be a great success with no injury to humans - just one dead camel.

Civil War Towards the end of the construction of the Bovis Pipeline, the PDRY president Ali Nasir Muhammad learnt his three colleagues on the ruling Socialist Party Politburo were plotting his assassination as he entered Government House.

It was 13th January 1986. He took appropriate action and ensured his own loyal bodyguard took the three colleagues by surprise and opened fire on them before they were able to carry out their intentions. Unfortunately, his action was only partially successful. Two were dead, but Al Beidh was able to crawl away to safety. The armed forces loyal to each of these politburo members then spent the next 12 days in an intense shoot-out. Unfortunately, Ali Nasir set up shop outside Aden, only two miles to the north of the Bovis camp and proceeded to fire shells into Aden. Five JTS staff were in the middle of a real battlefield. Not much fun and no description in their personal contracts as to what to do under such circumstances. Bullets and shells were flying overhead. With the help of binoculars, Tony very clearly saw tanks roaring into Aden with eastern bloc military in charge. It was an alarming few days which appeared to have no end.

Necessary communications When this was all going on, I answered the telephone at my home in Tipton Drive, Croydon. It was the Foreign and Commonwealth Office.

> "Mr Price?"
> "Yes."
> "I understand you have staff in Aden with a shortwave radio receiver."
> "Yes."
> "We have the Royal Yacht 'Britannia' standing offshore from Aden but have no means to communicate with any Europeans on land. Can you let us have details of your receiver waveband, please?"

How did the FCO get my telephone number?! The Royal Yacht, having recently passed through the Suez Canal en route for New Zealand, had just emerged from the Red Sea. With Her Majesty The Queen's permission, the ship was commandeered for an evacuation theatre in and around Aden.

Tony and his team continued to try to be 'invisible' when, after four days of sporadic fighting, a message suddenly crackled over the radio

> "HMS Jupiter calling John Taylor & Sons. HMS Jupiter calling John Taylor & Sons".

Tony jumped to attention. This was the first time he had any knowledge help might be on its way to get British nationals, or anybody else, out of this mess. Some form of modus operandi was discussed with an officer from the Navy frigate; the general idea was to push whatever foreign nationals could be found towards Khormaksar beach. All this was very different from the routine construction supervision of pipelines, reservoirs - and things!

JTS staff were in three separate locations, Bir Nasir, Al Mansura down near Aden itself, and Abyan, 82 km away at the wellfield site. Fighting continued in all three of these locations, confused and spasmodic because the Yemenis didn't really know which side they were on, so shot at anything that moved. The rebels continued to fire over the JTS camp into Aden. Occasionally, there were counterattacks as bullets whizzed back from Aden.

The evacuation During a pause in hostilities, Tony Harris took advantage to get from Bir Nasir to the Al Mansura camp and from there into Aden itself. He went from embassy to embassy, persuading staff, and any other foreign personnel in hiding, to go down to Khormaksar beach, from where they could be evacuated by wading into the sea, clambering into small boats and away to the Royal Yacht. The first surge of evacuation picked up 450 evacuees on 17th January 1986. The Royal Yacht then returned three days later to pick up 209 off a beach 35 miles from Aden, including our staff from the wellfield site. Tony stayed in Aden to help with other evacuations and took refuge in the Russian Embassy. The place was full of Russians and other eastern bloc nationalities hiding under tables or anything else they could find; their supplies were running out, and they were fearful for their lives – if the shelling didn't get them, they were scared of what a Yemini Arab might do if they were to walk into the Embassy and shoot the lot. Among them, he found three Britons who had not been able to get to an earlier evacuation. Like the children with the Pied Piper of Hamelin, they followed Tony, who collected some UNDP staff along the way and made for Khormaksar. Sniper fire was now a real hazard, and it was becoming too dangerous to leave from the beach. Coming under small arms fire, Tony organised a mass evacuation from the oil refinery at Little Aden across the bay, from where they were taken by launches to the Royal Yacht.

Return to the UK The Royal Yacht sailed to Djibouti. After a day or so, the British evacuees were flown to Heathrow. I was informed of their impending arrival by the Foreign and Commonwealth Office and told to meet the evacuees the next morning, 8.30 am sharp, at the Heathrow VIP lounge. The BBC was there as well as Lynda Chalker, Minister for Overseas Development, with whom Kay and I had a long talk while waiting for our colleagues to arrive. Kay and I were very proud to meet our team, who had all been through an ordeal they did not wish to repeat.

UK Government recognition The fighting in Aden only lasted 12 days before Ali Nasir Muhammad fled to Sa'naa in North Yemen, leaving al Beidh to rule the country. It is not often an event with which you are familiar is recorded in Hansard, but extracts from Baroness Young's speech in Parliament amuse me:

> "On the 13th of January, fighting broke out in Aden. The ferocity of the fighting presented grave risks to the safety of British subjects. In those

circumstances, and with the full agreement of Her Majesty the Queen, the Royal Yacht 'Britannia', which was just leaving the Red Sea, was ordered to remain off Aden

On the 17th of January .... the Royal Yacht took off 450 people, who were taken on 'Britannia' to Djibouti. .... On the evening of 17th January, Mr Arthur Marshall decided that he should withdraw all members of the embassy.

I should like to express my gratitude to all staff of the Ministry of Defence and of the Diplomatic Service, at home and abroad, who have been involved in this operation. I know, too, that the whole House will join me in praising the calmness and efficiency of our Ambassador in Aden, his staff, and their families throughout this difficult period. Their example has been matched by the fortitude of the British evacuees who helped to organise the evacuation of hundreds of other nationals and who set an example of disciplined behaviour throughout.

During this time, radio links had been set up between several Royal Naval ships and a shore-based radio. This radio link was broadcasting the BBC World Service and informing evacuees of areas in which they should gather, near to the beaches from which they could be lifted."

Fame at last, recognition in the House "of the fortitude of the British evacuees ...""! A silent recognition of Tony Harris's gallant deeds. Finally, as I was listening to the BBC's Radio 4 programme 'Today in Parliament', a smile came over my face when I heard a brief mention in the Baroness' speech that

"Radio links had been set up between several Royal Naval ships and a shore-based radio."

My eyes closed, and I dreamt of all sorts of ridiculous things, not least that with all our joint experience, perhaps Tony and I should set up a Land Agents & Consultants Management firm and call ourselves Fitzharris and Price – let's choose St James's Street as our head office[12] . Good night!

Al Mukalla Water and Sewerage Project

Al Mukalla, the Town Al Mukalla is located on the coast about 300 miles east of Aden and has been a fishing port for over a millennium. It is the largest settlement to the east of the country, a centre for the fishing industry

---

[12] Ref: Salmon Fishing in the Yemen by Paul Torday.

with a fish-canning plant and a fish meal factory. Fish products, tobacco, and other goods are exported, and boatbuilding is an important activity. It is also a marketplace for agricultural products from inland in the Wadi Hadramaut.

The Project We were asked to design a new water and sewerage scheme for the town, funded by Danish Aid (DANIDA). PWC told us to make it the contractor's responsibility to provide the resident site staff accommodation. While preparing the contract documentation, Tony became very enthusiastic about staff accommodation as he discovered the Danes manufactured air conditioned portacabins with all fixtures, fittings, furniture, utensils, kitchen equipment, indeed, everything appropriate for 'living' in the wild and all to a Danish standard of design. When the portacabins arrived, our Aden-based staff were envious of the luxury our staff in Mukalla were to 'endure'. However, it is hotter in Mukalla (the highest recorded temperature in August is 49°C), so air conditioning indeed was a real comfort.

The Project involved a water supply element (funded by World Bank), a major redevelopment of the wellfield, treated water storage, strengthening of the distribution system as well as a sewerage element. First time sewerage for the Town (funded by DANIDA) included a 1.5 km-long sea outfall.

We met the same technical difficulty with the development of the wellfield as we did in Aden. PWC had previously been advised that only 4 exploratory wells were necessary to prove the expansion of the existing wellfield. In practice, we were obliged to carry out investigations further afield to locate an adequate water resource. Twenty-nine exploratory boreholes were drilled, four of which were subsequently converted to production.

Ring Road construction, Mukalla

Housing on the town's waterfront was built right up to the rocky edge of the sea. We took a leaf out of the book of London's 19th-century sewer development along the Thames embankment. A significant dual carriageway was created on the seaward side of the shoreline housing as part of the Project. This would not only improve vehicle movement around Mukalla but also provide substantial coastal protection for the town. A trunk sewer was then laid in 'the dry' underneath this new coastal highway to collect wastewater from coastal properties and further inland.

The World Bank concluded in its final report:

> "*Consultant performance was generally creditable. They demonstrated a high degree of skill in interpreting hydrogeological information and provided good service to PWC*"

The evacuation The 13th of January 1986 uprising in Aden affected work in Mukalla. There was no fighting within 200 miles of the Mukalla construction site (because that was all concentrated around Aden), but the Mayor of Mukalla nevertheless instructed all foreigners to leave. HMS Newcastle and a British cargo ship, the MV Diamond Princess, were offshore waiting to pick up evacuees. There was a problem. The mayor forbade HMS Newcastle from docking in Mukalla harbour because it was a foreign warship. The shoreline is not like Aden, blessed with sandy beaches, but is rocky for miles in both directions. Eventually, on the 20th of January, 200 evacuees were airlifted by helicopter to the two ships standing by, before being transferred to The Royal Yacht. This act of desertion from the construction site produced interesting arguments later when interpreting the contract. The Danish contractor, E Pihl and Son AC, submitted a claim for reimbursement of extra costs for having left site. They cited "civil unrest on and around the site" as to why they were obliged to stop work, all in accordance with the terms of his contract. There was no civil unrest around the site. However, as the mayor had instructed all foreigners to leave his jurisdiction, the thought of just carrying on regardless might have been perceived to be cavalier by an outsider. We concluded our negotiations amicably after detailed discussions with PWC, our Aden-based client.

The Wadi Hadhramaut

Wadi characteristics The Hadhramaut Valley is a large plateau region in the east of PDRY spanning over 35,000 square miles and is generally hot and dry. It consists of a narrow plain about 2,000 feet above sea level flanked by 600-900 feet high vertical cliffs (The Jebel). The south-eastern end of the Hadhramaut slopes down to the Arabian Sea. The average annual temperature is about 27°C, rising in summer to 38°C. Average rainfall is a mere 3 inches per year. This tends to fall on only two or three occasions in the year resulting in heavy rainfall and significant flooding.

The local people The Hadhramis have been living in the Hadhramaut since the Stone Age, seeking out a living through the trade of incense, a valuable commodity around the Middle and the Far East. The region has been invaded several times, including by the Persians, Abyssinians and even the Judean faith for a time. From the year 1500, Seiyun had been the capital of this region until the involvement of the British, who controlled the Wadi Hadhramaut from Aden as one of its 'protectorates'.

Local society is tribal, with the belief they are descended from the Queen of Sheba and the Prophet Mohammed. The Wadi meanders along its whole length, which has the effect of eliminating any visual contact of one village with the next. This visual barrier caused each village to build lookout towers high up on The Jebel and permanently manned to warn that the neighbouring tribe were coming and on the rampage. Each tribe had been constantly at war with one another until 1937, when a truce was called, known as the "Ingrams Peace". Harold Ingrams was a British Consul based in Mukalla who persuaded the then British Ambassador Riley he should visit the Hadhramaut to get them to become part of 'Aden and its Protectorates'. Harold was instructed to make a nine-week reconnaissance trip with his wife, Doreen; first by sea to Mukalla, then by donkey to Du'an and the Wadi Hadhramaut, and finally by camel down the Wadi back to the coast. They were the first Europeans to travel throughout the region, and, on one occasion, local tribesmen threatened their lives. Doreen was the first European woman to enter Seiyun and Tarim. This pioneering journey left them in no doubt of the widespread popular desire (not least among women who had lost sons and husbands in blood feuds and tribal warfare) for an end to the anarchy bedevilling the Wadi. Harold's impressively detailed survey resulting from their trip (which Doreen helped him to compile) became the mainspring of closer British involvement in the Hadhramaut and led to it becoming a British Protectorate. He used his diplomatic skills to obtain a truce between the various sultans and heads of other individual tribes. Totally unprecedented in the history of the Hadhramaut, Harold and his wife, Doreen, had enabled peace to reign in the Wadi and bring stability to the region – the look-out towers along the edge of The Jebel are now obsolete structures as local hostilities remain dormant to this day. Harold Ingrams introduced the basics of administration, which then led to educational and developmental measures being put in place.

Shibam Town

The population in the Valley by 1980 was about 170,000, of which 45,000 were in the four densely built towns of Seiyun, Tarim, Shibam and Al Qatn. The valley has a good network of primary schools. Seiyun has a secondary school, a teachers' training school and a farm machinery training institute. The Wadi is green, thanks to the underground aquifer flowing from the Empty Quarter out to the Arabian Sea. Local agriculture is based on crops of wheat and sorghum, date palms and coconut groves, vegetables (mainly onions and tomatoes), sesame and alfalfa, and some coffee and frankincense.

Projects in the Wadi Hadhramaut A 180-mile road had been built from Mukalla to Seiyun to provide a link with the rest of the Country. JTS was instructed to engineer both water and sewerage schemes for the two main towns of Seiyun and Tarim (20 miles down the Wadi from Seiyun). My first visit was by car from Mukalla along the new tarmac road. It was enjoyable because the scenery was amazing, and we were very nearly the only vehicle on this feat of engineering. We stopped at Shibam, which is the most picturesque town in the Wadi. The narrow streets are only passable on foot, either side rising five storeys and more of mud walling, keeping out the light. From afar, the town really does resemble a medieval Manhatten or maybe a film set in real life.

Once in the Wadi, you are transported back to biblical times. The valley is over a kilometre wide, and my overall impression was how green and fertile it all is between two great cliffs on either side of the Wadi. Where there was no green, the ground was taken up with brick building, not like the London Brick Company south of Bedford. Mud was placed into twenty-four-inch square moulds about four-inches deep. The thin mud 'bricks' were then removed from their moulds and placed all over the ground to dry in the sun. This was the process for creating building materials for use locally up and down the Wadi – including up to nine-storey high mud brick 'skyscraper-like' buildings. While the team were undertaking the works, Doreen Ingrams, now well in her eighties, travelled to PDR Yemen. Tony Harris and the Ambassador accompanied her to the Wadi Hadhramaut. Her welcome by the more elderly residents of the Wadi was both extremely warm and exuberant.

Seiyun Seiyun is a town with a significant history going back to the 4th century. At the time of JTS's involvement, the population had reached 50,000. In modern Yemen, the town's administration is subservient to Mukalla (*the provincial capital*) on the coast. The water supply scheme for Seiyun consisted of appropriate standard solutions revolving around the development of a wellfield, chlorination; treated water storage, and the enlargement of existing reticulation systems. The sewerage scheme was based on 'ease of management' solutions to collect wastewater from the town with a minimum of pumping. Treatment was by using sewage stabilisation ponds. Fortunately, I had considerable experience in Zambia using such designs, which had been developed by GVR Marais at the African Housing Board in Lusaka. By 2006, the population of Seiyun had grown to 72,000

Tarim Tarim has also been inhabited since biblical times and is believed by some to be the birthplace of the Queen of Sheba and of Abu Bakr al Siddiq, the first caliph of Sunni Islam, who met with the Islamic Prophet Muhammed in Medina. The inhabitants of Tarim were traders sending frankincense northwards through Dhofar to Persia and beyond. JTS developed similar schemes for Tarim as those proposed for Seiyun.

Chapter 10: Mauritius

"Remember you are half water. If you can't go through an obstacle, go around it. Water does."
Margaret Atwood Canadian poet and novelist (born in 1939)

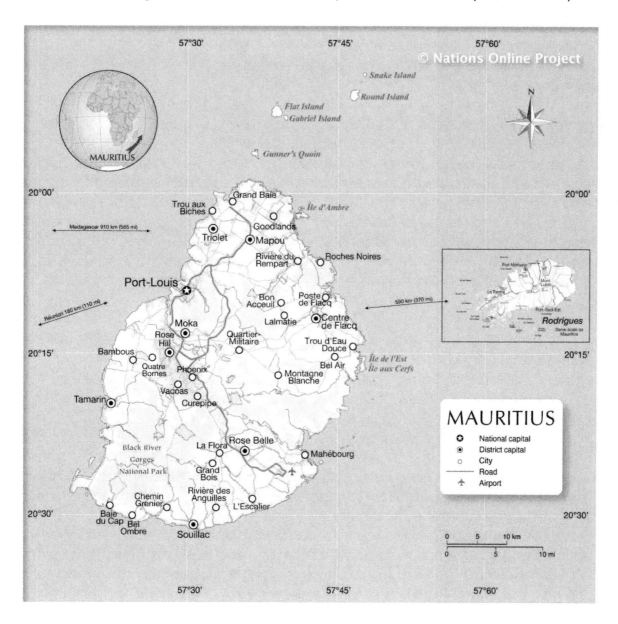

Introduction

Brief history lesson Mauritius is an island in the Indian Ocean over 1,000 miles off the east coast of Africa and about the geographical size of Surrey. There are no indigenous people. The Dutch arrived in 1638, named the island after Prince Maurice de Nassau, tried to farm, introduced several animals from the East Indies such as wild boar, the Javan rusa deer and mongooses; killed off the dodo bird; and left in 1710 because of cyclones, drought, and disease. The French landed several years later and called it Isle de France. There are two natural ports, one in the southeast developed by the Dutch, which the French called Mahéburg and the other in the west at Port Louis, which is now the Country's capital. The French used these ports as a launch pad to plunder East India Company ships as they made their way towards the Cape of Good Hope and Europe. The British and French fleets battled over the territory during the Napoleonic wars until the English successfully invaded in 1810. The Island remained in British hands until its Independence in 1968.

The geography The Island is an extinct volcano; thrust up from the Indian Ocean floor many millennia ago. It is pear-shaped in plan with the high ground at the centre, sugar cane production in the Northern, Eastern and Western Planes and a series of mountain peaks that represent the remains of the extremity of the volcano's crater. The population in 1972 was about 820,000 (*compared with 1,300,00 in 2017*). The rainfall pattern is complex, with about 200-inches per annum falling in the centre, 60-inches in the Western Plaines and 36-inches in the Eastern Plaines. Cyclones forming in the Indian Ocean affect the Mauritian weather pattern between January and April each year and greatly increase precipitation during those months.

British rule The Island was a sick place to live, with regular epidemics of malaria, beriberi, cholera, and other tropical diseases. Apart from allegiance to Queen Victoria and the imposition of an English Governor, British rule remained very 'French' by retaining their laws and practices (Code Napoleon), their food and continuing with French as the main commercial language.

The Franco Mauritians had been royalist French farmers who fled Europe before or during the French Revolution. They controlled the sugar cane industry (virtually the only commercial enterprise on the Island in 1972). Only two of the controlling families today were from the UK; all other immigrants had been 'obliged' to come from India, Africa, and China to work in the sugar cane fields as slave labour, an obligatory factor that seemed to go with a sugar cane business in those days. The Country prospered over the coming century, slave labour was abolished, and democracy benefited from Harold Macmillan's 1959 'wind of change blowing over Africa' speech, in which he acknowledged the best option for Britain was to give complete freedom to its colonies. This paved the way to grant Mauritius Independence in 1968. Sir Seewoosagur Ramgoolam was the Prime Minister, and Sir Veerasamy Ringadoo his finance minister.

Moving the family to the Indian Ocean

Initial concerns JTS won the consultancy competition to undertake a Water Resources Study of Mauritius, financed by the UK Government's Overseas Development Agency (ODA). Our success was very much against the odds because the 'opposition' (Binnie and Partners and Howard Humphreys) were regular performers with our aid programme - and we had never before been invited. John Haseldine was the nominated Project Director, and now my bluff was called because I had nominated myself as Project Manager, and you can't do that by remaining in the UK. Our first marital home was a Wates-built terraced house at Tipton Drive, Park Hill, East Croydon. We purchased it in 1970 with £3,000 of hard-earned savings made while in Zambia and took out a £6,000 mortgage. At the time, we thought we would never be able to pay off such a huge debt. Rather than leave the house empty while we were in Mauritius, we found a tenant through an agency, signed an agreement for 12 months, and then tried to forget what damage they might inflict on our most treasured possession. I gathered up Kay, Anna (2 years 7 months), and Eleanor (10 months) and scooped us all across Africa and out into the Indian Ocean.

Departure It was a typical November day in 1972. London was in full mist, cold and the journey to Heathrow seemed a mammoth expedition in itself. We took a taxi to East Croydon station and caught the train to Victoria. BOAC had merged with BEA the month before to form British Airways. The newly vamped BA departure terminal at Victoria was smart, but I still had the feeling of déjà vu, for this was the same building I had used to leave for Zambia six years earlier. We had the clutter that goes with small children, together with what we thought we might need to live on a tropical island, about which we knew nothing. Today's young parents may not be able to understand how you can travel 6,500 miles across the globe with flannel nappies and powdered milk to support two young children. Somehow, Kay took it all in her stride, well supported by a cooperative flight crew who knew exactly how to make our 15-hour journey bearable.

The first step of the journey was overnight to Bahrain, where we were required, children in tow, to decamp into the airport lounge while the aircraft was cleaned and serviced. This enabled us to touch the Middle East for the very first time. We then flew 2,000 miles over the Empty Quarter of Saudi Arabia and across the Indian Ocean to drop out of the sky at the Republic of Seychelles, where, again, we were all obliged to leave the aircraft. The final lift-off took us yet another 1,000 miles southwards with nothing but Mauritius between us and the South Pole.

Fortunately, the pilot didn't miss our destination, and we landed at Plaisance Airport, situated just above sea-level on the Island's southeast corner. Plaisance may be an international airport, but its approach flight path falls short of international recommendations. Planes approach the Island from the west, pass over Port Louis, navigating carefully between two mountains before making a sharp right-hand turn to line up with the runway, which by this time is all too close. It may have been wet and cold at Heathrow, but what we now saw was a tropical island on a sunny afternoon with not a cloud in sight. As we peered out of the cabin windows during our descent, we could see the clear, bright aquamarine sea hemmed in by a strip of coral reef and the tropical vegetation coming up to meet us. We landed, eventually, on what appeared to be a local landing strip and stepped out onto the tarmac and into our new 'home'. We felt privileged to be working in such a comfortable environment. Compared with the November weather in London, we thought we had died and gone to heaven.

Arrival

Journey into the hinterland The taxi from the airport took us to Curepipe Town in the centre of the Island, 1,870 feet above sea level. Along the way, we climbed through villages with little or no economy. The locals appeared to be of Indian extraction. Their children were well dressed and with no apparent evidence of malnutrition, and in no need of encouragement to smile and wave at passers-by driving on up towards a more modern civilisation. Curepipe Town is relatively cool, and most main residences of the Franco-Mauritian fraternity were there (*they also had a seaside villa or 'compment' on the north coast, to where they would decamp during the winter months of July to September. These two locations were equidistant from their place of work in Port Louis*). The Island supported just four main hotels for visitors: Le Chaland near the Airport for cabin crew, Trou aux Biches (individual chalets on the northwest coast), Le Morne Brabant (on the south-west corner) and the Park Hotel in Curepipe Town. The first three were all on the coast and accommodated the modest number of tourists visiting the Island (15,000 per annum in 1972). The Park Hotel, on the other hand, was the hotel for the commercial traveller, whether he was 'in sugar', selling equipment to local industry such as the new South African Brewery at Floreal or for the fledgling rag trade. There were 'hotels' in Port Louis, but without exception, they were dives of varying degrees of disreputable human behaviour. The Capital City, therefore, was the only capital city I was aware of that had no hotel facilities for the unsuspecting European visitor.

The Park Hotel This was to be our home for the next two weeks. It was made of wood in a colonial style and was a good illustration of domestic architecture on the Island. The Hotel was owned by the Rodgers Group (*who, with Ireland Blyth, seemed to own all significant commerce and industry in Mauritius*). This Hotel opened its doors in 1947, probably coinciding with the time hotels were needed in Mauritius. There was a grass garden, well treed with jacarandas and flamboyant Royal Poinciana between the hotel and the road. For about an hour before dark, local nannies in their white and blue overalls would parade their charges in the garden and chat with one another. This made a charming charade from our bedroom window, and after a day or two, Kay was persuaded to join them.

"Why do you look so sad?" said a friendly creole nannie holding a Franco-Mauritian babe in her arms.

This was an excellent entrée from a friendly local. Kay said she was not sad; it was the only face she had. Simone introduced herself. Kay responded by telling her why we were on the Island and were looking for somewhere to live. By the end of a ten-minute conversation, Kay had learnt how single-handedly, Simone had defeated Hitler in Egypt and how she had been reprimanded on parade for giggling. She had decided there and then to forsake her existing employer and come to work for us as a maid for £9 per month. All that she required was two blue overalls and a white overall for meeting guests. It was a whirlwind 'debate' but, having already lived in Zambia, £9 per month seemed low by comparison and Kay was stunned into accepting her kind offer. As for the Hotel, alas, its days were numbered because it burnt down in 1980.

Quatre Bornes It was not long before we found a house nearing completion in Quatres Bornes being built by the lovely Raj Naik, who you could never take too seriously. He had no idea about house design and even less about furnishing his new investment. As a structure, it was far too large for us, but if we allowed some of the top floor to be the JTS Mauritius Office, it was perfect[13]. Kay took Raj under her wing and knocked the house into shape, although we failed to control his fascination with stippling the ceiling with wet plaster. He must have seen this technique in a book or somewhere in Europe, for it was certainly a first in the Indian Ocean. We ended up with three-inch-long stalactites 'dripping' from all over the downstairs ceiling.

We said goodbye to Curepipe Town and the Park Hotel, and our 'caravan' moved down the hill (towards Port Louis) to Quatres Bornes, taking Simone with us as our maid. It wasn't long before Simone summoned Kay to inform her that she was going to bring her daughter Mariange to be our maid.

"But we already have a maid", was Kay's response.

"Mariange shall come as your maid, and I shall be your nannie."

---

[13] *Raj's day job was at the Ministry of Health in charge of birth control. During the 1960s, Mauritius had managed to get on top of this problem and WHO recognised their achievement as a cause célèbre for the developing world. Over the next 15-years, Raj found himself promoted to be in charge of the WHO's birth control programme, first in East Africa and then eventually for the whole continent.*

Well, what was Kay to reply. She chose the least line of resistance and remained silent.

"*And Joseph,*" Simone was off again, "*and Joseph, my cousin, will come as your gardener.*"

In the end, it was a very happy family of Simone plus three of her relations. Their remuneration was unbelievably low. They were to be our 'staff', and you could trust them with your life.

Central Water Authority – the beginnings

While Kay was off finding somewhere to live, I had to start in earnest with the Study in hand. The potable water supplies serving Mauritius had been divided into two administrative centres. Port Louis Municipality managed the water supply system under their jurisdiction, served by a gravity feed from the Grande Riviére North West at Pailles. The Ministry of Works (MoW) managed all supplies for the rest of the Island. The MoW facilities were in the process of being handed over to a fledgling Central Water Authority set up by an Act of Parliament in 1971. Jean Nairac had been appointed General Manager. He had hoped to retire from his post as Chief Engineer MoW but had been persuaded by his Minister to stay on to be in charge of the CWA for its first 5-years to provide continuity and stability for the new organisation. He had an engineering degree from Cambridge and had spent two years in Artillery House with Binnie and Partners before returning to Mauritius to start his career as a water engineer. When I walked into the CWA Office on Club Road, Vacaos (a small unoccupied wooden government building), there were only five CWA employees. The local Mauritian staff were Jean Nairac, Harold Abraham (who was a long-term serving MoW water engineer) and a young accountant called Soobramanien.

Two British expat ODA advisors had been retained on two-year contracts to assist in the start-up of a modern island-wide utility; and to give as much support as possible to the local Mauritians who were well versed in the workings of the MoW systems. Mike Norman was a civil engineer the other ODA advisor was an accountant (*who, seemed, rather than providing advice to the CWA, seemed more concerned with discussing the higher 'daily rate' the ODA had given the JTS staff than the one he had been able to negotiate for himself*). When I visited this modest CWA office for the first time, nobody was either expecting us or had been informed of our appointment. However, Jean Nairac was both an anglophile and a gentleman. After a quick call to the British High Commission, he immediately set to with the task in hand, asking us what data we required and issuing instructions to his staff to collaborate with our team. Mike Norman was less enthusiastic. I am confident he had been looking forward to working alongside

149

Binnies or Howard Humphries, who had also bid for this project and, as a result, was giving us the cold shoulder. While we were trying to discover details of a plethora of facilities for which there was no written record, the CWA was coming to life like a moth out of its cocoon with its official start date still in the future (*1st July 1973*). Up until that date, the Port Louis Municipality would continue to manage its own water supply system, and the local CWA staff seconded to our team pleaded total ignorance about anything to do with their capital city.

JTS team and the workload

JTS team We were a young and inexperienced team, but nonetheless very enthusiastic. I was supported by two very young JTS engineers, David Sargeant and Bob Wagstaffe, and by two economists from Economic Consultants Ltd, John Fulbrooke and David Seldon, who were the glue to bring all our engineering recommendations together into a unified economic master plan. John Haseldene was to visit as our work progressed and Dr John Knill, a geotechnical Consultant from Imperial College, was on tap should we need advice on dam construction (which we did).

The project programme The ODA had outlined the task in the tender documents for the consultancy bid. Having arrived on the Island in November 1972, we had to provide monthly progress reports leading up to an Interim Report due end-March 1973. This Interim Report was a three-volume affair, two of which were support volumes (one to determine future water requirements up to the year 2000, which involved a detailed demographic study, an analysis of industrial and commercial demand, including an all-important appraisal as to how, when and where an Island tourism demand might begin to grow; the second support volume was a detailed hydrological study of the Island's surface and groundwater behaviour). Our Final Report was to be in two volumes and had to be ready by July 1973; the first volume was to describe the Immediate Works Programme, and the second to detail The Master Plan for Water Resource Development 1974–2000.

The potable water system of Mauritius as of 1972

General Nearly everybody on the Island had access to a potable supply in 1972, albeit, in the rural areas, it may only have been through a public tap. There were three separate systems of supply. First, the Port Louis system served the Capital. The potential for expansion was limited because the city was geographically constrained by sea and a surrounding mountain range inland. The two MoW systems were kept separate; the Mare aux Vacaos system was gravitational and had its main resource at the middle of the Island above Curepipe Town to serve the urban sprawl from Curepipe through Phoenix, Vacoas and Quatres Bornes terminating in Rose Hill and Beau Bassin. From there, a branch fed rural development along the west coast all the way to Le Morne Brabon in the Island's southwest corner. The Districts system also relied on gravitational feed and served rural development in the North, East and South of the Island.

Table 10.1   **Outline of the Mauritius water supply systems**

Water Supply Systems	Population served in 1972	Type of Supply	Treatment	Supply in mgd
Port Louis	120,000	River Intake	Slow Sand Filter	10
Mare aux Vacoas	400,000	Dam	Slow Sand Filter	20
Districts	300,000	Dam + boreholes	Rapid Gravity Filter	7

Note: mgd = million gallons per day

Our initial study had to start up quickly. Jean Nairac's friendly approach did not bring instant results. Once a week, we would 'uncover' an existing water resource to add to those already offered up by CWA staff. I can only believe their approach to us was learnt at school based on Francis Bacon's quotation of 1597, "knowledge is power". This was not very helpful to us when we were trying to assess the whole water resources of the Island; in fact, it was mighty frustrating at the time, but we got there in the end. The MoW system relied on treating water in the highlands at the centre of the Island and then distributing it to the far-flung corners of Mauritius in all-too-small pipes to service the demand in distant coastal towns and villages (*a metaphoric image being the resource was at the hub and conveyance reflected spokes of a wheel*). The availability of potable water at the coast had become a major constraint for tourism development on this idyllic island.

Port Louis The gravitational system for the Capital was simple. Grand Riviére North West poured huge volumes of run-off from the central highlands out into the Indian Ocean just south of the City. A river intake diverted water to a batch of revolutionary upward flow sand filters built in the 1920s at Pailles, some 4kms from the city. They seemed to work well for most of the year but failed every cyclone season when the river sediment load was meteoric. Raw river water was fed directly onto sand filters without facilities to settle out solids. This caused them to block and become ineffective within a few hours after the start of any heavy rainfall event. The cleaning process of the filters involved sending an operative into a purpose-made chamber beneath the upward-flow filters, where he would shovel out the silt. This process would have given any modern-day Health and Safety Executive a heart attack. Once filtered, the water was 'chlorinated' in a small room oozing with chlorine gas (an almighty explosion just waiting to happen). The lack of any storage facilities for the 'treated' water meant the chlorinated water was then measured and put straight into the mains to supply the city by gravity – not a pump or mechanical aid in the system. We were able to observe 10 mgd being regularly recorded as the flow left the Pailles plant. There was no storage in the city. The mains water pressure reduced the further away you got from Pailles. We visited many households at the extremities of the city distribution system who had not had water in their taps for years. Water usage at every house and commercial business in the city was metered. A detailed study of past meter readings showed, without doubt, the city could only account for 4 mgd. The balance of 6 mgd was apparently 'lost' in transmission. Leakage was evident by a plethora of weeping wet patches on the roads.

Mare aux Vacoas The MaV water resource was the Mare aux Vacoas reservoir which had been built in the 1920s. The dam impounded run-off from a small saucer-shaped catchment at the top of the Island where rain fell in abundance. The La Marie treatment plant was conventional slow sand filtration, and chlorination, after which the treated water was stored before discharging by gravity to supply a system of relatively small service reservoirs, each supplying an individual conurbation further down the hill.

Districts Most rural consumers were served by standpipes (over 1,300 'public fountains' on the Island in 1973). An impounding reservoir at Piton du Milieu in the middle of the Island to the north of Curepipe provided a resource to a 3.75 mgd 'package' plant sold to Government by the UK water treatment specialists Patterson Candy International (PCI) in 1955. This provided the type of conventional treatment you might find in the UK with sedimentation tanks, rapid gravity filtration, chlorination, and storage of the treated water. It was well built, and maintenance was generally understood. This source supplied the villages to the East and South-east of the Island. A similar but smaller PCI 'package' plant (2.25 mgd) had been built at La Nicolière, not to treat water from the adjacent impounding reservoir (which was for irrigating the sugar cane plantations in the Northern Plaines) but from spring water higher up the catchment. This plant provided supplies to villages in the North, which was augmented by a few local boreholes along the way. (*A decade or two later, impounded water from the dam was fed into an expanded La Nicoliére treatment plant.*)

152

Principal interim results

Port Louis Unaccounted-for-water at 60% of input for a capital city was beyond my experience. We were confident it was practical to bring leakage under control. We made a controversial recommendation, therefore, to suggest future demand for raw water to serve the city would be less than the 1972-recorded input. This policy was unacceptable to the CWA at first, but with strong support from visiting engineering advisers Brian Grieveson (ODA) and his World Bank counterpart, I was able to predict the demand for raw water could be halved over the coming 30-year period – a prediction that was unique among professional water engineers at that time. Because the City boundaries are constrained geographically by mountain ranges and the sea, we could not predict a huge growth in residential population and proposed 140,000 by the year 2000 (*The government 2012 census gave Port Louis population as 148,000, so we were about right*). Our recommendations for Port Louis were:

(i)	Pailles TW	New sedimentation tanks, reconstruction of the slow sand filter and chlorination plant and provision of treated water storage
(ii)	Conveyance	Increased capacity from Pailles into the City
(iii)	Treated water storage	Plaine Lauzun to serve the growing industrial sector Moneron Hill above the City's Champs de Mare Racecourse
(iv)	Leak Detection Unit	To reduce the 'unaccounted-for' treated water.

The Baptiste dam Another proposal put to us for consideration was the multi-purpose Baptiste Dam project. This involved:

(a) earth bank impoundment on a tributary of Grand Riviére North West in the agricultural area to the north of Beau Bassin

(b) tunnel through the mountain range to take the impounded water into Les Guibes valley

(c) steel penstock to allow the diverted water to drop 800 ft

(d) 8MW Les Guibes power station and tailrace.

Once the water discharged through the power station tailrace, it would be below the level of the Pailles treatment plant and not available to Port Louis unless it were to be pumped up to the treatment plant. As there was adequate flow in the Grand Riviére North West to produce a gravity feed to Port Louis, we proposed the Les Guibies tailrace water should be conveyed south of Port Louis to augment

153

irrigation of sugar cane plantations in the Western Plaines. This was an interesting project as it involved dam engineering, tunnelling, and a hydroelectric station. We carried out geological investigations to determine the best configurations of both the dam and tunnel. The Project was presented as a real benefit to the Nation in terms of energy creation and best use of river water (for agricultural production), which would have otherwise gravitated unused into the Indian Ocean.

The Pierrfonds tunnel We came across another project which I would have liked to introduce to the Port Louis potable water supply system – groundwater by gravity, an unusual and cheap resource. Keerpal Jawaheer was the MoW hydrologist (*six years later, he became CWA General Manager*). He took us to inspect the 'Pierrefonds Tunnel'. The Corp de Gards mountain rises up from La Ferme impounding reservoir to the south of Port Louis. This dam is used to irrigate sugar cane in the Western Plaines. Jawaheer had drilled exploratory boreholes in high land under the lea of the mountain to the west of Quatres Bornes and discovered considerable amounts of groundwater flowing westwards out to sea. The Ministry of Agriculture agreed to drill a tunnel under this relatively flat land and then put boreholes down into the tunnel to collect groundwater by gravity (as if the tunnel were a conventional adit). The exit of the tunnel was about 1,000 feet above La Ferme reservoir, and the groundwater was used to generate a modest amount of electricity before being discharged into the dam. There was potential to improve the yield of the adit to about 1mgd by drilling more boreholes. This groundwater was far too good a quality to be used just for agriculture. It should have been possible to send this water by gravity into the southern parts of the Port Louis distribution system with only a little chlorination for treatment. Unfortunately, Port Louis didn't need the extra resource prior to the year 2000, so the scheme still remains on file.

Mare aux Vacoas The existing system in 1972 was conventional with the benefit of impoundment and treatment in the Island's centre; the treated water could then be gravity fed to serve its mainly urban consumers. In reviewing rainfall statistics, which were voluminous, I was amazed to see the amount of rainfall that comes with a cyclone, the maximum recorded figure at the Mare aux Vacoas reservoir being 27-inches in one day. Our opinion was not a shortfall of resources, but a constraint in the conveyance and storage serving each conurbation down the hill to ensure consumers had a regular 24-hour supply. A conventional system requires a conventional solution to meet the increasing urban population. Non-domestic demand was modest, with a fledgling rag trade business, which had a potential for expansion caused by a significant increase in sales to Europe and beyond, good Indian management and a cheap labour force. The system served just one tourist hotel, Le Morne Brabant, at the extreme southeast of the Island and, alas, at the furthest possible point from the resource at La Marie above

Curepipe. Our proposals, therefore, were relatively predictable; increase slow sand treatment and treated water storage at La Marie and increase conveyance / treated water storage throughout the urban areas.

Districts This system was basically a rural water supply system controlled by sophisticated, but conventional, treatment and a significant constraint in conveyance over long distances from the point of treatment to the coastal villages. Improvements to the system were inevitably going to be focussed on increased conveyance and treated water storage close to centres of demand, with the possibility of increased treatment facilities if dictated by projected consumption. The area served was agricultural, with no real Government strategy to impose commercial or industrial demand on these regions. I 'invaded' various Government departments in search of potential proposals for future growth and came across a succession of failed planning applications for hotel developments around the coast from interested landowners and developers. I discussed this situation with senior civil servants, Raj Naik, my landlord and with Harold Abraham, who I discovered was one of Raj's cousins – should I have been surprised? It became clear the Government recognised the nation was blessed with the most wonderful beaches. The length of coastline was not boundless, and quite rightly they were anxious that if they approved a particular planning application, it might set a precedent to enable the limited number of beaches around the Island to suddenly turn into Torremolinos. There was also the not insignificant issue that all coastal regions were served by small-bore water mains from the centre of the Island, terminating in standpipes to provide an adequate service for the villages, (but not for a barrage of new hotels along the coastline) and the MoW had no plans to improve water supplies in the Districts System.

John Taylor & Sons – the catalyst for the birth of the Mauritian tourism industry It was my decision. I took each individual rejected planning application for a hotel complex and plotted it on a map of the Island. This produced about seventy 'dots' around the coastline, with a predominance around Grand Baie to the North, Flacq to the North-east, around Grand Rivière Sud Est to the East and around Flic en Flac to the West – the latter three places having particularly poor water supply facilities. I assumed that, over time, there would be increased political pressure on Government to approve such applications, whether it was for a 100 or a 1,000-bed hotel. I then built up a future water demand around the coast that was quite incapable of being met by the existing infrastructure. My team worked out what increased treatment facilities were required at Piton du Milieu, La Nicolière and La Marie, what new water mains were needed to convey treated water to the north, east, south, and west to serve this potential tourism demand and what treated water storage was required close to points of this new requirement. With this entire new infrastructure in place, the Mauritian tourist industry could begin to flourish.

Kay and I returned to Mauritius for our 30th wedding anniversary in 1999. What a transformation. Everywhere I said there would be a hotel at some stage in the future, there was now a hotel. But not only that, the Government's wish to control hotel development had been achieved so as not to reflect a Costa del Sol master plan. I can justly say the JTS recommendations were entirely responsible for the healthy Mauritius tourism industry today (tourist arrivals in 2014 over 1,000,000, projected to rise to 1,200,000 in 2016 – *compared to 15,000 in 1972*).

Dinner with a General Manager

Kay and I were invited to a dinner party with Jean Nairac. He lived in Vacoas in a wooden colonial-style house with a veranda and floorboards throughout. Jean and his wife represented the archetypal Franco Mauritian; Jean was the true professional, while his wife managed the household.[14] There were two other couples, one being the British High Commissioner and his wife and the other Franco Mauritians and long-time friends of the Nairacs. We were served throughout by Creole servants, all wearing white overalls and plimsolls.

My recollections of the evening were twofold. First, the food was unbelievably excellent, starting with a superb cheese soufflé made by Madam Nairac that did not deflate before we were invited to have seconds. Secondly, the ladies were asked to retire at the end of the meal. Once gone, Jean invited the men to look at the roses in his garden. We all marched out, and I started to lend a critical eye on his floribundas. Suddenly I noticed, quite by chance, the other men were lined up to provide the roses with an unconventional 'irrigation and fertilisation' technique. What was I to do other than comply with the assembled menfolk, as they all knew I was an international plumber.

Report production

The Interim Report We were obliged to present our Interim Report by end-March 1973. This meant we had a very tight schedule as we only arrived less than 5-months earlier. There were a lot of data to be presented, all to justify historical and future predictions of demand; and how that demand could be met in principle. It meant putting down on paper for the very first time a comprehensive presentation of all existing supplies across the Island and how (if necessary) such supplies might be augmented.

---

[14] Later, in 1977, I learnt how one of their nephews, Robert Nairac, had been abducted by the IRA in Northern Ireland. He first arrived in that territory in 1973 at about the time we were being entertained by his uncle. His first tour of duty was with the Grenadier Guards; but in 1977 he joined the Argyle and Sutherland Highlanders where he was assigned to a special unit called 14 Intelligent Company. He went missing and has never been heard of since.

Choice of printer The JTS Team were all-doers of engineering rather than report writers, so although we all worked hard, most of us were not wordsmiths. Our colleagues from ECL were used to report writing and gave the rest of us enormous encouragement in what to say and how best to get our point of view across to the reader. While all this report writing was progressing, I was conscious we had to get the stuff printed and presented to the Prime Minister. I decided to engage local consulting engineer SIGMA to undertake the printing of all three volumes of this Interim Report. They had helped us once or twice in surveying and other local activity during the early stages of the Study, and their Port Louis office included a comprehensive 'publishing' suite that was avant-garde for 1973. This allowed them to print A3-size report drawings and bind reports. It seemed a sensible decision. SIGMA was interested in helping us because they would understand first-hand what potential design workload might be coming out of the Report, for which they would be eligible. We were also paying them for that privilege.

The printing process I fed SIGMA with drafts Chapter by Chapter for them to type. I would then proofread their work before printing began. This whole process started slowly, naturally, as neither party was really au fait with what they were doing. However, the delivery schedule was slipping, which was unfortunately not an option. The British High Commissioner was due to present our Interim report to the Prime Minister at Government House, in front of TV cameras and the Press at a specific time on a specific day. We reached a threshold when it became clear to me we were not going to achieve this deadline; in fact, the printing was hopelessly behind. I had to come clean and go and see our High Commissioner, who was not at all pleased; he was darn right rude and said this was unacceptable as the timing of the Report Presentation to the PM was fixed and had to be met if we were to avoid a diplomatic incident. *That was civil service speak for 'pull your finger out and achieve what you were instructed and what you promised'.* I suggested a compromise that the High Commissioner present just Volume 1 of our Interim Report, which might itself be incomplete, on the understanding we retrieve that specific document and have it shredded. JTS would then submit the three volumes of the completed Interim Report before the week was out. As a diplomat, he saw a way out of his impasse and chose to adopt my outrageous proposal.

The Interim Report presentation to Government The day of the Presentation to the Prime Minister arrived. It was a boiling hot day with not a cloud in the sky. Dressed in a suit and tie that morning (as I was to be part of the Presentation Ceremony), I drove down from Quatre Bornes to SIGMA's office, which was about three blocks away from Government House. My heart stopped a beat as I entered their office. The noise of the printer was deafening, and organised chaos reigned on the print room floor. New pages were still being churned out at a rate that would have disappointed William Caxton. There were neat individual piles all over the place, each one representing an individual Chapter. A3 drawings still had to be folded and inserted into their rightful place in the volume. It was a nightmare scenario because I needed to be out of there by 11.30 am to hand over the rogue 'document' to the High Commissioner in good time before the Ceremony began at Noon. SIGMA was aiming for a single document to be paginated and ready for me to meet that target. But as the morning progressed, it was clear they were never going to achieve this. I took the decision to stop printing; collate the first five chapters that were already printed; add the same amount of any old, printed pages from 'wherever' in SIGMA's office and start binding the document in its apparent totality. I had to have 'something' to prevent the British from appearing to fail in their diplomatic duty, even though the whole production of the Study was a gift from the British Nation to our Commonwealth colleagues.

Now came the real test. Binding had to be glued and was not a simple matter, particularly for those at SIGMA who were not used to doing it on a daily basis. Time passed quickly that morning, my deadline of 11.30 am came and went, and the hands of the office clock were speeding up to mid-day. "It's ready" was a very welcome sound, but the clock registered 11.55 am. I snatched up the still warm document. I must say it did look like a learned tome (albeit only the first half would make any sense to a water engineer). I ran out into the street and sprinted as I had not done since my days at Lancing, round two street corners, down the side of the Government buildings and made my way to the front gate where a very nervous British Trade Attaché was waiting, ready to box my ears. The midday sun was beating down hard on those urban streets, and sweat was streaming down my face. I handed the rogue 'document' to him and wiped my face clean. We then reduced our speed to a dignified 'we know what we are doing' sort of walk as we entered the hallowed quarters of the Prime Minister's anteroom, where Press and TV cameras waited in awe to be the first to learn what gems of knowledge we were about to impart, all for the good of their Nation. The rogue 'document' was handed over to an equally nervous High Commissioner. No sooner had we arrived than the Government clock struck mid-day, and we were ushered into the presence of Sir Seewoosagur Ramgoollam, Prime Minister, and his Finance Minister, Sir Veerasamy Ringadoo. The High Commissioner made his presentation, including the brief I gave him outlining what we believed might be necessary to develop the water supplies in Mauritius. The PM responded with a smile in equal diplomatic tones. Cameras clicked, and the Press remained obedient and silent only to report on what was said by the two Nation's representatives.

During this whole charade, the rogue Report remained firmly shut. I retrieved it immediately after the event and walked back to SIGMA's office. The ceremonial volume was returned to its place of birth in preparation for a cremation. I gave the instruction "Shred it" and left for a happier environment up in Quatre Bornes. That evening, sure enough, the Presentation was part of the headline TV News of the day, but we only heard and saw the PM thanking the British Government for their goodwill to develop the Nation through improved water supply systems. Nobody quoted what might or might not have, been written in the back half of the Report. The rest of the week passed, and ten copies of the correct version of the three-volume Report were submitted to the CWA for them to digest. Copies were sent to the ODA in London and World Bank in Washington. The JTS Team had already started to get on with the second phase of the Study, and I had taken a firm decision to produce our Final Report in London.

Project implementation

Mauritian High Commissioner in London with Gwilym Roberts, Jessop Price and Dick Waller

Introduction The Firm received instruction from CWA in 1974 to undertake the implementation of the Baptiste-Guibes scheme. It was this Project that brought JTS back to the Island, funded by the African Development Bank in Abijan, Côte d'Ivoire. We signed a standard ACE Agreement and began our investigations in earnest. This Agreement was extended to cover subsequent instructions from CWA to undertake all the recommendations we had made in our 1973 Master Plan (*the real not rogue version!*) covering the whole Island. The expansion of the Firm's workload enabled us to maintain a significant presence in Mauritius until the mid-1980s, with over twenty expatriate personnel during the construction supervision phase. Immediately after signing the Agreement, the British Government agreed to donate funds for the creation of a leakage control unit in Port Louis to attack the recorded 60% 'unaccounted for water' in the city.

Leakage control unit Port Louis The Firm advertised for a leakage control Inspector and appointed Paul Walker. He had spent his whole career with the South West Devon Water Board and had taken early retirement in 1974 when the Board was absorbed into South West Water on the creation of the Regional Water Authorities. We also searched for a project manager to represent JTS in Mauritius and were very fortunate to retain Ian Staniforth. He joined Sheffield Corporation Water Department straight from school as a trainee engineer and later became an engineer with Preston and District Water Board. He spent 14 years learning the trade of all aspects of pipe technology, including everything to do with leak detection and concrete technology. He became chartered with the Institution of Civil Engineers, after which his managers recommended he should study for an engineering MSc at Sheffield University. This was his experience before he joined JTS in Mauritius.

CWA assigned us the upper floor of the old Decaen School, constructed in thick stone walls around a central courtyard. It had most probably been built by the French as part of their fortifications before British rule. The CWA operators were based on the ground floor, and we were quick to learn the limit of their technical aids to resolve leakage, joining two water pipes together and providing new connections. The Municipality had failed to provide them with the proper tools for their trade. Instead, their equipment consisted of an old metal file, a lump hammer, and an old flip flop. The unconventional process they had developed was to use the file as a chisel by banging it with the lump hammer to chip away at the crown of the existing metal pipe to form a 'crater' in the cast iron. Next, a circular piece of a flip flop was placed on this crater, and the ferrule was positioned on top, which was then given a further 'bash' with the lump hammer to fracture the remaining wall of the cast iron pipe. The flip flop was then used as a washer in an attempt to create a watertight joint. If this process failed, the operative would drive in a tapered wooden peg (of which he had a considerable supply in his bag) to stem the leakage flow. Invariably, this primitive process led to loose leaking connections across the city of Port Louis and a reticulation system peppered with bits of flip flops and wooden pegs.

This is the situation we found on our arrival. We immediately started work to reduce leakage and to set up a CWA Leakage Control Unit. The British Government arranged a loan for the purchase of ferrules[15] and tapping machines[16] to make permanent watertight connections. Valuable time was spent on training CWA operatives in the use of all the right tools for the job. This was essential if we were to make any headway in reducing leakage and restoring pressure throughout the distribution system. Paul Walker was in his element, dedicated to his art of finding leaks. He restored water pressure in pipes where there had been no water for decades in some parts of the city. The results brought great rewards to consumers and, quite rightly, huge praise to Paul from customers.

Master Plan designs Most of the design work was undertaken in London in the office we had taken behind the Army & Navy stores, across the road from Artillery House. Detailed survey information was gathered in Mauritius and sent back to the workforce in this 'back street' office. The design of pipelines was conventional

---

[15] A pipe ferrule is a device used to join pipes with different diameters.
[16] Tapping machines are used on existing pipes under pressure to install a valve to control the direction of supply in the reticulation system.

and relatively straightforward. The same was true with the reinforced concrete reservoirs across the Island, which were based on a modular design (rectangular in plan) to speed up implementation. One reservoir was built with a totally different technique. A tenderer (*Johnson Construction from the UK*) for the Priest's Peak reservoir, above the Champ de Mare Racecourse to serve the centre of Port Louis, had recently completed a slip-form construction for two sugar silos on the Island. They offered a competitive price using this technique, which was accepted. The reservoir was then constructed of circular walls with an appropriate height to achieve the same stored volume as the original designs determined by JTS. The whole process was unique to water engineering at that time, and implementation proved academically interesting to our supervisory team.

The remaining works were extensions to existing treatment plants; first to La Marie with pipeline augmentation down through Curepipe, Vacoas and Quatre Bornes and on down to the west coast and La Morne; secondly to Piton du Milieu with more pipeline capacity towards the east coast and down to Plaisance airport; and finally, to La Nicolière with extra pipe capacity to serve the north of the Island.

Baptiste-Guibes Scheme The first activity during JTS's presence on the Island for the project implementation stage was to carry out a considerable ground investigation and survey work. A contract was awarded to drill cores along the alignment of the proposed earth-fill dam, and the tunnel from the dam through to the Guibes Valley. The results were studied by Professor John Knill, who then determined the geometry of both the upstream and downstream faces of the proposed earth-fill dam as well as the dimensions of the impervious core at its centre. John Haseldine (Project Partner in charge), Prof John Knill and Ian Cookman (JTS senior mechanical/electrical engineer) all came out to familiarise themselves with the site, hold discussions with both the CWA and the Central Electricity Board (who had initially identified the project) on all project issues including those related to the 8 MW power generation plant and how that should be integrated into the Island-wide power distribution network. Once all this information had been gathered, data was fed to the JTS design team in London. Tender documents were prepared, which were then issued to a select list of tenderers. Our role continued to review tenders received and make a recommendation to the CWA

Meeting the Politicians

Introduction Mauritius is a relatively small Island where everybody tends to know everybody else. Raj Naik recognised the importance of our Study and insisted I went to see the Prime Minister and other relevant Ministers and tell them about what we were trying to do for the good of their Nation. He would make all the introductions, and then it was up to me to play the 'diplomacy game'.

The Prime Minister – Sir Seewoosagur Ramgoolam An appointment was made for me to visit Government House in Port Louis to see the Prime Minister. I put on a suit and tie and made my way down to the Capital. The Government buildings were all solidly constructed in karstic stone in the colonial style, protected by a large statue of Queen Victoria.

Sir Seewoosagur Ramgoolam head on a Rs2,000 note

The Prime Minister's personal assistant was waiting for me, and I was ushered into a huge room with the PM seated at the far end of the room behind a large 'Partners' desk. He was a small man with thick, dark-rimmed glasses. My first impression of this great man, who had brought his country to independence only a few years earlier, was that of him sitting with 'goggles' staring at me just above his desk line, making me think I was staring at Toad in the *Wind in the Willows*. He stood up, walked around his desk, took my hand, which he shook with a surprisingly weak motion which felt like he had really exhausted the handshake 'thing' getting around to every household on the Island to secure their votes and there was no strength left in him now to welcome visitors to his office. I was told to sit down and, to break the silence, I started on a pre-rehearsed assessment of the Mauritius water supply system, where there were constraints and what we were going to recommend was water for all to meet the needs of the end of the millennium.

"Interesting, very interesting", he kept saying whenever I had stopped for air.

It was clear to me nobody had ever briefed him about the paucity of supplies and why no developers had been allowed to move the country away from a sugar-based economy towards a more broad-based environment that might include tourism, textiles and other industries requiring good quality water, of which there was an abundance falling on the Island from the heavens.

"*Interesting, very interesting*", he kept on saying.

At the end of our meeting, he graciously asked me to come and see him each time I came back to Mauritius to update him on our progress – as nobody else was going to do that. And so I did, four times a year for ten years. On one of these occasions, he reached from his shelf and took down a copy of "*Speeches of Sir Seewoosagur Ramgoolam 1960-74*". On the inside page, he wrote

"*To my dear friend Jessop Price.*"

And duly signed it with a signature that had probably been put on every Act of Parliament since its Independence in 1968. During my first meeting, he recommended I see his Minister of Finance, Sir Veerasamy Ringadoo, who he told me was not a well man and only worked three days a week from his Government Office.

Sir Veerasamy Ringadoo, Minister of Finance Raj Naik made the necessary contact, and I was in like a shot. There are Mauritians who are short people and

Sir Veeraswamy Ringadoo

those who are very short people, and Sir Veerasamy was one of the latter; being probably less than five feet. Could his handshake be weaker than the Prime Minister's? It was! I repeated the presentation I had given the PM, and I got an immediate response that this indeed was going to be very good for the Nation, particularly as water supplies were about to be managed by a new Central Water Authority. He knew Jean Nairac and had every confidence that we would have his full cooperation and enthusiasm to formulate a Master Plan for the Island's water resources.

I met Sir Veerasamy many times after that, not always in his office. I remember going to the Trou aux Biches hotel one evening with Kay for an evening meal and to watch the spectacular sunsets you get on this side of the island. Sir Veerasamy was there with his wife and family, and he insisted on our going with them for a drink. Island life in Mauritius was sublimely informal, and everybody would try to put you at your ease. (*There was no Mauritian army, only a Special Police Force that seemed to contain law and order without being obtrusive.*) The last time I met Sir Veerasamy was in London on Oxford Street, outside John Lewis department store, taking a breather while his wife was spending his money. I asked him if he managed his country's finances in the same way, to which he laughed, and we both went on our way.

Sir Harold Walter I never met Sir Harold when we were doing the Study, but he was always on the TV News as Minister of Health. He was a lawyer with a wonderfully deep speaking voice, ideal for getting the point across when visiting a local hospital or talking to the public about what Government intended to do to eradicate disease and make for a healthier population (*that would soon top one million*). The Prime Minister advised me to see him on one of my regular trips to the Island.

Like all Ministers, Sir Harold had a huge office, and you had to walk across the room towards his desk before you could begin a useful conversation. He was a rotund man, and his sonorous voice echoed nicely around the vast space. Apart from the Minister's seated form, there was a sign behind his desk for all visitors to read that said;

"If you are not part of the solution, you are part of the problem".

During the conversation that followed, I learnt he had been Minister of Works in the 1950s and 60s and had intimate knowledge of the Mauritian water supplies (outside of Port Louis). He had been responsible for doing a deal with Paterson Candy International to purchase the new treatment plants at La Nicoliére and Piton du Milieu. He was very interested, therefore, in what we had proposed and in how progress was being made on all the projects on which we were engaged.

Lunch with Sir Harold Walter Kay and I were invited to lunch at Sir Harold's house in Curepipe. His wife was a very elegant and artistic high caste Indian lady. There was an interesting assortment of guests, including a pair of French lesbians, one dressed top to toe in white leather who owned a chemist shop on the Champs Elysées in Paris. I sat next to Sir Harold and learnt a lot about his personal life, including that his brother was the Priest-in-charge at Kingston-upon-Thames parish church, where I had sung with Louis Halsey's professional choir. We were deep in conversation about local and UK politics when he turned to me and said:

"Jessop, you should have been a politician".

Kay, who was sitting across the table listening to this conversation, made an immediate response in support of her husband:

"Oh no, Sir Harold, he is far too honest to be a politician!"

Ian Staniforth, the JTS Resident Manager, then spent a minute or two trying to minimise the damage:

"What Kay really means, Sir Harold …".

Sir Harold saw the humour in this repartee, being both thick-skinned and used to making other people feel uncomfortable when he was a practising Barrister. The amusing corollary to this story was that, in the following week, Sir Harold was lampooned in the L'Express (*the local Mauritian Daily*) for having instructed the Ministry of Works to widen the elaborate metal gates in front of Parliament that had been there since Queen Victoria was on the throne, to enable his newly acquired Range Rover to gain entry.

General Managers under whom JTS served

Jean Nairac Jean Nairac was the first General Manager of the CWA. He only undertook this role on the understanding he could retire after five years in post. We had an excellent relationship with him, and he was very appreciative of our presence. He understood that, without us, there would be little progress in developing new infrastructure.

Freebairn L Simpson In 1976, Jean Nairac said his goodbyes and was replaced by Freebairn L Simpson, a British ex-civil servant of long-standing and a personal adviser to the Prime Minister. Rumour on the grapevine believed his background was MI5, but we thought better than to engage in detailed discussions about his personal past. He had no background in the water sector and undertook a critical analysis of our work to ensure the JTS team was good for the country. His relationship with CWA employees was tense. They did not respect him because he appeared to lack technical knowledge and was imposed on them by Government. I am not sure which was the most damning indictment.

Civil unrest was quick to catch fire amongst the staff, led by the CWA hydrologist Keerpal Jawaheer whom we had met him in 1973, early in our studies. His office at the time was no more than a temporary 'shack' amid the sugar cane fields outside Quatres Bornes, made out of corrugated iron. It was he who had made us aware of the Pierrefonds Tunnel. We had no knowledge he had political intentions. Mr Simpson became tired of Jawaheer's conduct and fired him. There was an immediate reaction amongst the CWA Workers Union and the Water Works Employers Union. Mr Simpson was not prepared for this or to tolerate such activity. He took action to quell insurrection but at the same time confided in the Prime Minister this was not his idea of fun for a final posting before retirement. As a result, Simpson's reign of office came to an end in 1978.

Keerpal Jawaheer Mr Simpson's replacement was none other than Keerpal Jawaheer. To say he had no experience in management was true, but he was nonetheless determined to strike a blow to the status quo. Jawaheer was keen to distance himself from previous management. He saw JTS as the Consultant of choice for the two former General Managers; we were foreign, so expendable. He was quick, therefore, to consider targeting JTS, 'the interloper'. We were halfway through the implementation of a major capital works programme across the Island to meet demands up to 2000. Nonetheless, he still believed we should be packed off back to the UK, and a new non-British Consultant appointed who would be seen as his choice, his new broom, his concept for a new CWA dawn. He approached Sogreah, one of the two French Consultants in the international market who were only too grateful to follow an easy path to a long-term appointment.

Arbitration John Taylor & Sons v CWA

Cancellation of Baptiste-Guibies Scheme for Port Louis Jawaheer's first attack on JTS was to cancel the Baptiste-Guibes Scheme. We designed this Scheme with considerable help from our Mauritius office and had several visitors from London:

Professor John Knill from Imperial College to advise on dam alignment and on what to look for during the site investigation. He then reviewed all the rock cores from the contractor's drilling logs and recommended the optimum upstream and downstream slopes for an earthfill dam embankment.

Ian Cookman, JTS's senior mechanical/electrical engineer, came to discuss the hydroelectrical arrangements with the Central Electricity Board and how best to connect to the National Grid. I remember he was appalled at the huge amounts of diesel fumes from ill-tuned bus exhausts as they climbed up the hill from Port Louis to Curepipe.

Partner John Haseldine came to ensure the whole water engineering project was up to the standard clients expect from JTS, whose international reputation was rightly envied by competitors, whether from the UK or elsewhere.

Progress on the Scheme The Project had gone to international tender in 1976 under the auspices of being funded by the African Development Bank. We then reported on tenders received and made our recommendation to CWA. The Consultancy Agreement JTS had signed in 1974 was the standard Association of Consulting Engineers Agreement which provides for stage fee payments, all based on a percentage of construction costs. (This Consultancy Agreement was specifically for the Baptiste-Guibes Scheme, but later all work undertaken by JTS across Mauritius was undertaken as an addendum to this same document.)

The first payment for the Baptiste-Guibes Scheme became due immediately after we had reviewed the tenders received and made our recommendation to the CWA. An invoice for about £100,000 was duly submitted on presentation of our report on tenders. Cancellation of the Project led Jawaheer to insist no fees were due because no contractor had started work and no construction costs had been incurred. We had undertaken significant investigative work, the detailed design, preparation of considerable tender documentation and the analysis of tenders received. This first stage payment barely covered the Firm's costs. I was convinced whichever way the Consultancy Agreement might be interpreted, the validity of this first stage payment was watertight (based on recommended tender valuations).

Legal Advice In my opinion, the CWA was being totally irrational to refuse payment for all the work we had undertaken, so it was time to seek legal advice. We approached Guy Rivalland, a respected Port Louis solicitor. He read the Consultancy Agreement from cover to cover and saw no justification for Jawaheer's approach to ignore any Consultant's fees just because the CWA wished to cancel the Baptists-Guibes project, which was clearly defined in the Agreement. His very words to us were

> "They are trying it on in the hope you would just go away back to the UK like good little boys".

Guy went on to say there were two important factors in our case. First, there is no indication CWA has dismissed JTS; all the paperwork revolves around the cancelling of a project for which CWA had instructed JTS to act as their Consultant. Secondly, CWA was continuing to pay JTS for all the other much larger consultancy work to serve Port Louis, Mare aux Vacoas and the Districts systems. The Consultancy Agreement allowed for arbitration, and Guy advised we should formally inform the CWA we wish to move to invoke this clause, but all in accordance with Mauritian Law. This we did, and CWA was not at all happy with our approach to engaging the law. Eventually, CWA conceded this was an appropriate line of action, and Guy began the process of ensuring we would have every opportunity to win the argument that had been thrust upon us. Guy's recommendation was to appoint Marc David (a local barrister) and propose to CWA that our choice of Arbitrator should be a former Chief Justice of Mauritius. Marc David had the best reputation in commercial law on the Island. His obituary in the Le Mauricien in January 2013 described him as having:

> "A razor-sharp mind, devoted sense of duty and undoubted charm ....
> Very occasionally, Mauritius presents to the world an exceptional gift.
> Marc David was one of them. La creme de la creme!".

Guy chose for us a very good barrister, and it was definitely better to have him in our camp rather than in that of CWA. We agreed to the Arbitrator as Sir William Garrioch, who had recently retired as Chief Justice.

Preparation for the arbitration I spent some time going through our files and developing a dossier for our lawyers of every pertinent letter, memo, and event. First, there was the statement in our Report describing the Baptiste-Guibes Scheme, including the Project's supporting documentation (written when we were employed by the British Government). This was the only factual information available to the CWA and Government to request the African Development Bank to fund this particular Project. I then abstracted from our files correspondence with CWA inviting us to Mauritius to discuss our direct employment with the CWA, as they now had funding secured from the African Development Bank. The files were full of every instruction from CWA to go ahead with site investigations, detailed design, preparation of tender documentation, invitations for international tender and confirmation of the receipt of the JTS recommendation on tenders received. The dossier suggested an open and shut case in our favour, and Marc David was astonished as to why CWA thought it was worth their while going to arbitration. He was anxious to establish their lawyer's approach to the case.

The case in Court The case was eventually brought in front of Sir William Garrioch and lasted one whole week. CWA was asked, in the absence of a stenographer, to provide facilities for recording the whole process and make the tapes available to the Arbitrator at the end of each day. As they seemed unable to do this for whatever reason, we offered to produce the microphones and tape recorder. CWA's failure reflected their whole approach to this 'battle'. I was in the cross-examination chair for three whole days. On numerous occasions, I would present correspondence on a particular issue, for which CWA's barrister appeared totally ignorant - that was until Harold Abrahams (who was providing technical support) handed it to him from 'below his desk' and allowed an embarrassed barrister to proceed to question me on another issue.

The summing up of the two barristers was encouraging. Marc had a brilliant delivery, and a sense of drama learnt at the footstools of the London School of Economics and the Middle Temple. In very flowery language and with the determination of an out-of-work actor, he spent a good quarter of an hour extolling the virtues of JTS and asking the question as to why the CWA would put this eminent firm of consulting engineers to the trouble of approaching the law to secure fees due - something the Firm had never done before in over 110 years of history. The approach of the CWA's barrister was quite different. He rose to his feet and addressed Sir William Garrioch.

> "*I am advised by my client they wish me to formally withdraw their accusation that John Taylor & Sons were incompetent and negligent*".

Sir William made an immediate response.

> "*You can't do that! That is the very reason we are all gathered together in this Court*".

Sir William was clearly very cross. With all the wind taken out of the CWA barrister's sails, self-esteem evaporated, his closing speech limped to a halt fairly quickly. Sir William's judgement came within the week – "pay JTS" - but it still took another six months before we saw a penny.

Mauritius revisited

Holidaying in Flic en Flac When we returned to Mauritius in 1999, we stayed at La Pirogue Hotel down near Flic en Flac on the west coast. We enjoyed the company of our old landlord, Raj Naik, who lived only a few miles away in Quatres Bornes. He had visited London officially in his capacity as WHO Director of Family Planning, Africa, over the years, and he had come to visit us in Croydon several times. We travelled around the Island; it became very clear to me the tourist industry had mushroomed dramatically since I wrote my report on Water Resources in 1973. Where I had made a proposal for touristic development along the coast, there was now a hotel complex. My engineering proposals had been to construct masses of new pipeline conveyance from the Island's centre in all directions towards the coast. This provided water supply facilities to enable a fledgling tourist industry to grow into a major national asset. Yes, it is true John Taylor & Sons were the catalysts for the creation of what is today a world tourist attraction. Such is the power of water.

Journalist extraordinaire I was reading L'Express on the third day of our stay when I came across a centre-page spread about CWA. Apparently, there had been labour unrest amongst the workforce, and journalists had talked up the issues to the embarrassment of senior management. There were also funding issues that had impacted the new works programme. The writer clearly had a good understanding of how a water utility works and how CWA has evolved since its inception in 1972. Then, towards the end of the article, words suddenly shot out of the page at me like a rocket in full flow.

> "Oh, what a pity we cannot go back to the days when John Taylor & Sons managed the capital works programme for the CWA".

My heart stopped a beat. All I was able to say was,

> "Kay, have you read this?"

How could anybody write this after JTS had finished their work some fifteen years ago?

Meeting the Minister We bumped into Raj later that day and showed him the newspaper article. He was very excited and said we must go and see the Minister (of Energy and Public Utilities). He would arrange it. The next day I found myself suited and, in the hire car heading towards Government House with Raj sitting next to me. He made the introductions and left. The Minister viewed me with suspicion, thinking I was after some favour or other. I broke the ice by identifying my credentials and said I was astonished to read the newspaper article the day before. You could hear him metaphorically breathing a huge sigh of relief as I appeared to be on the same side as Government. He was comforted I knew the Island's water supplies in minute detail and was encouraged enough to invite his senior technical staff to join the meeting.

"What is your opinion about water privatisation?" the Minister asked.

For the previous twelve months, I had been employed by Three Valleys Water Company (owned by Compagnie General des Eaux) to specifically search for water privatisation opportunities in India, so I was well versed in responding to the Minister's question. Diplomacy is my middle name. Like a competent Consultant, I was able to spell out the advantages; to enable Government to source funding other than through the general exchequer, to bring international expertise to the Island and to relieve Government of direct day-to-day responsibility for providing a water utility service. I then outlined the disadvantages; the need to persuade the public that the Government was not to give away its birth right, to put in place rigorous regulations to ensure the private sector is not failing to meet the Government's specifications on quantity and quality of supply and, finally, to impose a legal constraint on charging the public for water supplied. All this seemed fairly sensible to the Government officials who seemed to agree with the *L'Express* journalist that it was a pity JTS was no longer on the Island to give the CWA their full support.

Hotline to Westminster The meeting was over, and I returned to the hotel a happy man. There was a message waiting for me at Reception when I got there twenty minutes later.

"Please phone Banon".

Jean Claude Banon was the head of Compagnie Générale des Eaux's UK business, and to whom I directly reported. His colleagues in Paris nicknamed him Lord Banon because he had been in the UK too long. I went to my room and phoned him at once.

"Paris has told me you had a meeting this morning with the Minister for Water. What is all that about?"

Clearly, the French seemed to have spies on every corner – including in the Minister's office. I had to explain I was on holiday; had read that day's newspaper article on the CWA; from 1972 to 1984, I was known as Mr Mauritius Water; and I always visited Ministers and the Prime Minister every time I visited (four times a year for ten years).

"Générale des Eaux and Lyonnaise des Eaux are jointly in discussions with Government to take over water supplies for the whole of the Island.

Paris is not amused that an employee from the London Office is talking with the Minister."

My response was that if Paris was serious about managing Mauritius water supplies, then, during their due diligence, they should have discovered they were fortunate to have an employee who knew more about Mauritius water supplies than anyone else in the world. What a pity Paris does not share with London its activities in Commonwealth countries.

"Enjoy the rest of your holiday but come and see me when you get back in the office."

I can't say I enjoyed the rest of my holiday as much as I should. When I got back to Old Queen Street in Westminster, I went to see Jean Claude right away. His face was stern, and I considered I was in for a rough ride because of pressure from Paris. I showed Jean Claude the L'Express article. A wry smile came over his face that was so endearing and usually made most clients concede to his requests. "*A storm in a teacup*" was all he could say, no apology. I didn't consider it a storm in a teacup, more, incompetence and jealousy between the two French mega water companies.

Chapter 11: Salalah, Oman

"It is chronic water shortage in the body that causes most diseases of the human body."
Dr. Fereydoon Batmanghelidj (Iranian Doctor)

Introduction

Location Oman holds a strategically important position at the mouth of the Persian Gulf and shares land borders with the United Arab Emirates (UAE) to the northwest, Saudi Arabia to the west and Yemen to the southwest, and marine borders with Iran and Pakistan. The coastline is formed by the Arabian Sea to the southeast and the Gulf of Oman to the northeast. The Madha and Musandam exclaves are surrounded by the UAE on their land borders, with the Strait of Hormuz (*a strategic pinch point for all shipping in and out of the Persian Gulf*) and the Gulf of Oman forming Musandam's coastal boundaries.

Colonial influence From the late 17th century, the Omani Sultanate was a powerful empire, vying with Portugal and Britain for influence in the Persian Gulf and the Indian Ocean. A decade after

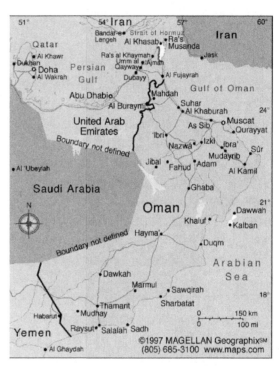

Map of the Oman, showing Salalah in the South

Vasco da Gama's successful voyage around the Cape of Good Hope and to India in 1497–98, the Portuguese arrived in Oman and occupied Muscat for nearly 150 years. In need of an outpost to protect their sea lanes, the Portuguese built up and fortified the city, where remnants of their colonial architectural style still exist. Ottoman Turks ousted the Portuguese from Muscat during the fight for control of the Persian Gulf and the Indian Ocean. Rebellious local tribes then drove out the Portuguese from Oman by 1650. The strategic importance of Muscat saw continued fighting, and by 1750, the local tribes were removed by the leader of an Omani tribe, who began the current line of ruling Sultans. At its peak in the 19th century, Omani commercial and political influence extended across the Strait of Hormuz to modern-day Iran and Pakistan and southwards along the coast of Africa as far as Zanzibar spreading the Muslim faith as they went. As its power declined in the 20th century, the Sultanate came under the influence of the United Kingdom. Historically, Muscat was the principal trading port of the Persian Gulf region and among the most important trading ports of the Indian Ocean.

The modern rule of the Sultans The rule of Sultan Said bin Taimur began in 1932 and was characterised by a feudal and isolationist approach. Notwithstanding this position, oil reserves were discovered in 1964, and extraction began in 1967. Various religious uprisings were put down in the 1950s, which had caused the Sultan to become erratic in governing the country.

The Sultan had sent his son Qaboos bin Said to the UK for his education studies at the Royal Military Academy Sandhurst and a year's service in the British Army. On his return in 1964, he was placed under house arrest at the Sultans' palace in Salalah. The people of Dhofar Province believed they should be allowed to bring the whole country into the 20th century. In 1965, they took up arms against the Sultan, supported by the People's Republic of China and communist insurgents from across the border in the People's Democratic Republic of Yemen. This rebellion threatened to overthrow the Sultan's rule in Dhofar and had a marked effect on Sultan Said bin Taimur who decreed it was forbidden to smoke in public, play football, wear sunglasses, or speak to anyone for more than 15 minutes. No one was safe from the Sultan's paranoia. This led Qaboos bin Said to depose his father in 1970 in a bloodless coup, after which his father was allowed to live at the Dorchester Hotel in London until his death in 1972.

The communist uprising was finally put down in 1975 with the help of forces from Iran, Jordan, Pakistan and the British Royal Air Force, Army, and the Special Air Service. Meanwhile, Sultan Qaboos opened up the country, embarked on economic reforms, and followed a policy of modernisation marked by increased spending on health, education, and welfare. Slavery, once a cornerstone of the country's trade and development, was outlawed in 1970. Sultan Qaboos saw his main home base as Salalah, the capital of Dhofar Province, with a 1975 population of 5,000.

Infrastructure for Salalah Town

Invitation to improve the water supply facility As part of Sultan Qaboos' reforms, Gwilym Roberts, JTS Partner, was called to the Wali of Dhofar's Office in Salalah in 1973, along with three other British Consultants. The topic was to undertake a water supply study for Salalah Town to meet the projected demands over the next 25 years. Sporadic fighting was still going on between the Omani army and communist infiltrators from across the border in PDR Yemen. The guerrilla war continued as there were still communist sympathisers holed up in various wadis surrounding Salalah Town. The national dress of Dhofaris, even to this day, is the proverbial dish-dash, a rifle and a khanjar (an ostentatious silver dagger with a curved blade shaped like the letter J) stuffed into a silver belt around their midriff.

On arrival at the Municipal Offices, instead of a hat stand and a coat rack, visitors were obliged to 'park' their armaments in the gun rack provided. Gwilym was still going to work in Victoria Street in in a bowler hat and rolled umbrella so needed no rifle rack. He outgunned the competition, and the Water Supply Study was awarded to John Taylor & Sons. Gwilym decided to give the work to the JTS Plymouth Office who were about to feel the pinch with the forthcoming formation of South West Water as part of the UK Water Industry reorganisation. Derek Coney was chosen as Project Manager, with his team of Devon and Cornish engineers who had never been out of the UK before.

Water Supply Master Plan Another British Consultant Halcrow, who seemed to do all engineering design in Dhofar Province with fees possibly containing an element of danger money, had undertaken a hydro-geological study of the Salalah Plain. This study identified the location of a new well field for the Town, the details of which were incorporated into the Master Plan. Population projections were problematic because Salalah has huge potential for encouraging tourism. A new deep-water port at Mina' Raysut was under construction, just 15 miles down the coast away from Iran and the Gulf States. This inferred industry might prefer to set up a regional centre there rather than relying on running the gauntlet of sailing through the Straits of Hormuz every time they wished to trade. Salalah was also the Sultan's preferred hometown. All these issues needed to be evaluated, particularly for when Dhofar Province is at peace with its neighbours. The recommendations for the rest of the components of a water supply scheme involved no sophisticated engineering solutions; treatment by chlorination at the wellfield, treated water storage and conveyance into town[17].

Detailed design The recommendations of the 1974 Master Plan were accepted by the Wali of Dhofar's Office. JTS received instructions to prepare detailed designs, go to international tender, supervise construction, and assist in the commissioning of all the works. Gwilym did not want to be involved, so I became the Partner-in-Charge and travelled out to Muscat to meet our Client, Ali Said Badar Rawas, the Chief Water Engineer at Salalah Municipality. Ali Said had an American engineer to run the water supply system and his youngish wife looked as if she had come straight out of an American TV soap. She wore the 1970s European fashion of hot pants to show off her long-sculptured legs, and her head supported the proverbial blonde hair to complete her glamorous image. As you can imagine, this didn't go down too well in this Muslim society. One day, while

---

[17] Peacetime came well before the end of the 20th century. As a result, hotels got built to meet the tourism demand, Mina' Raysut became a major container and general cargo port and a huge growth of expatriates (mainly from India, Pakistan, Bangladesh and the Phillipines) caused the rise in population to rise to 150,000 in the year 2000 and 430,000 in 2020.

she was travelling in her car within the municipality of Salalah, she was stopped by the police, who found a handgun in her handbag. It turned out she worked for the CIA. She and her husband were escorted to the airport and told never to return. Our engineers, led by Martin Francis a long-standing JTS man, were left on their own to establish the extent of existing water systems and what reinforcements might be needed to raise pressures and quantities of potable water around the Town. We had an excellent relationship with Ali Said, but he was not trained as an engineer. Like all managers of importance, his qualifications were proudly displayed in a wooden frame on the wall behind his desk:

> "Land Rover, Coventry
> Technician Second Class - Pass"

The wellfield Our London office had just taken on Dr Sally Letts, a hydrogeologist who had spent a couple of years in villages in the north of Oman as part of her studies with Durham University. She joined the team in Salalah and was a tremendous asset. First, she was able to identify the location of all necessary boreholes in the wellfield to give us the correct yields to meet demands up to the year 2000. Secondly, because she was fluent in Arabic, her ability to smooth the Client-Consultant relationship was worth its weight in rubies (*although I later discovered her local North Omani accent always brought a wry smile to the locals of Salalah*). A contract was awarded, and a drilling rig wended its way up onto the Salalah Plain. Successful drilling yielded ample water for the Town. Some of the team, who decided to swim in the Arabian Sea in their free time, recorded they observed freshwater springs on the seabed. This confirmed there were ample supplies of fresh water flowing from the Empty Quarter of Saudi Arabia. Our new wells were to tap this excess flow before it was lost to the ocean.

We met up with a team of engineers from America Water Resources Inc. who had decided to use Salalah as their base for an investigation into water availability up in the Jebel. This area is mountainous, barren land high up above the Salalah Plain and continues to the Saudi Arabian border and the Empty Quarter. They seemed serious enough and showed great interest in our proposals. Several years later, I had an illuminating conversation with a Croydon friend who was a helicopter pilot employed by Sultan Qaboos. He was instructed to pick up these water resource engineers to convey them to the Jebel for their investigations. Once airborne, the engineers gave my friend a swift command to change direction, fly low and head for the deep wadis on the Salalah Plain. Their engineering credentials were clearly written on CIA-headed paper, with interest not in water resources but focussed on flushing out communist terrorists who still remained in Dhofar, even though the war with PDR Yemen had officially ended two years previously.

The Yemen/Oman conflict is a forgotten campaign, probably because it was very much a guerrilla war between Marxist-indoctrinated Yemenis interested in colonising a peaceful, undeveloped Dhofar province. However, it had been described in an engaging book entitled 'Where Soldiers Fear to Tread' by Ranulph Fiennes (later to become Sir Ranulph Fiennes), who had been one of many British Army officers seconded to the Omani Army to assist in putting down this rebellion. The JTS Agent in Salalah was another such SAS officer who rather dismissed certain facts reported in Fiennes's book. He was not dismissive, however, of the extremely difficult engagement the continuous skirmishes represented. He pointed out several Omanis to me with the comment that he never knew from day to day whether they were loyal to the Omani Government or had changed their allegiance to the Yemeni revolutionaries – a serious issue if you are in close proximity to provide the locals with military support.

Travel to Salalah The Royal Airforce built a runway at Salalah during the Second World War as an alternative strategic staging post to Aden for their activities between Europe and the Far East. I always remember during my early flights to Mauritius via Bahrain, the captain would announce, "*we are just passing over Salalah*", which would mean absolutely nothing to most passengers on the plane - except me. You would have thought, therefore, that travel to Salalah was relatively easy. Not so. There were no scheduled flights to Salalah from anywhere because the Government perceived the Dhofar Province was a war zone. The only options, therefore, were to drive the 600 miles of dirt road, part of which could be in dangerous territory; or be a guest of Sultan Qaboos, who flew a daily chartered flight from the Capital to Salalah using the latest Boeing aircraft. On arrival at Muscat, having signed in to a comfortable hotel, I would wend my way to the official Muscat Office of the Wali of Dhofar to secure a boarding pass, which was more often than not first class. The flight was rarely half full but often had extraordinary passengers from Government ministers to two blindfolded hawks perched on a stick next to their minder in full Omani dish dash and headdress.

Accommodation There was just one hotel for businessmen, the Holiday Inn, a two-storey building with 200 rooms and a private beach of golden sands that seemed to go on to infinity in both directions. The hotel also had serviced detached townhouses (all airconditioned) along the beach, which were a godsend for three of the JTS staff and their families. Whenever I stayed, there were never more than four rooms taken, so I believed, incorrectly, this was my private space, which included a five-star restaurant. Today, Salalah is a significant holiday destination, with over 600,000 tourists visiting during the 2017 Khareef season (*June to September*).

Other Appointments in Oman Once the Wali was aware we were a Consultant who could be trusted, we found our contract extended to design a trunk water main from the new Salalah water system we had designed to serve the commercial port of Mina' Raysut, together with terminal storage of the treated water[18].

The British Government provided considerable support to the Omani Army, and there was an army camp outside Muscat full of British soldiers and associated staff to maintain an army on the move. JTS was invited to second a water engineer to this MoD camp. This initiative probably came through my Partner John Haseldine who was a colonel in the British Army Reserves. We sent Keith Hitchcock, one of our senior engineers who was a musician with a particular interest in music prior to the sixteenth century. His luggage contained the usual stuff for a two-year secondment but included a crumhorn, which he took out into the desert to entertain any passing camel. He often invited me to dinner in the officer's mess when I was passing through Muscat – an evening of excellent food and strange military behaviour in a foreign land.

The Omani Government gave us another assignment far away from Salalah in the very north of the country – the Musandam. We were to prepare a Master Plan for three towns in this strategic province, which overlooks the Straits of Hormuz. This point of geography enables Oman to control all shipping in and out of the Gulf. It also is the closest point of the Horn of Arabia to Iran, whose politics are very different to those of the Gulf States and Saudi Arabia. JTS was instructed to develop water supply schemes for the towns of Al Khasah, Timah and Kamzar. Access to the Musandam is restricted. I never visited the area but sent Eric Combes, a senior engineer with a good sense of engineering and sound writing ability, to draft our report. My role was to review his findings and submit them to the Government for their approval.

Meeting the Wali of Dhofar During one visit to Ali Said's office, I noticed he looked particularly upset. Ali Said explained the Wali had been taken ill and had been airlifted to a Muscat Hospital. The medical authorities thought it best he be flown to London to receive medical attention at the highly respected private Wellington Hospital, all at the expense of Sultan Qaboos. When asked what was wrong with him, Ali Said replied he had severe liver failure. Oman was a 'dry' country, so it was a little surprising to hear the Wali's complaint might be alcohol induced. I was due to fly back to Heathrow that evening, and on the spur of the moment, I suggested perhaps I could visit him at the Wellington tomorrow to send him good wishes from all his flock in Dhofar. Ali Said's face suddenly lit up; he thought it a

---

[18] Today, the port is called Port of Salalah and is a container and general cargo terminal. It is the main Container Transhipment Terminal of the Region and is perceived as at the crossroads of trade between Asia and Europe. As a result, 'Salalah Free Zone' situated adjacent to the port is developing as a new centre for heavy industries in the Middle East. All this shows the importance of establishing a good supply of fresh water back in the 1980s.

very good suggestion which ensured, on the one hand, I had made a commitment for myself on return to Blighty, but on the other hand, I had secured a happier client into the bargain.

The next morning, early, I was met at Heathrow by my usual driver to take me home to Cobham where we had moved to. But I asked him to re-schedule my route home and drive me to London down the M4 and drop me off at the Wellington Hospital. I had passed the Hospital many times as it was near Lord's Cricket Ground, but I had never had reason to enter its holy portals. As soon as I arrived, I asked Reception where I would find a patient called the Wali of Dhofar. My request was met with a quizzical smirk, but I was directed up several floors and into a private room. There was my client lying resplendent, but with a sorry look on his face telling me one place he did not want to be was here in London, in the Wellington Hospital - all so alien to his own environment back home in Salalah. He had no idea who I was, so I invoked my inner diplomatic self and told him I was in charge of the new development for the Salalah Water System.

"Your Eminence", I said (I wasn't too sure how to address a Wali). *"I have just got off a plane from Oman and I am pleased to bring you greetings from all your friends in Salalah who wish you well. You are very much missed in Salalah, and everyone hopes you will make a speedy recovery, inshallah. They look forward to your return in good health."*

I don't know if he spoke enough English to know what I had said but having glanced at the doctor and nurses looking after him, I thought it best to retreat backwards towards the door of the private room with as much respect as I could muster. I heard later he returned to his people in Salalah in good health and continued to administer his Province for many a year.

Official opening at reservoir site on Salalah Plain

Salalah Town water supply opening ceremony I received a formal invitation from the Wali of Dhofar for myself and Kay to attend the Opening Ceremony of all the works we had designed for Salalah Town. The Sultan wanted to open the scheme on National Day (18th November), which was only one week away. We had no alternative but to accept and my secretary, Brenda Norton, made a quick telephone call to the Omani Embassy in London to get the relevant

NOC (Non-objection Certificate) and other papers to enable us to enter Oman without a hitch.

Opening ceremony

It was an honour to be an official guest at this function. The skies were blue, and the temperature reached over 40°C by midday, but there was always a breeze on the Salalah Plain. The sand was yellow, and the local dignitaries looked resplendent in their flowing white robes, multi-coloured headdresses and silver khanjar attached to their waistbands. The event went smoothly with military precision, followed by invitations to meet everyone and everybody over a non-alcoholic drink and canapes out in the open of the Salalah Plain.

The day before, our agent had informed us there was always a camel race on National Day on the Salalah Plain, but he did not know either the time or place.

"As soon as I have information on the desert telegraph, I let you know."

The telephone went at 8 am. It was the Agent, and he was going to be with us in ten minutes to take us onto the Plain to watch the races. What a spectacle! It looked like total chaos with about twenty camels charging around, not appearing to be much in control at the start of the race, all mounted by child jockeys. Great wodges of Rials were exchanging hands at very 'unofficial' bookies. There was an elevated 'clothesline' to demarcate from where the camels should start. The starter had his pistol - as one of those locals who kept changing sides during the Yemeni/Omani troubles. All of a sudden, he blew his whistle; and they were off. We were all standing to one side of the track about 100 yards from the start. The excitement and shouting gathered pace, with the camels seeming to go at a terrific pace with an increasing sound of hooves thumping the ground as they came down the track. Then, without warning, the camel nearest to us veered off the conventional alignment and headed straight for Kay, knocking her to the ground. (*Help, help – thoughts flashed through my mind of Lady Legard from Benenden, who was trodden on by a camel in Egypt in the 1930s and was never the same again.*). Our Agent was mortified and, being a former SAS soldier, was quicker than I to lift Kay back to her feet, apparently unperturbed by the event; or totally embarrassed that a mere camel had got the better of her and she wasn't going to show any deflated ego. So ends my first and last experience at the races.

179

An Invitation to dinner

After the Opening Ceremony, Ali Said Badar invited Kay and me to dinner at his house. This was indeed an honour and one of the few times I have been invited to a client's home to mingle with family. We put on our best clothes and arrived by taxi at Ali Said's relatively modest house. Inside, we were ushered into a large room with sofas positioned at all extremities of what appeared to be the main living space of his home. We were introduced to his sons, many of them (!), the eldest of whom spoke reasonable English; for the rest, there was a great shaking of hands, nodding of heads and polite salaam alaykums.

Once the greetings were complete, we were ushered into one corner of the room and invited to squat crossed-legged on the floor. Kay was immediately told she was an 'honouree man' for the evening, for which she replied she was flattered and very pleased to be considered one of the family. Although we were about ten in number, the conversation was constrained to just the four of us bold enough to communicate in English. We spoke about the successful Opening Ceremony that occurred earlier in the day and how the Wali was very pleased with our work, Ali Said's work. He waxed lyrical about how he had enjoyed working with JTS on this project which, for him, was the beginning of his life's work. He mentioned Dr Sally and Martin Francis in particular, both of whom had helped him win brownie points with his fellow Omanis, particularly the local hierarchy, and that included the Wali himself. A large plate of food arrived, probably 750mm in diameter, containing a special local dish of lamb, rice, various vegetables, local herbs, and spices, all to celebrate this specific National Day. "*Tuck in*", said Ali Said, or words to that effect. Plates were provided, but no knives or forks. The protocol was specifically to eat with your right hand as your left is deemed to be unclean – a bit of a quandary for me who is left-handed – but 'when in Rome ….' (*thank you, St Ambrose*). Ali Said's cook had obviously been told to prepare a meal suitable for National Day and for a very important guest from Great Britain! He did his stuff for the food was delicious!

After the meal, Kay was asked to leave, and the eldest son took her to meet Ali Said's wives. None of them spoke English, so the son stayed to act as interpreter. What followed was a mixture of a lot of gesticulations and giggling, all in an attempt to communicate with this foreign lady. They plied her with little gifts, which turned out to be soap, shower hats and other such things that had previously been handed out by an international airline. Then a scale was brought out and very proudly, the senior wife, who was a portly lady, stepped on the scales and scored a resounding eighteen stone. Kay was then instructed to try to beat that. When only eight stone something came up, the ladies giggled again but were horrified because they believed that her husband was not financially able to support her. Thus ended Kay's only experience of being party to a harem in an Arab land.

Chapter 12: Ethiopia

"We forget the water cycle and the life cycle are one".
Jacques Yves Cousteau

Introduction

Location Ethiopia is situated in the Horn of Africa, to the east of the continent. It shares borders with Djibouti and Somalia to the east, Sudan to the west, and Kenya to the south. With over 100 million inhabitants, Ethiopia is the most populous landlocked country in the world and the second-most populous nation on the African continent. It occupies a total area of over a million square kilometres, and its capital and the largest city by far is Addis Ababa.

History The oldest skeletal remains of homo sapiens have been found in the region. It is believed that from there, humans migrated to the Middle East and beyond. Ethiopia can trace back its rule as a monarchy to the 2nd millennium BC. The ancient Ge'ez script is still used today by a nation that is predominantly

Christian (Ethiopian Orthodox Tewahedo Church)[19]. Warring rulers expanded the country over the centuries and defeated several colonial powers until the Italians came in the 1930s. There is a 13th-century document recording the visit of the Queen of Sheba to King Solomon in Jerusalem, by whom she conceived the Solomonic dynasty of Ethiopia founder Menelik I. This line has been handed down from king to king, and Haile Selassie (The Lion of Judah), who became Emperor in 1930, is believed to have been the 225th ruler after King David. He and his father were highly respected monarchs both at home and internationally. Ethiopia was the first independent African State to become a member of the League of Nations in 1923.

The monarchy was overthrown in 1974 by a communist military government led by Colonel Mengistu, supported by the Soviet Union. This soldier and politician became chairman of the Derg, the socialist military junta; he removed all opposition to his rule. It is well documented that Haille Selassie was assassinated by members of the Derg in 1975. This led Mengistu to become dictator of the People's Democratic Republic of Ethiopia in 1977, graduating to President in 1987 until his downfall in 1991. Mengistu is one of the most notorious African leaders of the 20th century, and his reign is infamous for its brutality, autocracy, and economic mismanagement. Today, he lives in Harare, Zimbabwe.

In the 9th century AD, a goat herder named Kaldi from the Abyssinian highlands noticed that when his goats ate berries from a particular tree, they became excited and energetic. Kaldi reported this to the Abbot in the local monastery. This discovery was shared with the other monks, and the knowledge of the energizing berries began to spread throughout the region. Thus, Coffea Arabica was born. Alas, although much coffee is grown in the country today, I doubt if the nation benefits hugely from the meteoric growth of coffee consumption throughout the Western World.

John Taylor & Sons involvement in rural water supplies

European Economic Community funding After several visits to Brussels to persuade EEC bureaucrats to let JTS have the 'UK ticket' for one of their Consultancy opportunities, the firm was nominated (along with six other Consultants from different member states) to bid for the Bahir Dar Rural Water Supply Project. The EEC had signed a Financial Agreement with Socialist Ethiopia in 1977 with a total commitment of US$8 million over a five-year period for the Project. (In the event, the success of those first five years secured funding for a further three years until 1983.) Tenderers were not permitted to visit Ethiopia. We had to rely on an atlas,

---

[19] Rumour has it, one of Jesus' disciples took a wrong turn southwards over a mountain range and landed up in a country called Abyssinia. He converted the locals who then remained insular for centuries. The rituals of this Ethiopian church are remarkably similar to those of the Greek and Russian Orthodox faith.

therefore, to try and define the project area. A carefully worded 'understanding of the project' was drafted, which turned out to be more political than of engineering content. Finally, we put forward our best 'team' for this unusual technical assistance assignment, together with man-month rates. Notwithstanding all the hard effort put into the written word from our base in Artillery House, London, the 'little grey men' in Brussels probably only considered the financial figures. Despite all that, we were successful. I was instructed to get on the next plane to Addis Ababa to negotiate our proposal with the Ethiopian Water Works Construction Authority (EWWCA).

Project area Our investigation was to cover a huge area in the Ethiopian Highland region (Gojjam and Gonder Provinces, about 150,000 sq.km) bounded by Sudan to the west, the Blue Nile to the south, Eritrea to the north and Wallo Province to the east. In the early days of the assignment, the project area was only accessible by road. Later, Bahir Dar Airport was opened to commercial traffic, and we were able to fly from Addis Ababa by Boeing 720s. The Project Office was based in Bahir Dar on the shores of Lake Tana (the source of the Blue Nile), nearly 6,000 feet above sea level in the Ethiopian Highlands.

Aims of the Project There were four main components of this Technical Assistance (TA) contract:

1. Establish an EWWCA Regional Office in Bahir Dar, including the provision of permanent office buildings and other appropriate facilities.
2. Develop water supply facilities in specific rural areas and improve the existing hydrometeorological network.
3. Establish a National Training Centre for EWWCA.
4. Operate and maintain completed facilities through appropriate budgetary and staffing provisions by EWWCA through the Regional Office.

Technical Assistance personnel The TA Water Engineer was to act as Project Manager and be responsible, together with the EWWCA Regional Manager, for setting up the organisation of a new regional office from scratch. Much work was needed to programme and budget the workload in the region, and this was to be initially carried out in Addis Ababa EWWCA Headquarters. As the project progressed, more time would be spent in the region by the Project Manager discussing day-to-day problems with his counterpart, the Regional Manager, developing construction programmes and reviewing project programmes.

The Project Manager was to be aided by a TA assistant engineer in the early years of the project. His duties included the determination of appropriate techniques for providing a water supply in each of the identified villages, leading the investigations, the design, and the construction, by direct labour force. Later, his duties would be transferred to Ethiopian counterpart engineers after training to undertake such work.

The team was to include a TA hydrogeologist responsible for siting boreholes and hand-dug wells using available air photography for his analysis. It wqs to be expected that more than half of the borehole sites should yield over 2.5 litre/sec, enough to supply 4,000 villagers with 25 litres per day, albeit from very deep boreholes.

The work of the team would be supported by a TA mechanic whose responsibility was to design, organise and implement an operation and maintenance service. With such a large project area, it was imperative to ensure thirty land rovers and four drilling rigs provided by the EEC were all in good working order. His duties were to include the training of Ethiopian operatives. Inevitably, the lack of their experience might cause unnecessary damage to engines, pumps, and valves of the completed works. He would set up a Pump Maintenance Section in the region therefore and would be involved in the workshop repair and maintenance activities.

The TA Drilling Superintendent was to be supported by an able and experienced counterpart. During the early years, the drilling capability was going to be limited to an old Speedstar and a Ross percussion rig which were both difficult to maintain and repair. Later, the project was to purchase two Halco rotary rigs, which would improve enabled progress and would provide training for operatives in conventional maintenance and repair.

Contract negotiations with EWWCA I arrived in Addis Ababa in 1979, very much in a foreign land. My purpose was to conclude a contract with EWWCA but wholly paid for by the EEC. Our proposal was a modest document, but the client homed in on the CVs of our Technical Assistance team. The staff proposed were well qualified for the project. Dr Davey, the hydrologist, had only recently joined JTS, but his academic qualifications greatly impressed the EWWCA officials sitting on the other side of the table. The TA Mechanic had an impressive CV, having had experience training young apprentices and managing workshops, but the clinch came when they read about his successes on his motorbike at TT races. Likewise, the TA Driller's thirty years' experience of doing nothing else but drilling for water, so he was more than acceptable to the EWWCA. The TA Assistant Engineer had a degree in engineering from a UK university and had a good ten-years post-graduate experience in water engineering, all with JTS.

We were then drawn into a detailed discussion about our proposal for the TA Water Engineer. He was not acceptable to the EWWCA because he did not have a degree.

"How can Mr Harris know anything about water engineering if he has not been to a university?"

Tony Harris had left school in the early 1950s and joined JTS as a young trainee engineer. It was not unusual in those days for somebody with high-quality engineering potential to become an apprentice in a firm of consulting engineers rather than going down the path of attending university. His 'experience' as a water engineer was entirely hands-on in a water engineer's drawing office. He had been the JTS Partners' prime assistant for all work the firm had undertaken in the 1950s & 60s in Aden, which was not a million miles away from Addis Ababa – so he was experienced in both water engineering and the region. Tony was the sort of person who was DIY-orientated and went camping on holidays. For me, he was the ideal choice to manage a very disparate project, or set of projects, across a large area some 1,000 km north of Addis Ababa. I very diplomatically explained Tony's background to my new colleagues at the EWWCA. They seemed unimpressed and continued to argue about Tony's lack of university background. I pleaded with them:

"In my opinion, Tony's lifetime experience is most appropriate to this project. Add to this, the benefit of his having visited and worked in Aden for ten years and more, a major city in this region, all leads to why I firmly believe he has an unbeatable track record for leading this assignment. Don't take a decision now. Let's all sleep on it overnight, and then perhaps I can come in tomorrow morning to learn of your decision."

They agreed to my suggestion, and I breathed a huge sigh of relief. We can all live for another day - just! In practice, the firm would have found it difficult to find a suitable replacement who might be prepared to live in the back-of-beyond from in-house, so I was anxious. The odd local beer was consumed with my evening meal that night, and I tried to sleep well. I then presented myself to the Managers at EWWCA first thing in the morning. I looked at them across the table, hoping to sense their response.

"Mr Price, we have thought long and hard about Mr Harris' suitability for this project up in Bahir Dar." Oh dear, they are going to turn him down. *"We are impressed by your team and having reviewed everything you have told us about Mr Harris, we are inclined to accept him as Team Leader for this TA."*

"Great News!" Wow, what a relief! *"We will mobilise the team and our resources without delay."*

Local hospitality

I met Tony in Addis Abba on one of my early visits. We were to motor up to Bahir Dar the next day, which meant starting at 5.30 am to arrive by the shores of Lake Tana before 6.00 pm, not only because after that time, a curfew was imposed, but also because the twenty-mile stretch before Bahir Dar was renowned for attacks from brigands and the like. Just as we were leaving in Tony's very distinctive red Land Rover with 'EEC Funded Project' emblazoned on its side, he told me we had a passenger called Susan, a nurse who lived at a clinic beyond Gondir. She had contacted Tony through the expatriate 'bush telegraph' last night to see if she could cadge a lift. Susan had received a message from a village headman at a place called Gebre Guracha about halfway to the Blue Nile from Addis who had told her:

"My son has a fever. Can you come and bring medicine?"

Having made our introductions, we were off on our way through the half-dark of dawn, out of the city's suburbs, past forests and up into the Ethiopian highlands. The road to the Blue Nile was a single tarmacked track. Traffic was light but mainly with overladen lorries. The trek through the mountain range was full of memorable scenery, with the sun still rising to cast strange and emotive shadows as we moved from one valley to the next. After we had driven for three hours or so, a man stepped out into the middle of the road waving his hands above his head, 'inviting' us to stop. It was the village Headman who had contacted Susan. He directed us towards his compound. Susan immediately went to see her patient while Tony and I were ushered into a large room full of people seated at long tables, all awaiting some meal or other. It was the Headman's name day (apparently, he has one every other week!), and he had invited his villagers to a feast. We were to be his special guests that day. Alas, we were the only people who spoke English, and we had not brushed up on our Amharic. So, there were lots of smiles and gesticulations to make ourselves understood. Eventually, we squeezed into two seats among the throng and obediently sat down as instructed. We were in for a treat.

My first Ethiopian meal was indeed an extraordinary experience. We started with a celebratory drink. It looked harmless enough, a clear liquid that looked like water in a non-too-clean glass. My first sip made me think it was over 60% alcohol content. It burned the back of my throat as though I was drinking pure vindaloo. I thought it best to postpone my next sip until I could accompany it with food, which I was politely told was to be homemade injera and wat. When this arrived, the wat (a chicken stew) came in a huge bowl, large enough for many, many good helpings. This was accompanied by the injera on a gigantic plate the size of a bicycle wheel. Both were placed in the middle of the table in front of us. I can only describe injera as a spongy pancake about half an inch thick which, when broken up to eat, had large air pockets giving the resemblance of, and tasting like sorbo rubber. The wat was exactly like vindaloo, presumably spiced up to kill all known germs. It was so hot my taste buds failed to recognise any fowl[20]. Clearly, the chef was indulging in foul play on us highjacked Europeans. The injera was a godsend because it was the ideal antidote to not only the wat but also the drink that we had been given. I was obliged to continuously breathe in through the mouth in an attempt to cool down my tongue, buccal mucosa membrane and throat. I thought it best to pace clearing my glass so at least I would have been seen to have consumed a component of this strange hospitality. No sooner had I emptied the glass than a kind villager quickly filled it up again – to the brim! I had no option but to continue my torture in silence and good grace. As we were munching away, the village Coptic priest got up and started off on a long speech. He looked as though he needed his mother to mend his habit because I saw large toes poking through the tip of his socks, and his cassock was holier than thou. He was a gentleman and clearly respected by all the assembled villagers, even though Colonel Mengistu ordered that all churches should be locked, and religion outlawed. I assumed the priest was saying, 'thank you for having me, thank you for the food, may you and your family all live to a great old age, etc. etc.' Then a man three down the table from him got up and started on another eulogy for the day. This ritual was repeated three or four times. I saw Tony looking at his watch in earnest. Somehow, we had to extricate ourselves from this feast without causing offence to our host and the rest of the village elders. I thought, cometh the day, cometh the man and stood up as soon as a villager sat down before anybody else had the opportunity to butt in. I drew on every sinew of diplomacy that my position as a Partner of JTS had taught me and said in English, which I knew only Tony would be able to understand:

"Sir, Mr Headman, Reverend, and villagers, Tony and I have been greatly honoured to have been so welcomed as visitors to your feast. This experience will live with us till our dying day. Tony lives in Ethiopia, but I am a visitor from London in the United Kingdom, far away. I, personally, have not experienced such fabulous local Ethiopian food you have so kindly put before us today; I must say this occasion has been extremely enjoyable. Your hospitality has been very precious to us, and we will have many happy memories of this meal and your company. Unfortunately, we must be on our journey, as we have today, to continue our travel over the Blue Nile and on to Bahar Dar, making sure we arrive before curfew at 6.30 pm. Thank you again so much."

---

[20] Years later, I came across an Ethiopian café in London's North End Road in Fulham. I couldn't pass by without enquiring within. I sat down and asked the waiter for an ingera and wat. His face was a picture; first his eyes nearly popped out of their sockets in total surprise and then a wry smile came over his face. *"No sir, not on menus.*

And with much waving of hands and smiles and thank yous, we backed away and made for the red Land Rover.

The Blue Nile

We continued our journey. The land fell away suddenly, and there, about a mile below us was the Blue Nile. Looking down, we could see the road wending its way down the escarpment as a series of multiple hairpin bends. Tony said it would take us an hour to drive down to the river and another hour to climb up the other side. He was right about the timing, but what a majestic sight. When we arrived at the bottom, the only evidence of man's interference with nature was a narrow bridge across this mighty river, and two soldiers with guns at the ready positioned at either end of the structure. Thankfully, we were waved on and started our climb, this time on a dirt road all the way to Bahir Dar. We arrived while the light was failing but before curfew. As we passed the outskirts of town, I couldn't help but imagine highwaymen behind every tree and at every corner. In practice, there were none. Tony drove to the Government Rest House where all the team were staying (the only local hotel, the Hilton, had been commandeered as a prison the year before). We were very dusty after our 1,000 km drive, so I quickly had a shower and went down to meet the team. To my horror, I heard Tony having a shouting match with the manager because he had no hot water in his room. Oh dear, I hadn't used much, but apparently, there isn't much hot water to have at the best of times.

Project results

Difficulties encountered The technology involved in developing individual village water schemes was not rocket science. But the logistics for securing success were fraught with unnecessary difficulties. If you were a manager, you had to be a politician. If you were a politician, you had to cow-tow to the military regime that had demolished the dynasty of Solomon a few years before and assassinated Haile Selassie. This made local managers very wary of being seen to be supporting our small band of foreign support. The team regularly had land rovers highjacked by the military for months on end, only to be returned to our compound when they couldn't be made to work through a lack of spare parts – where our TA mechanic was able to put them back into service. Tony's successor as team leader was kidnapped and held for a couple of months in Sudan until he became sick with some rat-related disease. To my eternal shame, because communication between London and Bahir Dar was virtually non-existent, I did not learn of this 'happening' until I next saw him in a London hospital some nine months later with a liver complaint.

Tony took me to see a typically completed village water scheme. The borehole was in the water compound. A formidable lady, large in stature, was in charge of administering 'fair play'. All you saw on the ground was an elevated water tank and rows of basins where the ladies of the village would come to wash their clothes and collect water for their own domestic use. There were no pipes distributing supplies outside the compound. This was a huge improvement over what the ladies were used to, walking most of the day to a water hole, collecting water of dubious quality, and returning to their village with a pot of water on their heads. Providing water was definitely a lady's responsibility in this society. The men folk appeared unsupportive of the government's project to provide the village with this essential commodity, even though it is a necessary requirement for life. In fact, they were generally against this new invasive action being brought into their lives. I was told,

> "What are our women going to do all day now that they will not have to travel to fetch water for us. They will all become promiscuous."

We couldn't possibly enter into such a discussion except to say we were only implementing government orders.

Villagers would go to their village hall at the beginning of each month and purchase their 'monthly allowance'. The administration would give them tokens, each token being equivalent to a 'pot' of water. Then before the ladies could collect water, they had to approach the compound keeper and hand over the requisite number of tokens to meet their needs for the coming month. They would then do whatever washing they needed to do and fill their pot of water, place it on their head and walk home. It all seemed to work. The borehole produced clean water in the village (instead of gathering dirty water from a watering hole that may be ten miles away), and water was distributed to the villagers in a fair and equitable way. The system had the potential to improve the villagers' health and thus enabling an improvement in work productivity around the village. The scheme involved technology at its simplest.It produced life-changing improvements over their previous method for collecting water. It was an appropriate solution to enable a village to ease their way of life into the 20th century and perhaps make them become more prosperous.

Project achievement JTS had team members on the ground in Bahir Dar for eight years. In that time, we were able to bring safe water to so many small villages where people had lived for centuries without any natural local water resource. By the time we left, we had set up an operational EWWCA Regional Office in Bahir Dar and provided safe potable water to over 375,000 villagers in the Gondar and Gojjam Provinces. No big technological achievement, but a huge logistical success for so many.

History recorded I was honoured to be invited to present a paper in Dublin on this project in 1985 to the 14th International Seminar on Case Studies in Technology Transfer organised by the Federation Europeene d'Associations Nationales d'Ingenieurs (of which I was a member) and the Institution for Engineers in Ireland on their 150th Anniversary.

Chapter 13: NED - The Essex Water Company

"The people are like water and the ruler a boat. Water can support a boat or overturn it."
William Shakespeare (Richard III)

Introduction

The invitation In 1987, my Partner, John Haseldine, called me into his office to ask if I would like to be considered for a non-executive directorship (NED) at the Essex Water Company (EWC). I was slightly taken aback because this was neither a question I had been asked before nor had I even begun to think it might be appropriate for me to receive such a summons any time soon.

Background to the UK water industry The UK Water Industry was developed over the decades by the private sector, particularly during the 19th century. Government set up the Metropolitan Water Board in 1903 to serve London by amalgamating nine private water companies. However, in the mid-twentieth century, there were still over one thousand private or municipal water companies serving the Nation. Government decided to regularise the water and sewerage industry, and in 1974, ten Regional Water Authorities were set up as parastatal bodies to absorb the majority of private water facilitators. This left 29 private statutory 'water supply-only' companies to remain active because their finances were managed on a non-profit basis (and quoted on the London Stock Exchange). The Essex Water Company was one of these, and by the 1980s, it served around 1.5 million domestic consumers in East London and the whole of Essex, as well as industries on the north bank of the River Thames, such as the Ford Motor Company in Dagenham and development associated with Tilbury Docks.

Non-executive Directorships and John Taylor and Sons Consulting engineers had a history of being retained as NEDs to these water supply-only companies. JTS had been well represented in the 1900s by Godfrey Taylor, his son Oliver Taylor, John Calvert and by Godfrey's nephew John Haseldine. Oliver retired from the Partnership in 1974 and found himself in demand by these water supply-only companies. He became a non-executive director of West Kent WC, Bournemouth & District WC, Tendring Hundred WC, and the Essex WC. However, the Essex WC was more adventurous in developing its facilities with whatever new technologies were becoming available, particularly in computerisation. Olly was finding a lot of this was outside his expertise and found the new youngish managing director difficult to engage in any technical conversation that encompassed Olly's own experience. He looked, therefore, to his cousin, John Haseldine, to find a successor. After a very brief meeting with John, I found myself invited to meet the

Essex Water Company Chairman at Claridge's to see if I might be a suitable replacement.

The Interview The Chairman, Admiral Sir Andrew Mackenzie Lewis KCB, was a charming gentleman – Lord Lieutenant of Essex and a former Second Sea Lord (1970-71). He explained the Company was managed by a small but nonetheless strategic Board. This was made up of himself, supported by a lawyer (Mark Farrar, a Partner in the Queen's solicitors Farrar & Co), a farmer (David Evans, representing the substantial agricultural community within the Water Company's area), an independent water engineer (Oliver Taylor) and David Parr, the EWC Managing Director. It was the independent water engineer post Sir Andrew was looking to fill. I don't remember exactly how the conversation went, but tea at Claridge's was an unforgettable experience I was on my best behaviour, demonstrated I was indeed a water engineer, young enough to understand evolving technology in the water industry (impressed I had been on Government committees related to developing computerisation in the water sector – so that was all good), and had a perspective not restricted to the UK water industry, but across the Globe. As a sailor, this later point appeared to be of interest, as I am sure we must have got on to the subject of Aden, Mauritius, Kuala Lumpur, and other places he had visited in his previous life. After this short tête à tête with a very senior former naval official in surroundings fit for royalty and the most glamorous of visitors from Hollywood, I became a non-executive Director of a Company that began its life at Grays, near Tilbury Docks in 1861 (the South Essex Waterworks Company) and the Southend Waterworks Company in 1865. The merger of these two companies to form the Essex Water Company came in 1970.

The Company

Map of Essex Water Company Area

Company water resources The Company supplied over 300 MLD throughout Essex, which is the driest county in the UK, having rainfall of around 600mm per annum, as opposed to the national average of 920mm. The previous South Essex WC had negotiated a bulk raw water supply with the East London Waterworks Company (*now part of Thames Water*) in the 19th century, which still exists today. This resource comes from the Lee Valley, and South Essex WC installed a treatment plant at Chigwell to service the growing industrial demand along the River Thames. Originally, the two Water Companies relied on boreholes drilled along the Thames Valley, but early in the twentieth century, these were beginning to become saline through excessive over-pumping. The Companies were forced, therefore, to depend on river abstractions from further north in their supply areas. Over time, this meant their water resources became more distant from their main centres of water demand:

- 1932 - The Stour Scheme. Government approval was secured in 1928 to abstract water from the River Stour at Langham Mill on the Essex-Suffolk border with a treatment plant at Langham. Water was also abstracted from the Rivers Chelmer and Blackwater. Some of these abstractions were downstream of Chelmsford's sewage outfall (2014 population 170,000) – so this 'water supply-only' Company was obliged to build and maintain a sewage outfall diversion so that all water abstraction points were upstream of the Chelmsford purified sewage waste discharge into the river.
- 1940's – River Stour Scheme. Government approval was secured in 1935 to abstract water at Stratford St Mary (less than two miles downstream of Langham). This also involved laying eleven miles of 36-inch raw water main to a new impounding reservoir at Abberton and a treatment works at Layer de la Haye, all completed in 1939. The two Companies were advised by consulting engineers T & C Hawksley (*today part of US Consultant Montgomery Watson Harza*) and Binnie, Deacon & Gourley (*today part of US Consultant Black & Veatch*).
- 1957 – major expansion with the building of Hanningfield impounding reservoir to serve the east of the supply zone, with advice from D M Watson.
- The 1970s - Ely Ouse Transfer Scheme. Surplus raw water that would otherwise enter the Wash (and then flow out to the North Sea) is diverted from Denver in Norfolk southwards to Abberton and Hanningfield impounding reservoirs. This 'surplus water' is transferred across the watershed from the River Great Ouse during periods of dry weather and discharged into the headwaters of the River Stour. When this surplus water is needed down in Essex, the direction of river flow in Norfolk is reversed to Blackdyke in order to achieve the diversion.

Meetings Once a month, I would leave the safety of my office in Artillery House, Westminster; take the Underground from St James' Park to Tower Hill; walk down through the underpass; round the side of the Tower and on towards the Thames and the Tower Hotel in St Katherine's Way and took the lift to a Suite on the eighth floor. My fellow Directors would be waiting for me to start the meeting at 11.00 am prompt. Plate glass windows looked both downstream towards Essex and Kent and upstream with a view of Tower Bridge. The Suite must have represented the nearest the Admiral could achieve on terra firma to being on the bridge deck of the jewel in Her Majesty's fleet. Sir Andrew managed meetings with naval precision, finishing at 12.30 precisely so he could go down to the Lobby to meet our guest(s) for the day and bring them up for drinks and a substantive lunch in our Suite – with alcohol. I would then struggle back to Westminster on the tube in the hope the effects of a good Chablis or Burgundy would have worn off enough to allow coherent management 'back at the ranch'.

The content of meetings would always deal with discussing employees' pensions and human resource matters, about which I could bring little to the discussions, but I learnt a lot, the content of which I was able to bring back to the Acer Consulting table. I was to learn Abberton Reservoir was a very special place for wildlife, particularly for wildfowl. I was no twitcher and therefore was more of an observer than a contributor to these non-engineering matters. Nonetheless, these Board discussions eventually led to Abberton becoming a Ramsar Site (Wetland of International Importance for birds), a Special Protection Area (SPA) designated under the EU Birds Directive, and a Site of Special Scientific Interest (SSSI). Apparently, the Reservoir site is used by a number of wildfowl species, including Coot, Gadwall, Great Crested Grebe, Goldeneye, Mute Swan, Pochard, Shoveler, Teal, Goosander, Tufted Duck and Wigeon to name but a few. It is also home to an inland breeding colony of Cormorant of European importance – even after 'Brexit'.[21]

On matters of engineering, I found my fellow Board members hung on my every word. I was comfortable when dealing with capital investment projects because that was my training. Operation and maintenance were a different issue, and although I blustered my way through early meetings, meeting up with various Company operatives taught me a lot and made me a better, more practical engineer as a result.

Annual review Once a year, the Directors of the Company would have an 'away day' held at different parts of the supply area. The Review always started the evening before at the Milsoms Hotel in Dedham, near Colchester. We would take a private room and discuss the needs of tomorrow's Annual Review. Sir Andrew and Mark Farrar would spend the day with David Parr, the Managing Director, to learn of any impending issues that need Board resolutions during the coming months. David Evans would direct his attention to personnel matters to ensure the

---

[21] It is reported the RAF used Abberton to practice low-level flying in preparation for the 'Dam Busters' attacks during the Second World War.

Company's workforce was happy in their work and that their remuneration structure was generally acceptable to all. For my part, a senior engineer was assigned to me for the day, and we spent our time visiting engineering installations, learning about difficulties in operation across the Company's 'patch'. All the time, I was gleaning knowledge about operations and maintenance that enabled me to talk knowledgeably at future Board meetings; as well as growing my own experience to bring to my 'day job' at Acer Consultants.

Privatisation Margaret Thatcher signed an Agricultural Directive in 1987 with the then EEC to limit certain contaminants entering river systems. In the small print, there was a reference in this Directive which applied not only to agriculture discharges but also to liquid domestic/industrial waste. When she returned to London and asked the UK Water Industry how much all this would cost, she got the response - £4bn! Government just didn't have that sort of money to spend on the water industry at that time, so she recommended privatisation, which eventually happened in 1989. During 1988, corporate predators approached the other 28 'private' statutory water supply-only companies with the intent of getting a foothold in the proposed new privatised industry. For months, nobody seemed to be interested in acquiring the Essex Water Company, even though we were the largest such undertaking. Then, within a twenty-four-hour period, we were approached by the two large French companies, Genérale des Eaux and Lyonnaise des Eaux. Sir Andrew believed we should follow a policy of (a) inviting the Company who first contacted us for a discussion and (b) preparing a comprehensive list of all our demands prior to any such meeting in case an Offer be put on the table. The Chairman of Lyonnaise des Eaux was invited to dinner in a private room at Claridge's. After a sumptuous meal, the Frenchman was invited to tell us what he had in mind for collaboration between our two Companies. His speech responded to our requirements virtually word for word, which meant that discussions were short and convivial. We suggested Lyonnaise put an Offer to the Company in writing which, if acceptable to the Board, we could present to our shareholders for their approval – or not. Within a few months, we became the UK-arm of the mighty Lyonnaise des Eaux.

Resignation After a Board Meeting in 1990 that had progressed in its usual way, I was called in for a private conversation with Sir Andrew. Rather sheepishly and with great embarrassment, he confided,

"I understand you have become a Director of Acer Engineering Ltd".

"Yes," was my reply.

I proceeded to tell him of the significant coup Acer Consultants had secured to form a joint venture consultancy with Severn Trent Water (as a minority shareholder) to carry out engineering design not just in water within the confines of Severn Trent's area but across the whole capability of Acer Consultants, and not just in the UK but around the World.

Sir Andrew came straight to the point. His bosses in Paris were not happy with this 'development' by Acer Consultants as they saw it as "doing business with the opposition", even though this arrangement was a consultancy and not the 'bread and butter' stuff of a water utility. He went on to say the French had asked for my resignation and handed me a letter to sign there and then.

Sir Andrew was a true gentleman and arranged I would be paid a full two-year salary as recompense for what he perceived as an ill-advised decision from the Continent.

So ended a three-year hands-on experience in management within a water utility.

Chapter 14: United States of America

"Thousands have lived without love, not one without water."
W. H. Auden

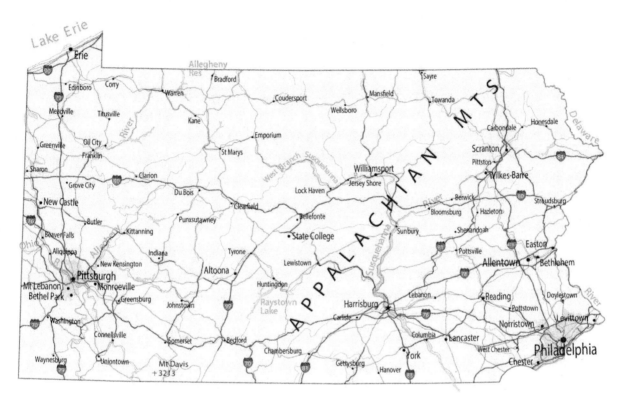

Map of Pennsylvania

Achievement

Signing the Contract Chapter 6 describes the success of acquiring PSC Engineers & Consultants Inc. for one dollar. I visited Bryn Mawr, Philadelphia, in early December 1991 to sign the purchase papers. Sitting across the table were Roy Stahl, PSC's General Counsel and John F Boyer Jnr, the PSC Chairman. Both sides signed the sale documents. As soon as the ink was dry and we had exchanged pleasantries, I could see the relief in their faces that, at long last, the water company had off-loaded its loss-making consultancy. John F Boyer Jnr reached for his side table and very kindly handed me a book entitled Reflections on Water. A Centennial History of Philadelphia Suburban Water Company 1886-1986 and wrote on the frontispiece:

To Jessop Price.
May our first meeting be the beginning of a continuing relationship with water.
John F Boyer Jr

I did not have a similar book to present to the Chairman, although, if I had thought about it earlier, I could have brought with me a glossy A5 brochure entitled John Taylor & Sons 1869-1969. It remained back in Blighty.

After the presentation, I thanked them both profusely and made my way into an adjacent room to meet Rennie Quinn, Managing Director of Severn Trent International. I immediately concluded a second deal with him to transfer a water operation subsidiary of PSC Engineers & Consultants Inc. to his company, as Acer Consultants was not in the operation and management business. When the job was done, we headed back to the hotel to toast our success and the beginning of new operations in a new continent, all with huge potential.

Bill Klaus – non-executive I was nervous about taking over a business of 300 engineers and architects practicing across the Eastern Seaboard without the Acer Group having any experience of working in the US. I persuaded Eric Bridgen (Acer Consultants' CEO) to retain Bill Klaus as a non-executive director of our new company, Acer Engineers & Consultants Inc., based in Lancaster, Pennsylvania. Bill was a senior Partner of the Philadelphia law firm Pepper, Hamilton & Scheetz LLP and had been our legal representative during the purchase process. It seemed a logical suggestion to make. After five years of operation, Bill made this comment about recording the work achieved over that time[22]:

> *"Upon its acquisition, we found an almost moribund business, which its prior owners had allowed to atrophy. The engineering staff were demoralised and looked around for other work.*
>
> *By a combination of personal skills, Mr Price managed to turn the company around. He quickly instituted financial controls and reshuffled the internal leadership. Most important, he put in place a business development program which began to bring in more and larger projects and personally energised the professional staff.*
>
> *Today, the Company is prospering as never before, is three times the size at the time of acquisition and continuing to grow."*

---

[22] Letter to Barry Horn Watson, Counselling Director, ICM CareerCare Services 17 12 1997

First visit to Philadelphia and Lancaster, Pennsylvania

Brief history Philadelphia was founded in 1682 by William Penn, an English Quaker. It became the hub for insurrection against their English masters, and it was where the Declaration of Independence was signed in 1776. Many key events occurred in Philadelphia in those days, including the preservation of the Liberty Bell. Philadelphia remained the nation's largest city until being overtaken by New York City in 1790. The population today is about 1,500,000, and it is the home of many U.S. firsts, including the first library (1731), hospital (1752), medical school (1765), stock exchange (1774) and business school (1881). It became a member of the Organisation of World Heritage Cities in 2015.

Introduction to Acer Engineers & Consultants Inc The day after the acquisition, I was called to PSC head office in Bryn Mawr to meet the President of our new firm, Arthur Morris, who had driven to Philadelphia from Lancaster. Arthur had been born in the North East of the UK but moved to the US with his parents when he was twelve. He was a qualified engineer, but before becoming President of the company, he had served as Mayor of Lancaster. He was, therefore, a huge asset in terms of political contacts. Over the coming months, I was soon to learn how important this is in the US context if you are to hold on to existing clients and gain new business. Roy Stahl introduced me to Arthur. I have never been introduced to anyone before who refused to shake my hand when it was offered. This was a first. The reason for this soon became very clear. Arthur had neither been told his company, PSC Engineers & Consultants Inc., was up for sale nor that it had been bought by an English company. Oh dear, an awkward silence pervaded the room, and I could see steam rising from the red hairs on Arthur's head. Anger was not directed at me, but the sheer unbelievability of his predicament involved not just Roy, but John F Boyer Jnr was called in to explain Arthur's predicament. A difficult half an hour was had, with me lying low in the corner while the former owner and the President of my new company battled out an extraordinary charade, the conclusion of which could only be a fait accompli.

Initial study of background documentation Eventually, Arthur Morris shook my hand, gave me an embarrassed smile, and we left on the understanding he would meet me at Lancaster airport the next day. He left by car to return the way he had come, and I sought refuge in my Bryn Mawr hotel, clutching documents given to me by Roy Stahl, including those related to the historical accounts of the consultancy. I went down to the hotel restaurant that evening with a few of those papers to read over dinner and to enjoy a private meal. I chose a corner table so as not to offend any of the other guests. The restaurant served me an excellent meal with a nice bottle of wine, all of which was appreciated to the full. The dinner was an appropriate antidote to the content of the papers I was to read through the three courses. After most of the guests had left, I asked the waiter for the check (Oscar Wilde was right when he wrote, *"We have really everything in common with America nowadays, except, of course, language."* [23]). I duly signed the document put in front of me and made my way up to my room via the lift. As soon as I entered the room, the phone rang.

> *"This is the restaurant here, Sir. Is everything alright? Did you enjoy your meal?"*
> *"Yes, thank you very much. The food was excellent."*
> *"Sir, are you sure, because you failed to leave a tip."*
> *"Oh, goodness me, yes, of course. Please add ten per cent to my bill."*
> *"It is usual, Sir, to leave fifteen per cent."*
> *"Oh, right"*, and in total embarrassment, I went on to say, *"Oh yes, of course. Please add fifteen per cent to my bill."*

Wow! How different can life be in this part of the English-speaking world?

Introduction to Lancaster, Pennsylvania Lancaster was the capital of the US for one day in 1777 and the capital of Pennsylvania from 1799 to 1812 (when it moved to Harrisburg). The first long-distance paved road was constructed between Philadelphia and Lancaster in 1795 at a staggering cost of $450,000. There are a few well-known former residents of the city, including James Buchanan (the 15th US President) and Robert Fulton (who created the first steamboat). FW Woolworth started his career in 1879 by opening his first 'Five and Dime' store in Lancaster.

I was met the next day at Lancaster Airport by Arthur Morris, who had quietened down by the time he had returned home Our meeting was in no way an embarrassment. He divulged his family background, how he was born in the UK and that his father obtained work at Armstrong World Industries (floor tiles, among other things); he spent his formative years in this very town. I happened to mention this was not my first visit to Lancaster as I visited briefly in the fall of 1953 as part of the St Paul's Cathedral Choir tour of the US. He was amazed and replied:

> *"Well, you must have sung in McCasky High School auditorium, which was built in the early 1950s as a state-of-the-art concert hall. Let's go. I can take you there, and you can sing to me from the stage."*

And that is what we did. He drove us to the school and, having been Mayor, he knew the head teacher well, and permission was granted for us to visit the auditorium. I was not going to remember the precise detail of the building and its facilities forty years on. It was a strange experience to revisit one of the fifty venues we had sung in all those years ago. So, I went on the stage and gave a rendering of the first two lines of Mozart's O Isis und Osiris before I got embarrassed!

---

[23] *The Canterville Ghost, 1887*

I was introduced to all the staff in the Lancaster office, which was located in what we in the UK would call a light industrial estate. I chatted with some of them to get a feel as to how they felt I should approach dealing with this aging company. It was a lot to take in on my first day. Arthur said he had a presentation to make in the evening to a potential client, would I like to come? I was never going to say no, so he picked me up from the Holiday Inn hotel, which was within easy walking distance from the office.

Nothing would prepare me for what was to come. I quickly learnt the US water industry was like the UK's but pre-1974 (maybe a good deal earlier in some cases). There were no rural district councils or local boroughs in the US where several villages might get together to share infrastructure facilities. Every community is responsible for its water and sewerage facilities – and all other facilities as well. If you were a citizen of a village in the middle of nowhere, then you would depend on their elected officials to supply all 20th-century facilities to the best of their ability.

That evening, we visited a 'village' with a population of less than 1,000 souls. They needed both a new water supply and to upgrade their wastewater system. Arthur took me by car, and we stopped outside the village fire station with a gleaming modern fire engine waiting for a call from within the village's bounds. To get to our meeting, we had to walk past this burnished beast and through a door that led to a room no grander than a village hall. The councillors were seated around a large table to accommodate them all, awaiting our turn to give a presentation. I was introduced as the owner of the consultancy from London, and away Arthur went with his proposal. He was good, and I was encouraged for the future of the company. Having said his piece, we politely upped and left. In the car, going back to my hotel, I asked him if he thought we wanted work from such a 'small' client. His response was:

> *"Probably not, it was gifted to one our competitors anyway, but local politics dictate we have to be seen to be offering our services where appropriate, and there was an important politico who lived in this particular village."*

I was clearly at the bottom of a steep learning curve.

The Amish One aspect of Lancaster, with its population of around 55,000, is that it is slap in the middle of Amish country. The Amish are a religious sect who stem originally from Switzerland and Germany. They emigrated to the east coast of North America in the early 1700s and eventually landed up in Lancaster County. The sect is an ultra-Protestant community that believes in no embellishment of any kind; for instance, buttons on clothes are seen as showing off, and electricity is Satan's way of allowing the human race to see in the dark. Strange behaviour to me in the 1990s, but they are lovely people. The Amish men are regularly seen driving a horse and cart into Lancaster Town to lodge their cash at the bank (*clearly, they understand they do need money to live. Rumour has it the families are really rich, but their faith does not permit them to flaunt their wealth*).

There is a 1985 film called "Witness" with Harrison Ford that describes the lifestyle of the Amish. Arthur mentioned a couple of our staff had been film extras, which I thought was a good omen! I took the car one evening after work to travel out of Lancaster on the road towards Philadelphia. I was intrigued by the names of some of the villages not very far away, three examples being '*Paradise*', '*Intercourse*' and '*Bird in Hand*'. It soon became clear I had motored into the heart of Amish country. Horse-drawn buggies were going hither and thither. The farms were very active, even at that late hour. I will remember to my dying day the spectacle of one farmer standing on his horse with the setting sun behind him, controlling five other horses to plough the land. No mechanical plant was anywhere near this part of the County.

Regular visits

The journey For two years, I travelled to Lancaster once every month for a working week. I would travel down to Gatwick Airport on a Sunday afternoon to take the American Airlines flight to Philadelphia. From there, I would be met by a chauffeur and driven the 70 miles to Lancaster in one of those stretched limousines, together with a drink's cabinet and TV. All very grand, but Arthur had done a deal with the limousine company, which justified the cost over that of a flight. I was always amazed at how slowly these vehicles travelled and felt they would speed up at some stage to outwit a passing pedestrian. The route via West Chester (a client) was to become very familiar after a while as I made this journey over thirty times, sometimes in bright sunlight and sometimes seeing a picturesque deep snowy landscape out of the limousine window during winter visits. I was deposited at the Holiday Inn in Lancaster and, more often than not, welcomed as a long-lost friend. Usually, they gave me the best room because when you arrive on a Sunday evening, the hotel is virtually empty. Breakfasts were memorable, in part because of the healthy fresh fruit on display, but also because of lashings of unhealthy crispy bacon oozing with tasty fat that I could never resist, especially as Kay was not looking over my shoulder in the morning.

The changing of the guard I walked to the office and made myself available to Arthur Morris. He would have a schedule of activities organised for me for the week; to meet the odd client, talk to the staff, organise an agenda for a board meeting on a Thursday (which would be attended by Bill Klaus and section leaders from within the company), and discuss the development of a business plan. It was this latter topic that frequently reminded me that Arthur had not forgiven his former parent PSC for selling on the company without his say-so. After about twelve months of treading eggshells, Arthur flared up, said he had had enough and walked out of the office – for good. This was an embarrassment all round. I couldn't manage the company on my own, and what would clients think, as Arthur clearly had a good working and political relationship with them all. I quickly upgraded Arthur's number two in the company on the understanding we would advertise without delay for a new President.

Fortune was on our side. An application came in from an engineer who lived and worked in Philadelphia. Eric Bridgen came over with me to present a solid front to this candidate. His name was David Child, and he was perfect for the job. Very presentable, strangely enough, another water engineer born in the UK but who had spent his whole working career in the States. Eric asked David how old he was. There was a pregnant pause, after which he replied:

"You are not supposed to ask me that question."

It was the law, and we had missed that in our eagerness to have a replacement president. David stayed President until I was no longer part of the company and made several visits to the UK to attend management meetings in our UK head office.

One year on

To begin at the beginning again Substantial activity occurred during those first twelve months. The focus was first on a continuous campaign of getting to know the staff both from a technical and administrative point of view. The company went through a period of consolidation in 1992, which brought a degree of stability to the operation and substantial improvement in its financial performance.

Personal letter to staff I decided to write a personal letter to all staff members. It was just coming up to Christmas, and I wanted the staff to feel they had really supported their new owner. Some of the letter is reproduced here to demonstrate what was achievable in only a 12-month period.

> *"... Company costs have been cut by 30 percent; the level of work we have won has gone up by 10 percent; and the all-important utilization factor (that weekly indicator you have all come to love and hate) is rising as we change our approach to meet the requirements of changing times and improve our commercial awareness. Your achievements have enabled the Board to recommend bringing forward the annual pay increase by two months.*

"What about the immediate future? I believe this company is now positioned for an expansion program, both geographically and in added value with new technological skills .... We have already tasted success with our appointments to advise both Lancaster and York County Solid Waste Authorities.

"Our first significant Geographical Information Systems contract with the City of Coatesville is a leap forward ... linked with mapping, hydraulic modelling, and surveying, it enables us to use our wit to offer valuable 1990s technology and provide a commercial edge to woo future clients.

"I see a beginning to technical cooperation between Acer offices and personnel across the Atlantic and beyond. Acer UK ... has opened up opportunities for us here in the US.

"I congratulate you all and urge that you continue to strive for technical excellence ... we all have a responsibility to win new business, and we must evolve our practices to improve efficiency. These two factors are going to be high on our agenda for 1993."

I then ended my draft by saying, *"may I take this opportunity to wish you all a very happy Christmas and success as we move forward into 1993."* My secretary piped up and said:

"Mr Price, you can't say that!"

Alas, another incident of American and UK societies having a very different understanding of words and sentiments. I changed the wording to:

"I wish you every happiness during the coming Holiday Season. I hope that you will enjoy yourselves and take a well-earned break to recharge your batteries. My best wishes to you all for 1993."

Baltimore, Maryland

One of the company's large clients was the City of Baltimore Department of Public Works. From time to time, they would call upon our company to give advice on the City's two large wastewater treatment plants at Black River and Patapsco. David Child visited them regularly as the city was only 55 miles to the southwest of Lancaster. He reported back on one occasion that he had had a serious conversation revolving around the increasing number of complaints the City was getting on odour nuisance surrounding their two wastewater plants. I expect elections to be coming up, and councillors need to be seen to be addressing real issues. David was quick to respond that, in our UK office, we had Arthur Boone, one of the world's experts on odour control. Indeed, Arthur had been chosen by the US Environmental Protection Agency to write the official guidance document on this very topic.24 Arthur came to work for us in the late-1980s and was able to provide us with all his background knowledge and experience, particularly in wastewater treatment and associated issues such as odour control. He was the ideal man to put in front of the Baltimore client. The

client was intrigued by this prospect, and on my next visit, Arthur accompanied me out to Lancaster and on to the crucial Baltimore visit. He was well versed in speaking at international conferences, so found it easy to convince this client they needed us to counteract their customer complaints. A contract was quickly prepared and signed by both parties. I then left Arthur to visit the wastewater plants and allow his recommendations to evolve to solve the odour problem according to parameters pertaining to both Baltimore plants.

Patapsco wastewater treatment plant

Boston, Massachusetts

The US needed our company again for specific expertise of which we were world leaders. This time, it did not relate to water engineering. Instead, the major project was in transportation engineering to build a tunnel in Boston for their expanding rapid transit system. JTS had merged with Freeman Fox & Partners in 1987, who had designed some of the longest span bridges anywhere, as well as roads, rail and all things related to transportation. The new expanded Acer Group could offer Acer Engineering & Consultants Inc. this kind of expertise. The Massachusetts Bay Transportation Authority (MBTA) were searching for tunnelling expertise for a tricky extension of their Boston rapid transit system.

Our proposal was not to build the railway as a conventional tunnel but because a critical length of the tunnel had to cross the Charles River and had to pass within

---

24 Arthur Boon had spent most of his working life as a research engineer at the UK's Water Research Centre at Medmenham, Buckinghamshire before it moved to Swindon. This institution was world renowned for research into water and wastewater treatment techniques and was the UK water industry's lifeline to keep pace with new developments.

one metre of an existing live railway tunnel, we proposed constructing this section as an immersed tube tunnel. This technique involves building the 'tunnel' structure as prefabricated manageable lengths in a dry dock. The ends are then sealed, and each segment prepared to be floated out on the river. During the preparation of the segments, a channel would be dredged in the riverbed to the required depth and tolerances to receive the segments. Once the prefabricated segments have been floated into their correct position over the dredged trench, they would be filled with water and sunk into their final resting place. The water is then evacuated, and a watertight seal secured between one segment with the next to create a dry tunnel through which to provide the associated apparatus for a rail line under the Charles River. The advantages of this technique include speed of construction, minimal disruption to the riverbed, safety, and flexibility in the overall tunnel profile, which was very relevant in Boston, where the new tunnel had to be aligned so close to an existing live rail tunnel. The Acer Group had used this technique successfully three times in Hong Kong to join the Chinese mainland road network with Hong Kong Island and in Australia.

Doug Morton was our lead engineer with this specialist knowledge, and we airlifted him from the Guildford office to Boston to talk to the MBTA. His knowledge and Scottish drawl impressed, and we secured the contract to design and supervise the construction of this tricky crossing under the Charles River – hoping not to find too many empty tea chests left there since December of 1773 (by the Sons of Liberty in Boston, Massachusetts as part of their tea party). The company opened an office in Boston. Doug stayed for twelve months to project manage the construction of the crossing, which proved successful. He was supported by about half a dozen staff, a couple from Guildford and the rest from the home office in Lancaster. I visited Doug just once to observe the technical progress of his speciality. It was important, too, to make him feel one of our team and not out on a limb to face alone those descendants of tea party fame.

Conclusion

Most of the company's clients were in Pennsylvania. The list was very impressive and included Lancaster, Harrisburg, Ephrata, Allentown, Easton, King of Prussia, West Chester, Myerstown, and York. A geographical expansion to secure new business seemed not just possible but indeed practical, which bodes well for the future. I was to remain in charge of the Lancaster operation for five years until my skills were required to look after the Group's business in the Middle East. The end of my regular stays in Lancaster always started at Friday lunchtime, when I made my way back to Philadelphia by stretched limousine and boarded an AA flight to Gatwick. From there, I was met by my regular taxi driver and driven back to Cobham.

Presentation by David Child, President of Acer Engineers & Consultants Inc. of a Eulogistic Statement in Recognition of the effort put in by the Chairman to turn the Company around.

Chapter 15: The Far East

"I believe that water is the closest thing to a god we have here on Earth. We are in awe of its power and majestic beauty."
Alex Z. Moores (American Author)

Malaysia

Introduction The country is, by definition, in Southeast Asia, located on the Malay Peninsula and the island of Borneo (population of 32 million). There have been Indian and Chinese influences on these lands for over two thousand years. By the 16th century, the Europeans began to arrive, first, the Portuguese took charge of Malacca, followed by the Dutch in the 17th century. Penang Island was leased to the British East India Company in 1786, followed by Singapore (in 1819) and

Malacca (in 1824). By the beginning of the 20th century, most Malay States came under British rule, while others accepted the British as advisers. Malaya was invaded by the Japanese army during the Second World War and occupied for three years. In 1948, Singapore became a separate country. The remainder became known as the Federation of Malaya, which restored the autonomy of the rulers of the Malay States, but under British Protection.

For twelve years, ethnic Chinese rebels allied themselves as part of the Malayan Communist Party and launched a serious guerrilla insurgency campaign fought by troops from Commonwealth countries In 1957, the country became independent and renamed Malaysia.

Local representation JTS formed an alliance with Bina Runding Sdn Bhd, a Malaysian firm of consulting engineers based in Petaling Jaya, Kuala Lumpur. It was owned and managed by Toh Ah Se (who liked to be called Mr Toh). He was a true gentleman, an astute businessman and understood local politics when it came to water engineering in his country. We were often invited to his house for an evening meal, and he and his wife were the perfect hosts. His one complaint concerning his own career was that Malaysian law dictated Chinese Malays were prohibited from owning companies outright. He was obliged, therefore, to invite two 'sleeping' Malay partners to take a 51% share of his business. Mr Toh often found this arrangement frustrating but recognised it was a necessary evil to allow him to practice in his own land. We had our own Area Representative, David Yaw, based in Kuala Lumpa, to help him focus on JTS activity and meet those technocrats in the water industry, state by state, across this fabulous country. David was a marketeer 'par excellence' and I learned a great deal from him on how to put together an unbeatable proposal. David's responsibilities were to search for consultancy work in Thailand and Indonesia as well as Malaysia and to keep a close watch on contracts issued by the Asia Development Bank in The Philippines.

Leak Detection One of the first projects JTS secured with Bina Runding was to examine why certain urban conurbations were recording huge 'unaccounted for' water in their distribution systems. The World Bank came to the rescue. Our successful leak detection work in Mauritius was well documented in the hallowed portals of their HQ in Washington, DC. Visiting World Bank technical officers were able to persuade State water undertakings (JKRs) that this was a good 'housekeeping' activity. Paul Walker had just completed his work in Mauritius and was redeployed to work on investigations in Malaysia. Whereas their distribution systems were in themselves well designed, in terms of pipe sizes and treated water storage, we often found inflows into treated water storage reservoirs to be less than the outflow. This had the effect of inflows passing straight over the tank floor to flow out into distribution without being able to be stored. When examining the number of customers served by each reservoir, it became clear there was over

60% of flow unlikely to be being used by customers and was therefore leaking out of the distribution system below ground level. Enter Paul and his 'magic', and soon pressures were returned to distribution systems, and reservoirs were able to fill again to help give customers the continuous service for which they were paying good money.

Kluang water project Johor Bahru is a town across the straits from Singapore. The local JKR entrusted JTS with a project to convey a large volume of water to this prestigious conurbation from the town of Kluang, all in the southern half of Peninsula Malaysia. We carried out the survey work, designed a 30-inch steel pipe, prepared the drawings and tender documents, and the client then put the project out to tender. Once awarded, the contractor mobilised and placed his order for the manufacture and provision of the steel pipes with Stewart and Lloyds (S&L) of Singapore. S&L were a highly respected steel pipe manufacturer and tended to operate in countries that formerly had British rule. I had come across them in Zambia, where they had a good reputation.

During one of my visits to Malaysia, I noticed the 30-inch diameter pipes were beginning to arrive and were strewn by the side of the road from Kluang, waiting for the contractor to dig a trench and carefully place the steel pipe at depths determined by JTS, all surrounded in a sand bed to give permanent protection to this considerable investment. JTS had a fastidious resident engineer on site who checked everything as the project progressed. Each pipe was six metres long, made up of three two-metre lengths welded together. He checked the welds and then the thickness of the steel plate. To his horror, he noticed that, whereas the pipe thickness at each end of the six-metre length was to the correct specification, the middle section was always registering a thinner plate. This was totally unacceptable. He explained his deep concerns to David, and we concluded this was a fraud of mammoth proportion. We immediately took Mr Toh into our confidence. We thought he might wish to sweep it under the carpet because local politics could prove 'troublesome'. Not a bit of it. He quite rightly insisted we inform JKR senior management without delay. The end of this story saw Stewart & Lloyds' Singapore managing director being immediately given his P45.

Nationwide Water Project The winning of this project is described in Chapter 6. Our role in this project was purely advisory to the various JKRs across the Nation, who were themselves the project managers to make sure Biwater of UK constructed everything according to their contractual obligations. I came out to Malaysia with Bob Owens, a very senior and experienced JTS project manager, who had just completed a similar assignment for the Santiago sewage master plan project in Chile. He was called to the Federal JKR offices for his first meeting and was handed the draft of a contractual letter for our approval before they issued it to Biwater. It was brief and referred to specific Sections and Clauses within the Conditions of Contract. Bob was far from being amused as this draft was a clear

Dam constructed in the Nationwide Project

instruction to terminate the contract – forthwith. Their argument was that the Malaysian Government had paid Biwater US$30 million (all in accordance with the terms of the contract) for which they could only see one kilometre of relatively small diameter pipe completed – and they didn't think this was good value for money. In any event, the Malaysian technocrats didn't want this contract in the first place, and now they believed it had gone 'belly-up' all at the expense of the Malaysian people.

We advised that paying Biwater up-front funds was to enable them to buy plant, materials, and equipment which we assumed they may well have purchased. Our recommendation was to request Biwater to justify the up-front payment had been used entirely on this Contract rather than supporting other financial commitments around the world or at home in the UK.

My concern, however, was focused on the political nature of this project. As explained in Chapter 6, Maggie Thatcher had cancelled free education in the UK for rich foreign diplomats and politicians. The Malaysian Prime Minister (Mahathir Mohamad) objected strongly and decreed a 'buy British last' policy for all government contracts. This ruling had lasted for 5-years, after which time diplomats from both countries began to argue enough was enough. This Nationwide Project was seen by both Governments as a means to let bygones be bygones so that trade between the two nations could flourish again. The Federal JKR's attempt to cancel this contract could indeed have all sorts of political implications way beyond Biwaters' perceived performance. I was to travel back to London that night, but before I did, I believed I should meet with the British High Commissioner. I went to visit him at his official residence in the centre of KL. UK taxpayers support this gated grand home in the centre of KL, with its immaculate lawns with flower beds to match, all tended by a fleet of local gardeners. The driveway turned a corner, and a magnificent colonial home with umpteen bedrooms came into view, the outside of the building having recently been whitewashed. A member of the household staff met me, and I was ushered into the presence of this senior British diplomat.

We had a few opening pleasantries before I got down to the kernel of why I had asked to see him urgently outside of office hours. He knew how important this Contract was between the Federal JKR and Biwater because a few months earlier, he was involved in securing a commercial 'peace treaty' between the Her Majesty's Government and that of Malaysia.

"Commissioner, I am well aware you know the purpose of our role in the Biwater Contract, which is to advise the Federal JKR as and when they ask for advice. Today, we had the first such request. JTS has been asked to approve the text of a letter the Federal JKR wishes to send to Biwater. The draft was short, unambiguous and invokes a particular Section and Clause of the Conditions of Contract. Biwater will realise this is none other than a Letter of Cancellation."

"Oh! Round Objects![25] Why would they want to do that?"

"Their argument is the Federal Government paid Biwater US$30 million upfront. 12-months on, all they can see on the ground in Malaysia is 1.6 km of pipe having been laid. Based on this scenario, they don't believe the Contract is in the best interest of the Malaysian voter. They have a right to stop the Contract and don't want to pay Biwater another dollar."

"It would be a total disaster if the letter should be issued."

"I agree, Commissioner. It needn't be issued if we can persuade the Malaysian Government that Biwater needed upfront payments to purchase materials and plant, such as pipes, pumps, and generators, to enable them to manage the Contract effectively. Biwater estimated they needed these funds up-front, and that is why it was included in the Contract, signed by both parties."

"That all sounds reasonable. What can I do to help stop this draft letter?"

"The technocrats in Federal JKR firmly believe this letter needs to be sent. I believe Biwater is performing within the terms of their Contract, so they need to be persuaded there is no fraud. The Malaysian Government needs to be confident a contractor such as Biwater, with a respectable international reputation to uphold, is unlikely to commit fraud in this highly political Contract. My recommendation to you is this; if there is any hope to prevent the letter from seeing the light of day, it will only be achieved by urgent Government to Government discussion.

"I'm catching tonight's flight to London. Can you possibly arrange to see the Minister of Public Works first thing in the morning to clear up this

---

[25] A well-known Principal Private Secretary has often been quoted to say "Who is Round and to what does he object" when reviewing a filed document where the previous reader had shown in the margin his violent disagreement.

unfortunate misunderstanding?" He said he would, and I headed for KL airport.

My flight landed me at Heathrow very early the next day, and I was out of the airport by 7.30am. I decided to go straight to Artillery House in Westminster. I gave Maureen at Reception a wave and made straight for my office. Within a minute, the 'phone went. It was Gwilym Roberts, Senior Partner - would I see him right away.

"I have just had a very irate Adrian White, Managing Director of Biwater, on the 'phone. He made just the one request, an instruction really. Fire Jessop Price from the Partnership. What has been going on in KL?"

Adrian has got the wrong end of the stick, and clearly had no idea of our role on this Nationwide Water Project. He was under the impression JTS drafted this letter and that we were trying to persuade the Federal JKR to issue it without delay. We were purely advisers to Government and had no jurisdiction to manage the Biwater contract.

I explained to Gwilym we had been asked to 'approve' the Federal JKR's Letter of Cancelation. We told them to back off for the time being while we investigated the facts to justify such a letter. I knew how highly charged this Contract would be if British companies were to escape the 'Buy British Last' policy imposed by the Malaysian Government some five years previously. Having told Gwilym I made a plea to the British High Commissioner to sort this out at his level of authority, he smiled and told me he had no intention of responding to Adrian White's request.

I lived to work another day.

Old Kuala Lumpur During my many visits to KL, I usually arranged to 'drop in' to the old part of the city, which exuded colonialism of former tea planters and rubber merchants. My first encounter was with a very old-fashioned British pub. I raised an eyebrow or two when reading a notice by the entrance door informing the visitor, *"no durians served here"*. I believed this to mean there was a ban on a local tribe called Durian, of whom I had no knowledge. Not a bit of it. Durian is a fruit native to Malaysia which has a terrific, sweet taste (if you are into sweet things), but it comes with the most nauseous odour that pervades the whole room when it is being consumed – hence the need for the notice!

Two streets became dedicated to market stalls during evening. You could buy anything there, from textiles with designer labels to household goods of every kind. I enjoyed walking up and down the aisles. My attention was usually drawn to two or three stalls dedicated to wristwatches. There were all sorts on display. On my first visit, I was tempted to buy a Gucci watch. It had a very simple but well-designed face and a leather strap. The trader was quick to try and make a deal.

> *"That's a lovely watch, sir. A genuine fake. To you, a mere 50 Ringit"*
> (about the equivalent of £5).

This came home with me strapped to my wrist. The family was amazed. During my next visits, my daughters gave me long lists of 'requests' from their school friends at Croydon High for every 'designer' watch you can think of – Rolex, Tissot, Breitling, Tag Heuer, Cartier, Longines, to name but a few. On one occasion, I think I returned with about fifteen watches in my bag. My flight always arrived at Heathrow between five and eight in the morning. I was always one of the first to go through customs, and I became conscious of having to run the gauntlet of a few keen officers who had probably been tipped off about a passenger(s) bringing in drugs or precious stones. I daren't declare my 'contraband' for fear of having my fakes taken away from me! I kept a strong focus on the exit and walked nonchalantly like any tired businessman returning after waving the flag for Britain over the past week. My 'innocent face' has ensured I never got stopped for bringing anything into the country, be it watches, fruit or silver jewellery for my long-suffering wife.

One place I always visited with David Yaw was a restaurant called the Colosseum, which probably started off in the 1920s as a hotel for Planters coming to KL for a weekend's leave. It had that sort of atmosphere, and rumour had it many a writer of the likes of Graham Green and Somerset Maugham used to stay there to soak up the atmosphere and write part of their novels whilst resident. By the time of my first visit, the 'specialité de la maison' was a sizzling steak that arrived on a metal plate. The explosive sounds generated from kitchen to table and the cooked meat were a true delight, even if not too good for one's health. I was back in London having my haircut across the road from the office in the Army & Navy Stores when a young man sat down in the chair next to mine and gabbled away to his hairdresser with much enthusiasm, describing how he had just returned from KL and had an amazing experience at an old restaurant called the Colosseum.

> *"I was blown away by the sizzling steaks"* were his final comments before
> he started to concentrate on his new tonsorial hairstyle!

A wry smile came over my face as my 'tonsor' continued to complete my blow wave.

Thailand

Songkhla Lake Basin We regularly paid visits to the Asian Development Bank (ADB) in Manila who were responsible for awarding consultancy contracts on all manner of technologies, including the environment and water sectors. The task had to be done, and we did win a couple of contracts in Indonesia. The largest assignment we secured was in Thailand, the Songkhla Lake Basin Planning Study. Songkhla is the largest lake in Thailand, down in the southernmost part of the country, close to the border with Malaysia. The Lake is divided into four separate sections covering over 1,000 sq km. It is strangely shallow throughout, with a maximum depth of no more than two metres. Water quality is affected by its varied environmental characteristics, with mangrove swamps to the north, a central portion where the Lake is predominantly fresh water, and finally, a brackish water section close to a 75 km spit protecting it from the Gulf of Thailand and the South China Sea.

For centuries, the Lake had been the lifeblood of local fishermen who secured a reasonable lifestyle within a very rural community. The growing problem facing the Lake was industrial growth with undesirable effluent being discharged without treatment, turning the shallow waters anaerobic, resulting in a catastrophic effect on fish life.

We decided to bid jointly for this Project with our colleagues in Australia (*Sinclair Knight and Partners*), with whom we have had a relationship for over ten years. This enabled us to pick up both the Australian and British tickets when being assessed by the ADB – definitely a plus point. We put forward Bruce Sinclair as our project manager. He was a founder of Sinclair Knight & Partners but was soon to retire. He fancied this challenge in Thailand as his last professional assignment, which no doubt gave us a considerable number of brownie points as he was well-known to the ADB. Our project office was in Hat Yai, which I visited a couple of times to meet the client, assess the magnitude of the problem and point Bruce in the direction of the considerable JTS experience in dealing with industrial effluents and discharging effluents into large volumes of water mass.

Considerable environmental measurement was undertaken as part of the Study to augment that already available. The results showed:

1. Depletion of dissolved oxygen (which is a significant indicator of the health of the aquatic system and explains why parts of the Lake suffer from algal blooms in the dry season, which get washed away during the rains)
2. Variation in salinity causing problems to aquatic life

3. Chlorophyll a eutrophication due to over-fertilisation of nitrogen and phosphorous mainly from paddy fields but also from aquaculture by the fishermen themselves.
4. Human and industrial waste was an ever-increasing problem.

Our final report attempted to explain that, up till now, the Lake system had looked after itself, becoming gradually polluted as the dry season progressed, which was generally then washed away during the brief period of rains each year. However, with the growth of Hat Yai, particularly industrial growth, this cycle of 'spasmodic equilibrium' was being attacked, and government regulation was needed to be imposed as a matter of urgency. Our Report was presented to the Thai Government, its findings acknowledged and acted upon as much as local politics would allow.

Chapter 16: From Heaven to Hell in the Corporate World

"For my people have committed two evils; they have forsaken me the fountain of living waters, and hewed them out cisterns, broken cisterns, that can hold no water"
Jeremiah 2 v13

The Partnership

Appointment A business partnership is a marriage in all but physical consummation, something which Henry VIII would not have approved. John Taylor & Sons had always offered Partnerships to engineers in their 30s every five to ten years or so, which was a good strategy for providing continuity. This was unlike all other UK civil engineering partnerships in Westminster, which relied on engineers who had already proven their engineering ability by overseeing a major project (such as a resident engineer on a dam, airport, or hospital project). Consequently, such new Partners were usually in their late 40s to mid-50s.

Presentation of the Queen's Award for Export Achievement by the Lord Lieutenant of Greater London the Baroness Phillips: Received by John Calvert, John Haseldine and Gwilym Roberts

When I was made a Partner of John Taylor & Sons with Nick Paul in 1974 (as the twelfth and thirteenth Partner since the firm began in 1869), we were both committed financially to the success of the firm. The existing Partners did not require either of us to put in capital. John Calvert CBE, our Senior Partner, said he would retire in three years' time and would not accept any part of the firm's profits during the intervening period as his wife, Barbara Calvert QC, was earning far too much money working in the Temple. It was agreed all the remaining Partners would partake in equal amounts of annual profit share to enable us younger Partners to build up capital in the firm. This was a very generous policy and one that made for a happy working environment which was reflected in a very supportive staff who remained with the firm for years.

Gentle prosperity During the next 15 years, the firm's general policy was that if the drawing offices were full, we must be doing well. This philosophy proved itself by becoming one of a handful of 'Consultants of choice' in water engineering across the globe. We won the Queen's Award for Export Achievement in 1978, and Partners became presidents of professional institutions and members of Government committees; generally, we were well thought of throughout the profession. The Partners were advised to change the business into a corporate entity, as our bankers (the Midland, now part of HSBC) saw the Partners as 'men of straw' when compared to our liability in respect of the firm's turnover. Eventually, we were persuaded this might be true, and John Taylor Consulting Engineers Ltd was born in the mid-1980s. Immediately, the bank wanted to lend us more money. We could not understand this at the time.

The merger

Acer Consultants Ltd was born JTS grew to 400 strong engineering staff, after which growth plateaued both in terms of the number of employees and where in the world we were working. A chance meeting over lunch at St Stephens Club between Gwilym Roberts and a Partner of Freeman Fox & Partners (specialist in suspension bridges, roads, railways, and all things related to transportation) sowed the seed of a possible merger of two well-respected firms. FFP worked in a totally different discipline and geography from JTS. We were strong in the Middle East, whereas FFP were leaders in the Far East, particularly in Hong Kong. After a few months of due diligence by both parties, Acer Consultants Ltd (ACL) was formed in 1987 by the total merger of the two organisations. This produced a modicum of scepticism from our friends across the profession. Ten years later, however, most forward-thinking engineering Consultants had decided for themselves to merge or acquire specialist expertise to enable themselves to face the next 100 years with as much commercial acumen and engineering excellence as they could muster. In the meantime, ACL staff had grown from 800 to 2,000. We began to work in new territories such as the former East Germany and USA. Our workload in the UK also mushroomed in both the transportation and water sectors.

The take-over

I was in Eric Bridgen's office, my CEO, in 1991 when the phone went. He was his usual confident self, putting the caller at ease. When he put the phone down, he said in total amazement:

> *"That was Charles Montessori from Lazards. They have been instructed by Welsh Water plc to enquire if we were interested in selling our*

company to the newly formed private water company quoted on the London Stock Exchange."

Our huge expansion since 1987 had caused the company to have significant cash flow problems. Eric and Terry Baughan, our Finance Director, saw this approach from a merchant bank as a lifesaver. A year later, I found myself with Eric on a Sunday morning at 21 Holborn Viaduct, London in the offices of Lovell, White, Durrant, our lawyers. The purpose of this visit was to sign the sale documentation by midday on behalf of the shareholders of ACL. We were now part of the Hyder Group (parent of Welsh Water plc). We were obliged to change our name to Hyder Consulting Ltd by diktat from on high as soon as it was practical.

Control by parent

When and how to account 1992 started a very different existence for the Firm, with controls imposed by a corporate organisation. Welsh Water's experience had never really ventured beyond the border with England. Once acquired, the plc began to try to understand our business and what made us a world leader in our engineering disciplines. They saw us as boffins who had little training on how to run a profitable business. 'Concerned' turned into real suspicion, however, when they delved into 15 contracts ACL (now Hyder Consulting) had with the Department of Transport to design new and expanded motorways around the UK. Each contract was likely to last about ten years - feasibility study, promotion and planning approval, detailed design, contract awards and construction supervision. Some of this work was paid on a time basis while the remainder was charged on a percentage of construction cost (estimated and then final). In order to minimise the peaks and troughs in potential income over the period of the contract, the various consulting firms' auditors across the board (including all the 'big five' KPMG, Deloitte & Touché, PwC, Arthur Anderson, and Ernst & Young) had agreed with Her Majesty's Revenue & Customs to spread the income equally over the ten-year period. When Welsh Water got around to understanding this, they were horrified. Their accounting practice could not permit such an approach. The kernel of Welsh Water's argument was that, at certain times across each DoE contract, Hyder Consulting would be recording profit that had yet to be earned. They blamed PriceWaterhouseCoopers (PwC), Welsh Water's auditors, for not having identified this during the Acer Consultants due diligence and imposed a penalty on PwC by withdrawing payment for services so rendered.

Hyder Consulting accounts were adjusted to reflect the more conservative approach adopted by the plc. As a result, the consulting firm failed to make profits for the next three to four years. Welsh Water also developed an increasing scepticism of the commercial integrity of senior management of their consulting firm.

Human Resource management – or not Personal relationships became broken between Welsh Water Board members and Hyder Consulting management. All the former Partners of JTS and FFP were called to a meeting in London. We were interviewed individually by Welsh Water's CEO, Graham Hawker, Paul Twamley (Finance Director) and John James (former Finance Director of Laura Ashley and now Welsh Water Board member). One by one we filed in. They all looked glum when they returned and would only say they had been sworn not to divulge what was said in their face-to-face discussio. Eventually, it came to my turn, and I entered the 'lion's den' with some concern. Only John James spoke:

> *"We were going to fire you, but clearly, you have friends amongst your colleagues we have interviewed so far - so we are not going to!"*

I left the room in a strange place mentally. Nobody to my knowledge, had ever thought of firing me before. What a total lack of understanding of people management, first to suggest they were going to remove me from the business, and then to counter with a throwaway line to suggest by some luck or Damascene conversion they had changed their mind in the previous quarter of an hour. Later, John Webb, who had been FFP's man in Hong Kong for the last ten years, confided in me that our dear owners had wanted to get rid of me, but he told them categorically

> *"You can't do that. He is far too important not only by being in charge of the water sector business within the consultancy, chairman of our USA firm, and board member of our very profitable Severn Trent Water joint venture, but also he is in charge of winning new business across all disciplines - and is good at it too."*

I was very grateful to John Webb for his eleventh-hour support, but my understanding of Welsh Water competence was shattered and never did recover. Both Eric Bridgen and Terry Baughan were asked to clear their desks, leave the office, and not return. John James was made Chairman, replacing Sir Geoffrey Howe, and Stuart Doughty was brought in as CEO and a Welsh Water Board member. Stuart was an experienced engineer from the construction industry, having been a director first of Tarmac and then John Laing plc.

Corporate control Like all large commercial entities, we were obliged to participate in corporate games. In November 1995, I was instructed to meet with Brian Fitzgerald (Welsh Water) in our Bristol office to complete a written questionnaire with six other senior employees of the Hyder Group. We were all to undergo a Kaisson Personal Profile, whatever that means. I got up at 5.30 am and

221

drove the 110 miles along the M4 from my home in Surrey, to Bristol to be on time and ready for a day's 'adjudication' starting at 9.00 am before travelling back home that evening.

The day had come and gone, and I thought nothing of it until I was called in to see the Welsh Water HR director in May 1997, some 18 months later what he had to say left me traumatised, so much so that I called Stuart Doughty and asked to see him as a matter of urgency. I explained I had been presented with the findings of this Kaisson Personal Profile, which were extremely worrying. I said:

> 'He does not demonstrate a strong inter-cultural mind set. This could reduce his capability in roles where it is important to be sensitive to the differences between cultures. Whilst he has the necessary experience to market the business in both new and existing marketplaces, his capability is likely to be limited by his somewhat limited inter-cultural mind set.'

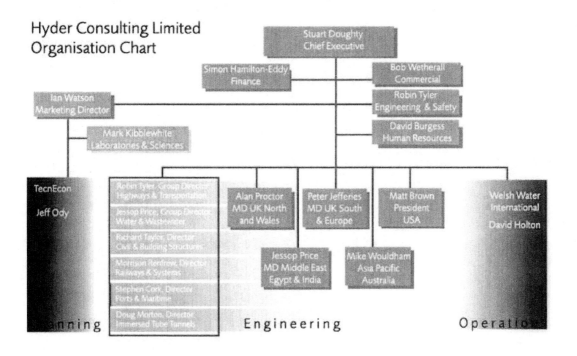

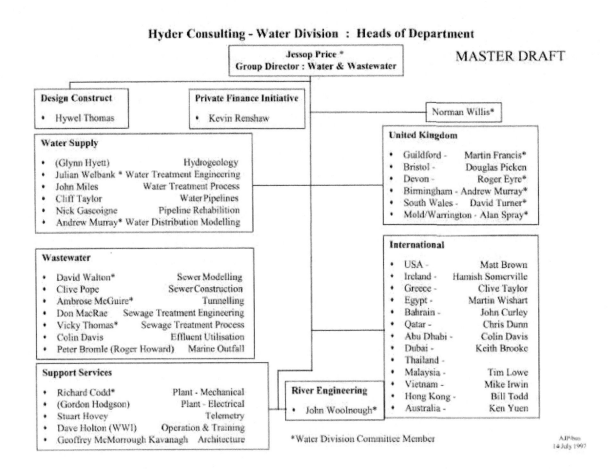

Hyder Consulting – Water Division : Heads of Department

Jessop Price *
Group Director : Water & Wastewater

MASTER DRAFT

Norman Willis*

Design Construct
• Hywel Thomas

Private Finance Initiative
• Kevin Renshaw

Water Supply
• (Glynn Hyett)   Hydrogeology
• Julian Welbank * Water Treatment Engineering
• John Miles   Water Treatment Process
• Cliff Taylor   Water Pipelines
• Nick Gascoigne   Pipeline Rehabilitation
• Andrew Murray* Water Distribution Modelling

Wastewater
• David Walton*   Sewer Modelling
• Clive Pope   Sewer Construction
• Ambrose McGuire*   Tunnelling
• Don MacRae   Sewage Treatment Engineering
• Vicky Thomas*   Sewage Treatment Process
• Colin Davis   Effluent Utilisation
• Peter Bromle (Roger Howard)   Marine Outfall

Support Services
• Richard Codd*   Plant - Mechanical
• (Gordon Hodgson)   Plant - Electrical
• Stuart Hovey   Telemetry
• Dave Holton (WWI)   Operation & Training
• Geoffrey McMorrough Kavanagh   Architecture

United Kingdom
• Guildford -   Martin Francis*
• Bristol -   Douglas Picken
• Devon -   Roger Eyre*
• Birmingham - Andrew Murray*
• South Wales -   David Turner*
• Mold/Warrington - Alan Spray*

International
• USA -   Matt Brown
• Ireland -   Hamish Somerville
• Greece -   Clive Taylor
• Egypt -   Martin Wishart
• Bahrain -   John Curley
• Qatar -   Chris Dunn
• Abu Dhabi -   Colin Davis
• Dubai -   Keith Brooke
• Thailand -
• Malaysia -   Tim Lowe
• Vietnam -   Mike Irwin
• Hong Kong -   Bill Todd
• Australia -   Ken Yuen

River Engineering
• John Woolnough*

* Water Division Committee Member

AJP/hsn
14 July 1997

"*Help*". I said to Stuart. "*We both went to Morocco ten days ago, didn't we do well enough? I am just returning from Pakistan, where I had to deal with a Singapore CEO and a Pakistan Government minister. I am travelling this weekend to Saudi Arabia to present proposals to two Saudi Princes and the Mayor of Jeddah, not to mention dealing with Dimitri Dondos and his Greek team. After reading all this claptrap from Kaisson Personal Profile, are you sending the right man?*"

And that is not all. The Kaisson report went on to state:

'*His strategic mind set is also less strong. This is likely to affect his capability in business unit management roles.*'

I said to Stuart, "*Heaven forbid; my working relationship with Harvey Binnie and his management team in Dubai, and the same in the US, has enabled me to turn around significantly both companies in terms of cash and profitability. Notwithstanding that, I had a meeting with John*

223

Banyard (the scourge of all contractors working for Severn Trent) and came away with a cheque for £750,000!"

Finally, Kaisson wrote:

'Reduced levels of openness could affect his capability in situations where a high degree of responsiveness to change is needed.'

"Stuart, you know I was a JTS Partner for 15 years, voted to take over FFP and readily accepted the new role as a subsidiary of a plc. Apparently, I have gained a reputation amongst my not so fortunate colleagues who have fallen because of plc mania as being a real survivor - not a characteristic of somebody who can't respond to change."

There were many other issues, but Stuart was very pragmatic.

"I have been in very similar situations to you during my time in plc environments. Ignore them. What is important to me and to those in senior management within Hyder Consultants is that you just carry on doing what you are doing, because you are doing a fine job."

So I continued in my various roles as an adviser to the Group Marketing Director, Commercial Leader for all of Hyder's Business in the Middle East and the USA, as well as Group Director for Water and Wastewater Business throughout the world. This included updating our knowledge so we could aspire to be a world leader in the technology and assure our clients, both existing and future, we were model technocrats and their a 'Consultant of choice'. I prepared regular Middle East Business Plans to demonstrate Hyder's necessary future performance in the Region to achieve our hopes and aspirations for the future.

The end is nigh

First to go – Stuart Doughty The firm prospered under the leadership of Stuart Doughty, and we developed new potential across the world. He put me in charge of all our business across the Middle East on the understanding I would improve profitability; and in Boston, USA, we engineered an immersed tube tunnel with his support. All was looking good. We took prestigious Nash offices in Cornwall Terrace on Regent Parks Outer Circle, which Welsh Water also saw as being suitable for their 'London pad'. Then in 1997, Stuart came into the office with a face like thunder, having been at a Welsh Water Board meeting all day. He told me the Chairman had instructed him to stay a while after the meeting; and then promptly fired him with an order to clear his desk at once. What annoyed him most at the time was that he had sat all day with his fellow Board members, whom he thought of as his friends, when all that time, they knew he was to be ousted from the company.

Appointment of new CEO Stuart was replaced by Tim Wade, who had been a fellow Director of Hyder Consulting. Tim had been Managing Director of Wallace Evans, a small consultancy business owned by Welsh Water at the time of our acquisition, the staff of which were absorbed into Acer Consultants. He was then on the Welsh Water payroll, and for reasons best known to himself and Welsh Water, he never transferred to Hyder Consulting's payroll. Tim had been fired by Stuart in 1996 for failing to bring Hyder Consulting's business in the Far East and Australia (for which he was responsible to our Board) into profitability. So, although he was fired by Stuart, he never left the Group and went back into Welsh Water's Cardiff offices.

I immediately called on Tim to congratulate him on his new appointment. I went on to say I would fully support his leadership, and he need not have any doubts about my integrity to remain in a fully focused role. It was not in my DNA to be the leader of the company, but rather to concentrate on being a supportive lieutenant.

It's terminal The next day, Tim called me into his office. He told me to come in, close the door and sit down.

> "I have been instructed by our owners that the Middle East business has now reached a satisfactory level whereby it can be managed from Dubai, rather than London. Your post as MD Middle East has therefore disappeared. To this end, your presence in the firm is no longer required and I must ask you to clear your desk and leave without delay."

On the one hand, I felt sorry for Tim because he knew my worth and was only administering an instruction from Welsh Water's head office. John James had been itching to come up with some justification to fire me since his failure to do so five years ago during the 'night of the long knives'. On the other hand, this was it; I was out of a job in my fifties, which is a difficult age to be taken on by another organisation. I also hadn't had to apply for a job since 1969.

To say I was mortified is an understatement. Apparently, the instruction to Tim neither mention my responsibility as leader of all water engineering business within the firm nor my role as the leader of all new business. But go I must, because the plc saw me as one of Stuart Doughty's boys and therefore dispensable. Worse was to come. When I read the letter of dismissal, they had generously offered me six months' pay in compensation, which was at variance to my employment contract, which identified a two-year figure. I contacted Stuart, who was appalled at my predicament.

"What are they playing at. I will put you in touch with Allen & Overy, a City law firm I am using to fight my case with Welsh Water. They specialise in employment law."

I went up to London to the Allen & Overy office in Black Friars Lane, one that I must have passed a thousand times when I was at the Choir School. The meeting was amiable, the lawyer had read my contract and confirmed it was watertight. She believed I had a strong case against my previous employer. Eventually, the correct amount of compensation, minus Allen & Overy's fee, found its way into my bank account.

A new dawn

Help required I was out of a job and not sure what to do. I was put in touch with a head-hunter, ICM CareerCare Services in Victoria, who made me fill in lots of forms to fully explain my competence (or otherwise) as an Engineer, a Manager, a Businessman and anything else I could think of. They also wanted to contact certain people who I thought might give me a glowing reference. Back came a host of letters, including the following, which gave me hope that it would be unbelievable for me to be out of employment for more than a few days.

William R Klaus, Senior Partner of Pepper, Hamilton & Scheetz LLP, Philadelphia
"Jessop Price served as Chairman of the Board and Chief Executive Officer of Acer Engineering and Consultants Inc. The assignment was most difficult not only because, on acquisition, we found an almost moribund business but also because he was responsible for large projects and project development in other countries as remote as Vietnam and India while somehow finding time to run this new company. By a combination of personal skills, he managed to turn this company around."

Sir John Grey KBE CMG, our former Ambassador to Lebanon, France, and Belgium
"I have pleasant memories of dealing with you over a number of years, and I am particularly grateful for the interest you showed me when looking at various ideas in the Middle East."

David Neil-Gallacher CEO British Water.
"It's not for me to question the right of any organisation to re-structure, but to dispose of someone as respected and experienced as you seems crazy .... We do sometimes hear of developments in other companies

which could offer openings, and I shall certainly be instrumental in bringing you to their attention."

Eric Bridgen, former CEO of the Acer Group
"Jessop and I worked together for some years during a period when the Acer Group quadrupled in size over a three/four-year period. I found him to be intellectually robust, a man of high integrity, professional but not slavishly so and with well-developed interpersonal skills"

Hope is eternal, eventually In practice, it was over a year before I found anybody who would take me on. Eventually, I met with Jean Claude Banon, CEO of Compagnie Générale des Eaux's English operation, which included Three Valleys Water Company and the Essex Water Company, of which I had been a Director some ten years earlier. He kindly offered me a job to win new business from the Indian sub-continent into this global water and wastewater operation. This company was later called 'Vivendi'.

Chapter 17: India

"A coconut shell full of water is a sea to an ant."
Indian Proverb

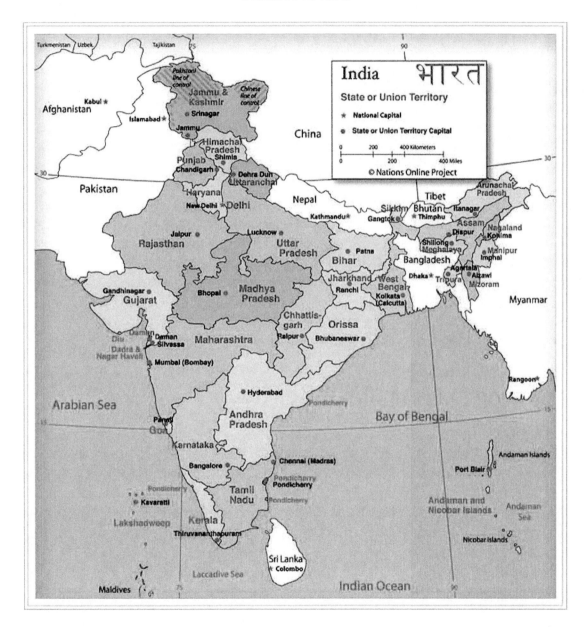

Introduction

India has an exciting history that goes back millennia. What is now called India is the seventh largest country in land mass and the most populous democracy in the world. Homo sapiens arrived from Africa 55,000 years ago, and for centuries they were hunter-gathers. Towards the end of the years before Christ, caste stratification developed and Hinduism, Buddhism and Jainism emerged, which caused a certain degree of order within the multiplicity of societies. In the Middle Ages, Christianity, Islam, Judaism and Zoroastrianism put down roots in the south and west of the Indian subcontinent. Later, the various societies were overrun either by Muslim armies or by the Moguls. In the late 16th century, the East India Company began to sign treaties with various leaders of local states and increased its influence to secure a strong trading and military presence. It was only in 1858, after the rebellion of certain rich landowners, that the British Government took over from the East India Company to exert crown rule and to unify the conglomerate of Maharajah-controlled lands and those of other Princes. Modern India evolved through British rule during the late 19th century. Today, the country is divided into 29 States with autonomous rule, but all are ultimately dependent on the Federal Government in Delhi. The English were the catalyst for major investment in infrastructure across the board, including in the urban water sector.

Independence came in 1947, and with it, the partition on religious grounds of India, Pakistan, and East Pakistan (now Bangladesh). Today, India is the heart of South Asia, bounded by seas on two sides and the Himalayas to the north.

After 1947, all infrastructure (particular the water sector) was financed and managed by either Central or State Governments.

The population of India in 2020 was 1.4 billion.

Background to the Indian Water industry

Underfunding I spent fifteen years with JTS searching for new work and undertaking assignments throughout India. In 1998, when I began employment with the French Company Vivendi (formerly known as Compagnie Générale des Eaux), the population of India was less than one billion. The country then supported over 30 cities with populations in excess of one million; and of these, six had a population greater than five million – Mumbai (*Bombay*) 15m, Kolkata (*Calcutta*) 12m, Delhi 11m, Chennai (*Madras*) 6m, Bangalore 5m and Hyderabad 5m. (This compares with the UK situation where there were only five cities in 2020 with populations greater than one million: London 11m, Manchester 3m, Birmingham 2m, Leeds-Bradford 2m, Glasgow 1m). Each Indian city had expanded both organically and by migration from rural areas to the 'bright lights'.

The provision of water supplies for both domestic and industrial sectors was a State matter. Successive State Governments had to wrestle with priorities of demand on the public purse. The softer areas of demands such as health, social service and education, tended to have a political priority over budgets submitted by committed engineers for the expansion of their city's water supply system. There never were any 'votes for sewage' in the 20th century in India or anywhere else!

Infrastructure problem for Indian conurbations Issues associated with the size of Indian cities relate to a 'developed' rather than a 'developing' world. This, coupled with a situation where 30% of the population in larger cities live under canvas on pavements (and where customers believe they have a right to a free supply of water), presents an almost insurmountable political problem for all State Governments to solve.

Deterioration of assets During my visits to India between 1980 and 2001, I witnessed chronic underfunding, resulting not only in delays to constructing new facilities but also in serious neglect of maintaining the existing asset base. The water engineering workforces across the country had become debilitated, and the same was true for the assets they operated. Skills learnt by operatives during their training years had often not been put into practice because management was obliged to manipulate available subsidies for maintaining a basic service rather than to finance an efficient operation. This resulted in the artisan workforce not always being given the proper tools of the trade; for instance, they were skilled in the art of using hammers and chisel to make 'watertight connections' into distribution mains instead of using conventional tapping machines. This practice would accelerate the deterioration of assets. The authorities provided a low-quality service to its customers in all urban water distribution systems (together with a limited sewerage system).

Customers For years, the Indian urban population has had to put up with intermittent levels of service provided by their State Government because there was no yardstick for comparison. The status quo had been and continued to be too easy to accept. Customers were unaware therefore that to deliver quality drinking water to the customer's kitchen tap, piped distribution systems needed to be continuously pressurised. This standard is mandatory in Europe and America. However, intermittent supplies to every house or public standpost were (and are) endemic in India. As a result, urban water supplies in India have led to an erratic service. When water does become available, its quality is appalling because pollution is sucked into 'leaky' water pipes when internal pressures fall below zero, only to be flushed out to every customer when supplies resume.

Customers have acted Those who could afford the investment had overcome the intermittent public supply by constructing ground storage tanks on their property to capture water from the city main whenever it was available (and they often sank a well on their property to augment their available water resources). These more well-off customers were incurring energy costs to lift the stored water into tanks in their roof space to secure their own 'continuous supply'. However, such customers were mindful to always boil the water before use, which would remove unwanted pathogens that might seriously endanger their health.

Most people were less well-off, however, and relied on either the intermittent State Government supply or a supply delivered by private tanker to each part of the city, which could prove expensive. They also invariably placed in the house a multitude of pots and pans under taps which were left permanently on to combat the uncertainty of supply, to capture water when the intermittent supply suddenly 'went live'.

Availability of water resources Notwithstanding the poor service delivered to customers' taps, the quantum of water resources abstracted from the natural environment for most of the big conurbations in India was equal to, or even exceeded, the equivalent per capita availability in most European cities. The figures recorded in the OECD 1997 annual report gave the raw water availability in litres per capita per day (lcds) for Bangalore as 140; similar figures for Mumbai (Bombay) were 260 and for Delhi 270. These compared favourably with England and Wales (175), France (150), Belgium (140) and Germany (135).

The distribution system If water resource availability was reasonably satisfactory, why was it the customer receives an intermittent supply or no supply at all? There was only one answer to this question – unacceptable transmission losses between the treatment plant and the customer. Most State water undertakings were admitting to 40-50% leakage along the way (*what manufacturer could possibly remain in business if they threw away that amount of product before it reached their customer?*). With supplies being intermittent, I learnt operators regularly responded to those in political authority by turning strategically placed valves to redirect water flow for their benefit rather than responding to the needs of the general public. This situation was tragic and the root cause of why State Governments alone were (and are) unable to resolve this issue.

Revenue One of the prime reasons for poor quality service in the Indian domestic sector was because the customer pays virtually nothing for this standard of service – and the issue of raising tariffs was a hot political issue with voters. Tariffs varied from State to State, but generally, the consumer was being asked to pay between Rs 2-4 / m³ (this was equivalent to £0.03 - £0.06 / m³). These rates were about two orders of magnitude less than similar charges in the UK. Because the tariff was so low, unpaid charges were often perceived by management as not worth chasing up.

The mindset of managers focussed, therefore, on two issues. First, it was rarely worth disconnecting customers who chose not to pay. Secondly, even though domestic supplies were metered, the total revenue from tariff collection was perceived as a 'fixed' sum. Managers then searched for ways to increase subsidies to the water sector through various arms of State Government – with little success.

Individual house meter readings formed the basis for revenue collection. Meters were not made sufficiently robust and regularly became damaged because they were not able to manage the silt and trash swilling around distribution systems. Daily pressure surges due to intermittent supplies also put extra stress on meter components, causing them to fail – and in most water undertakings, there were no backup services to maintain meters. Added to all that, there was also plenty of evidence of vandalising meters and meter reader abuse; it was said some meter readers deliberately bypassed certain properties for a fee, so those customers were never billed.

John Taylor & Son's relationship with India

The beginning John Taylor's sons, Brough and Midgley, were both made Partners in 1882. On the death of their father in 1891, Brough became Senior Partner, and both began to undertake assignments overseas. Brough advised the Shanghai Waterworks Company and prepared a scheme to augment and treat existing water supplies to St Petersburg from Lake Ladoga; (*he was strongly advised to leave the country immediately as World War I was about to start – so he came home, first travelling by train to Vologda and Archangel and then by boat into the Arctic Ocean transferring to a steam packet boat in Vardo, Norway, which then landed him in Newcastle*).

Midgley spent more time overseas advising water authorities in Auckland, Singapore, Port Elizabeth, and Bombay, where he advised the Waterworks Corporation over many years and acted as their London agent for the supply of mechanical plant. (*I remember tidying up the basement in Artillery House with senior Partner John Calvert. We were throwing away anything that had no commercial value to the firm's current operation. We came across a cable from Midgley to the Bombay Waterworks Corporation advising his arrival – "Please meet me at Quay D on 3rd June 1905*). All this travel was made by the fastest means possible – by boat; travelling from Tilbury Docks to Bombay to advise his client was a three-week journey. This meant he was away from his London office for a good two months or so. While in Bombay, he also advised the authorities in Kanpur, Pune, Shimla, and Surat.

World Bank assignment - the 1970s (*Maharashtra State population 80 million*). My regular visits to the World Bank in Washington, DC bore fruit when we won a World Bank-funded contract for the design of a new water treatment plant at Temghar to serve the very northern areas of Bombay (now called Mumbai). Water was to be abstracted from the Ulhas River. The client was the Maharashtra State Waterworks Corporation, and our recommendation was to design and implement conventional sedimentation plus rapid gravity filtration plant for treating river water, whatever its quality, particularly when there was a heavy silt load during monsoon season. My senior engineer on this assignment was David Wallace, who had a good understanding of what we were to design, a process to be easily understood by those who would operate the plant. He focussed on having channel flow between individual units rather than conventional pipework. This would assist in seeing precisely how water travelled through the plant. First, raw water flowed through screens (to eliminate trash abstracted from the river) before passing on to sedimentation tanks. The settled water flowed to rapid gravity filters. The filtered water was then sent first to the chlorination plant (to eliminate any 'bugs' left in the filtered water) and then on to treated water storage tanks. Here, the treated water would be held for a good 24 hours before being discharged into trunk mains for onward distribution to customers. For all this work, we had teamed up with Perfect Engineering (later renamed Shah Technical Consultants Pvt Ltd), with whom I was to have an over twenty-year relationship, first with JTS/Acer/Hyder until 1997 and then with Vivendi UK until my retirement in 2001.

On 15th February 1999, a mission from Maharashtra State Waterworks Corporation came to London to visit British Water. There, they met members who formally welcomed the mission. This was followed by a questions and answers session. We all had to introduce ourselves and identify our interest in meeting this professional team of engineers and administrators from one of India's major water undertakings. It turned out I was virtually the only one to have experience in the Indian water industry. When I mentioned I had been responsible for the Temghar water treatment plant, their senior manager immediately stood up and said:

> *"The Temghar filtration plant! Yes, it is still going strong after 15 years of operation, and it works very well!"*

A nice feather in my cap, but I was unsure how my fellow English water engineers and scientists sitting around the table viewed this outburst of praise, as this was clearly a meeting to secure future contacts and assignments for themselves.

Setting up a local office I viewed India as having enormous potential for JTS. We had a good working relationship with our local Mumbai consulting firm, but the country was huge. So how do you identify prospects and gather information to be there, on the spot, when opportunities arise? The Partners allowed me to set up a local office with Dr Karim Alibhai in charge. He had come to London for his tertiary education, and we learnt of his skills when he was a lecturer at Imperial College. It turned out Karim was an ideal candidate for us; Indian-born, highly intelligent, technically skilled in our disciplines and a good communicator. I spent several years with him trying to win business in this vast country.

Madras non-revenue water project – funded by World Bank (*Tamil Nadu State population 55 million*). The firm won this contract first to identify, then to control, unaccounted-for flow between treatment plants and the customer – which could be either through leakage or illicit connections. As implied in previous chapters, this type of contract is to instil good housekeeping on the water utility. It is important to repeat no business can afford the cost of extracting raw water at source, treating, and storing it and then 'throwing away' half the product before it reaches their customer. However, it is a very diplomatic exercise to convince operatives that their lifetime's work is unacceptable. Our first port of call was to see the General Manager of the Madras Metropolitan Water Supply & Sewerage Board (MMWSSB). She was a very educated lady and blamed the British for the shortage of water in the city. She started our meeting by saying:

> "*The East India Company chose to set up shop here in 1835 at Fort St George. There was no significant river running through the village. What buccaneer in their right mind would wish to settle a staging post here? Yes, I blame Major General Robert Clive, your Clive of India, for today's problems He created a significant urban development that has turned into what is now the City of Madras. Can you think of any other city in the world without a river? This has caused us so much trouble over the years. Today, we rely heavily on the River Cauvery for our raw water, which has to be brought 200 km to our city. Farmers in the upstream Karnataka State often suck the river dry before it arrives anywhere near Madras.*"

I thought I was at the end of a colonial ambush, but she did have a sparkle in her eye. Her 'lecture' was the very reason for having a positive outcome from our project. I was soon to learn the educated elite in India love the British, and the feeling is reciprocated. This project gave Dr Karim a good reason to continue to search for work in the country. I was to return to Chennai later in 2001 to enter into a much grander contract that was to last way beyond my retirement.

It is who you know and not what you know Bribery and corruption, as we know them in the west, has been endemic in India since time immemorial. When visiting a Maharajah or any person of elevated status, you could not get past their threshold without bearing a gift. It did not have to be substantial, just commensurate with their station in life. Jump forward to the 1980s, and what I learnt was contacts around government circles had their price. Civil servants were paid a low salary on the understanding it would be made up by the influence they could bear on anybody, and everybody, who needed their support. One such visit was made by me (for free, I might add) because we needed encouragement from within the Bangalore Water Supply and Sewerage Board

(BWSSB) for proposals we had in mind to improve the existing distribution systems (customers could only rely on a two-hour supply in their taps – every other day).

I arrived in Bangalore with Karim on a Friday evening and checked in to the Oberoi Hotel. My room was on the 4th floor with a balcony looking out onto the swimming pool area and a spectacular tree that towered up past the 6th and maybe the 7th floor. The staff had placed a huge bowl of fresh fruit on the circular table where I sat to prepare for my morning meeting. Also on the table was a polite notice:

> "Monkeys are an occasional problem in Bangalore.
> For the safety of your belongings, please close the balcony doors and windows when you are absent from the room."

I thought nothing of it at the time, went to bed but left the window open to allow fresh air into the room. At 7.00 am, I was awoken by the sound of movement in the room. There, at the window, was a Bonnet Macaque monkey, cocking its head slightly to one side as if to say, shall I or shan't I go in. He decided the former. His movement was swift and focused. He picked up the banana from the bowl of fresh fruit and vanished as quickly as he came.

It was Saturday morning. Karim and I were recommended to see Hari Khoday, a leading light in the local distillery business. We had been told he was a 'king maker' because of his influence with both politicians and the electorate. It was rumoured whatever politician came to him for his support before an election had the best chance of succeeding to become the next Chief Minister of Karnataka State (*population 45 million*). We were driven to his house in central Bangalore. It was grand but in the colonial style. There was a doorman who ushered us into a room full of people from all walks of life, waiting their turn to see the great man with their specific life problem. Men and women from the rural areas were seated in their 'best' working clothes and were identifiable from those who had come straight from their middle-class houses in the Bangalore suburbs. I was mortified when Mr Khoday's secretary beckoned us to come in right away, thus by-passing all these very honourable people who had real needs for which they sought real help.

Mr Khoday was charming and very interested in learning about Bangalore's water supply predicament. However, he believed the politics of the day were such that any chance of a meaningful cataclysmic change in the way the BWSSB ran its business would only lead us up a blind alley. To sum up his advice to us, he said:

"Your proposals are definitely needed, but with today's political climate across government and the State water industry, they have to be considered premature."

We thanked him for his candid advice and retreated gracefully. Whereas it was not what we wanted to hear, at least we should not be wasting our time banging our heads against a brick wall. Time to regroup and look for a more fruitful opportunity in this great country.

Controlled entry Because I was visiting India at least three times a year, my secretary Brenda Norton, organised multiple visas for me from the Indian High Commission in the Aldwich, London. On one occasion, Karim called me to make a quick visit, during which I would sign a contract for a water and sewerage project to serve 2.4 million population in Bombay (*Mumbai*) Maharashtra State. I was more than happy with this because it meant I could legitimately excuse myself from a Hyder corporate jamboree in Hong Kong, organised for the same time. I hated that sort of event. (*I worked in Surrey. Why was I being asked to go halfway around the world to meet the same colleagues I worked with every day?!*) Brenda booked my ticket to Bombay, and I prepared myself for the trip. I awoke the night before in a sweat with the thought that my two-year multi-entry visa may have expired. I checked in the morning; and it had. Six weeks before! I was on the phone immediately with Karim. A quick management decision was taken for me. I would travel as planned. My responsibility was to get on a flight at Heathrow, and I requested Karim to ensure I could get out of Bombay air terminal – free.

I arrived at the Heathrow check-in desk, and, of course, they insisted I could not travel because I had no visa. It was time for me to use my trump card:

"Will you please call your manager?"

The manager duly arrived. I explained my predicament and offered him my passport, which clearly had entries to demonstrate I was a regular visitor to India. The problem for him was that if I was refused entry at Bombay, the airline would be responsible for putting me on a plane and returning me to whence I came, which in this case was Heathrow. The solution he proposed was for me to purchase an onward ticket from Bombay to – anywhere! I immediately organised an onward flight to Hong Kong, in the knowledge that maybe I might have to attend the firm's jamboree after all. The ruse worked, and I was on the flight to Bombay.

I was nonetheless a bit nervous, knowing how things can be 'arranged' in India. However, I was confident if anybody could persuade the Indian immigration authorities to let me in, it would be Karim.

The flight arrived in Bombay at about 10 pm. I disembarked from the Boeing 747 and saw Karim hovering on the other side of immigration. He waved to suggest I should sit down and wait to be called. The full load of 747 passengers passed by where I was sitting, all 350 of them. They were on their way to freedom of entry to one of the largest cities in the world. I sat alone in 'no man's land' waiting for some positive action. My stay continued much longer than I had anticipated, and my isolation felt as though I was about to be treated as some fugitive. Eventually, I was approached by an immigration official. He gave me a glum look and told me to come up to the immigration booth. I was handed a scrappy A5 piece of paper that demonstrated I had a temporary visa for 48 hours, during which time I must contact the Chief of Police in Bombay. I was in. Karim looked shattered, with perspiration dripping from his brow. I had put him through an ordeal which was not easy for him to manipulate. But he had secured success when all the odds were against him; and I was extremely grateful for his trouble; and relieved that I didn't have to travel to Hong Kong for the corporate navel gazing and bun fight!

The next day, we both visited the police headquarters in Bombay, a splendid Victorian building that clearly had been built to house officers of the British Empire. Eventually, we were ushered in to be interrogated by the Chief of Police. Karim explained he had obtained a letter from the Chief Minister in Hyderabad, requesting immigration authorities to waive the formality of needing a visa for Mr Price as he could personally vouch for his integrity and good behaviour. The Chief looked at Karim and, with a wry smile, said:

> "My dear Karim, Andrah Pradesh is the wrong State! The Chief Minister from Hyderabad has no jurisdiction here, this is Maharashtra State, and I see no letter from our Chief Minister."

Karim's face was a picture of absolute horror because we were not on comfortable ground at all.

> "It's all right Karim, I am going to permit Mr Price entry to Maharashtra but only for a short while. Let me put this to you. If an Indian National were to arrive at Heathrow without the appropriate documentation, what do you think would be the outcome? He would be repatriated to India, wouldn't he?"

Of course, he was right. He asked for my passport, wrote the appropriate words on a blank page, signed it and provided his big stamp with a flourish to make sure we knew he was in charge here. There was nothing else to say. I thought about asking for the latest cricket score to ease relations (knowing all Indians are mad about the sport) but thought better of it. We thanked him profusely for all his trouble and understanding and made a rapid retreat to the awaiting Indian Ambassador's car (*all cars in India in those days were the Morris Oxford model of the 1950s*).

Hyderabad, Andrah Pradesh (*State population 65 million*). Andrah Pradesh State was 'dry'; very different to its neighbour Karnataka State, where Khoday Distilleries and Kingfisher Brewery were significant Bangalore employers. However, State Government rules were pragmatic. If you were a guest in Hyderabad, you could be served alcohol in the hotel bar.

Hyderabad was a city to definitely explore opportunities, as it appeared to be the only State where civil servants were being obliged to jump into the 21st century. The Chief Minister was the charismatic N. Chandrababu Naidu. First, he had deposed his father-in-law and then passed an edict that all civil servants would be supplied with computer facilities, whether in cities or in outposts of the State. Out would go hard copies of files, whether correspondence or collected data and in would come 'Word', 'Excel' and other more sophisticated programmes. This was a huge transformation for anywhere in the India of the 1980s.

Chandrababu Naidu

But that was not all. Chandrababu Naidu was envious of what he saw down south in Bangalore, which was promoting itself as the California of South Asia – not because of facilities provided by the State, but as a result of the motivated private sector resident in Bangalore itself. Chandrababu Naidu learned Bill Gates was coming to Delhi to promote his technology to the South Asian Market. Bill was not giving interviews, but Chandrababu Naidu used his political standing to secure a ten-minute slot with this great entrepreneur. To Bill's amazement, this top politician got out his laptop and personally proceeded to give him a PowerPoint lecture, using every computer trick at his disposal. The Chief Minister's message was to persuade Microsoft to set up their South Asia headquarters in Hyderabad and not Bangalore - which was the rumour doing the rounds at the time. Bill listened for forty-five minutes and nearly fell off his chair at Chandrababu's cheek, courage, and competence in putting forward his case. Within a few years, Microsoft Corporation Research and Development was set up in Hyderabad; (and in 2020, there are many individual hi-tech industrial parks surrounding the city).

Chandrababu Naidu was a person who was going to change the whole concept of living in his State, whether it was in cities, towns or even in rural areas. We got to meet him and made it clear his urban electorate only had piped water for two hours each day or less. Our presentational skills were clearly not up to his standard, as we were unable, within the brief time allotted, to persuade him to transform Hyderabad's water supply system. He was adamant this was not one of his priorities; and so, as in Bangalore, we 'moved on' elsewhere to find someone – anyone – who might take India's catastrophic water distribution systems seriously.

Uttar Pradesh (*State population 130 million – twice that of the UK*). I was a regular visitor to Delhi over the years. The Delhi Capital Territory is surrounded by Uttar Pradesh State, which has three big cities; Lucknow (*population of 2.5 million*), Varanasi (*population of 1 million*) and Agra (*population of 1 million*). Water and wastewater for the whole state are managed by Jal Nigram. It was pertinent, therefore, to visit their offices in Lucknow. The managers were excited by such an appointment as no foreign consulting firm had made it to their offices before. They were conscious of the undertaking's failings in providing a continuous water supply service and seemed eager to take us to visit both Varanasi and Agra.

Business visit to the Taj Mahal with UP Jal Nigram personnel

We inspected the Jal Nigram facilities in the three cities, but I think they were more interested in showing us tourist sites within their jurisdiction. Varanasi is seen by many locals as the spiritual capital of the country. It was an extraordinary sight to observe Hindu pilgrims bathing in the River Ganges' sacred waters. It has to be said the waters were highly polluted and having total immersion was not the most sensible thing to do from a medical perspective. While this activity was going on, there were fires burning on the shoreline performing multiple funeral rites, all as a business. Bodies were then allowed to float on rafts on the river, where the current took them downstream and out of sight. The following day they encouraged us to visit Agra, and after a quick tour around the water treatment plant, we were off to Agra Fort and that great 'wonder of the world', the Taj Mahal. Agra was the first real city in India and the capital of the Mogul Empire. Agra Fort is situated on a strategic promontory above the Yamuna River and built around 1565 by the Mogul Emperor Akbar – definitely designed as a fortress with over 2 km of the perimeter wall, 20 m high and all surrounded by a moat.

His grandson Emperor Shah Jahan spent the last eight years of his life imprisoned by his son Aurangzeb in this magnificent structure. His 'crime' was being too lavish with his son's inheritance. From the Fort, Shah Jahan would have been able to gaze over the Taj Mahal, which he built as a mausoleum for his favourite wife, Mumtaz Mahal. It is the most amazing building, much smaller than photographs would have you imagine. The relative dimensions of all components of the structure had been masterly designed. The architect is not known for sure, but it has been attributed to a Persian named Ustad Ahmad Lahori. (*Shah Jahan's son prevented him from spending any more money to build an identical structure in black marble on the other side of the Yamuna River as his own mausoleum.*)

1998 – 2001 The Vivendi experience

Employed by the French The French conglomerate, Compagnie Générale des Eaux, had changed its name to Vivendi to encompass not just water operations but also waste collection (Veolia), power, Canale Plus, Universal Studios and many more profitable avenues. After I 'left' Hyder Consultants, I was employed by Vivendi's UK arm, General Utilities plc, at 37-41 Old Queen Street, Westminster - not a million miles away from Artillery House and St Stephens Club. My role was to secure new business in water and wastewater operations on the Indian subcontinent. The geography of my workplace was not just India but encompassed Pakistan, Bangladesh, Sri Lanka, and Nepal. The French had tried without success to gain entry into this market. A discussion in Paris concluded that, as these are all Commonwealth countries (except for Nepal), the Group could give the task to Jean Claude Banon (JCB), who was in charge of the London office, to see if he could crack this hugely potential market; hence my appointment as Commercial Director, International Water Division.

Government control versus private sector participation

Would India ever accept private sector participation in the water sector? I attended numerous conferences around India. The technocrats loved to talk about the future of their water sector, and knowing the quantum of necessary funding would never be made available, they were often outspoken in their proposals. Private sector participation was promoted by some but, at one conference I spoke at, was stoutly rebuffed by a local politician:

> "*If you persuade us to privatise our water supply systems, may you come back in the next life as a lizard*" He paused and then added, "*in the desert!*"

I tried to explain that continuous underfunding of the urban water sector had created situations where State Governments just do not have the financial ability either to 'catch up' on the expansion of existing facilities or to provide funding for the improvement of assets they already own. World Bank had suggested (*in the mid-1990s*) that India needed to spend US$65bn equivalent on water and wastewater infrastructure in the next decade alone, but only 10% of this amount was available through planned Government spending.

Should a water utility be perceived as a public service activity with continued State Government subsidy or as an industry that has a product with customers to serve? I pointed out there are instances of government excellence as a water utility provider, quoting Singapore as an example. However, improvements generated by a switch from public to private operation in India could be the catalyst to bring about necessary changes in reforms of bureaucratic and procedural matters to meet the demands of the 21st century. A crossover to the private sector would require a strong focus on customer relations. Such focus appeared absent across India in the 1990s water sector.

Once the private sector is able to provide a sustainable public water service (for which customers are prepared to pay a fair tariff), the 'profit' earned would be taxed to provide a revenue stream for State exchequers. This situation should have been a welcome quantum leap for State Governments compared with the financial environment in which the water sector found itself at the end of the millennium, where obligatory State Government subsidies can only provide poor public water service.

I then illustrated my point by drawing attention to the English and Welsh experience. The UK Government used to subsidise the water sector (*prior to privatisation in 1988*) to the tune of US$1bn equivalent per annum; ten years later, the UK Government was receiving billions of dollars equivalent per annum in taxation from the privatised regional water companies.

Private sector skills There are three principal skills the private sector could bring to the Indian water business to secure a long-term relationship with both State Governments and consumers alike:

1. Raising finance, both as equity and debt
2. Utilising contemporary management and technology skills to turn a subsidised activity into a self-sustaining service
3. Introducing appropriate technologies to solve engineering and administrative problems. This would enable managers to manage, and no longer would they be tied to the 'apron strings' of State Governments.

241

India needed a transformation in its water sector

Introduction Wherever I went, and whenever I spoke at conferences or in the quiet comfort of water managers' offices, I always began explaining, as diplomatically as I could, that their existing distribution systems were corroded and leaked like a sieve. In reality, they already knew this through their own evaluations of existing assets and their own intuition but were blinded by pride and refused to acknowledge such catastrophic problems ever existed.

I rehearsed as diplomatically as I could that private utility operators are good at renovation and the operation of existing assets - these were private sector skills State Governments should be encouraged to adopt in India. In reality, this would not be achieved without necessary administrative reforms.

Options for private sector participation In the year 2000, there were several privatisation options State Governments could have adopted if they would only allow the private sector to support administrations to undertake their responsibilities. The end goal was mutually focused on supplying a continuous and sustainable water service to customers. There was enough experience for me to justify the practicalities of the following options:

1. Build, Operate and Transfer (BOT). This model would provide a new component to a water system but isolated from existing apparatus. The private sector would provide the finance, construct the particular facility and then be responsible for its operation for, say, twenty years. The private company would then receive payment over that twenty-year period for such a 'service' on an agreed basis per m^3 supplied to the utility's existing system. State Governments had already looked at this model and had organised tenders on five separate occasions:

    Andrah Pradesh in 1995 – 124 km pipeline to deliver 450 MLD[26] bulk supply to Hyderabad
    Tamil Nadu in 1997 – 180 MLD water and sewerage project to supply Tirupur
    Goa in 1997 – bulk water supply project
    Karnataka in 1997 – Cauvery Stage IV 500 MLD water supply project to Bangalore
    Maharashtra in 1998 – Pune water and sewerage project.

    Alas, all five projects were deemed un-fundable once tenders had been received and the contracts were abandoned.

---

[26] MLD = million gallons per day

2. Management, Leasing or Concession Contracts. Renovation and operation of existing treatment and distribution assets would gradually improve levels of customer service. This option could be attractive to the private utility operator and a common-sense priority for good 'housekeeping'.

3. Provide New Supplies. Pouring more finance into 'bolt-on' new works would increase availability of resources at the outskirts of a city. These increased flows would be discharged into a distribution system that needed to be continuously rehabilitated. I recommended this option should only be considered as a 'phase two' solution of a long-term strategy.

The way forward

Change in philosophy I contributed to a glossy quarterly magazine called 'Indian Infrastructure', which is still published today. At the turn of the millennium, it focused on articles related to the oil, gas, and telecommunications industries. I suggested to the Editor that the magazine should expand its readership to serve the water sector. He agreed and immediately made me their 'correspondent! I wrote several articles which were really good marketing tools for the Group. They had titles such as 'The Indian Water Industry. A Cinderella Business' and ' Setting the Urban Water Agenda for the 21st Century Through Private Sector Participation'.

Government support There was little apparent enthusiasm in India to secure a water industry run on business lines, except within the most enlightened State Governments. Quite the opposite. Politicians were fearful that water tariff increases were synonymous with political isolation. This argument would be valid if tariff increases took place in an environment of continued poor level of service. I regularly beat the drum advising State Governments they must come to realise a water utility service has to be run on business lines if there is any hope of improvement, whether this is then run by the public or the private sector. I was encouraged that State Water and Sewerage Boards generally felt that, having carried out their own evaluations, the water sector displayed weaknesses crying out for reform. Their 'masters' were not prepared to sanction any such programmes because of a lack of political will and funding.

Vision for long-term financial self-reliance I sought to present my predictions as to how continuous improvements in water systems in India might take place. I often used to quote:

"Weak cost recovery is the root cause of both low standards and low coverage of water systems." [27]

This so reflected the situation in water supply systems across the Indian nation. Existing levels of tariff did not reflect, in any respect, the cost of service provided to customers.

For long-term sustainability, systems have eventually to be directly financed by the customer. For this to be achieved, it is inevitable tariffs have to be raised, but gradually. The growing 'middle class' in India had the ability to pay a substantially higher tariff, but their willingness would most probably be constrained by wanting to see a clear improvement in the levels of service. I was brave enough to point the finger at politicians to suggest they do the community a disservice if they perpetuate the concept that water should be free. Their lack of action would eliminate the customer's option to have a sustainable service. This last point was generally accepted by technocrats in the audience but went down like a lead balloon with the decision-makers – I believe it was the kernel of what had to be said in India at that time.

The private sector would only be prepared to participate in the Indian water sector if an environment were created to provide long-term stability. This required local 'champions' in each city with the vision to create a substantial improvement in the delivery of what is so often described as an unacceptable standard of a State Government service.

Finance I have probably overemphasised that water was virtually free to the domestic sector across conurbations in India. The following four financial issues needed to be resolved, however, if the private sector was to assist State Governments in providing a sustainable service.

Tariff The customer was paying for their water service, either through tariff or indirectly through general taxation (State Government subsidy of domestic water). In practice, the water service was costing the taxpayer, in practice, up to ten times the tariff (under normal accounting conventions). What the customer did not realise was that, without their consent, State Governments were deliberately constraining budget availability to the water sector because of competing pressure on their exchequers. There will always be those amongst the urban poor who would qualify for a subsidised service. Appropriate recognition would need to be put in place to address such issues, as State Governments work

---

[27] UK Government: Department for International Development's Guidance Manual on Water Supply and Sanitation Programmes

towards realistic sustaining tariff structures acceptable to public and private sectors alike.

Sharing the risk State Governments need to accept the private sector does not always have the ability to control risks related to revenue collection, country macroeconomics (such as devaluation and roaring inflation), political issues and other force majeure. Reducing risk shouldered by the private sector would assist in reducing project costs and therefore reduce the financial burden imposed on the customer by increasing tariffs and by reducing State subsidies.

Security of payment The private sector would need to have confidence that, through the appropriate sharing of risks, State Governments would permit normal trading conditions regarding payment for their services. Such confidence would require a contractual obligation, whether payment came directly through the water rate or from a State Government guarantee (*a 'take-or-pay agreement' where a State Government commits to buy a predetermined quantity of water at an agreed price*).

Regulation The policing, or the lack, of legislation, has been the cause of bad practices that prevent Indian water engineers from performing. This is true whether it relates to the control of water abstraction from the nation's resources, the provision of a predetermined quality of water at the customers' tap, or the quality of purified effluent discharged to a watercourse. I pointed out that the private sector would need to have a clear understanding of:

- What regulatory rules would be in place to reflect an improving level of service?
- What State organisation would measure performance?
- What constraints might be imposed by, or on, State Governments related to their ability to make structural changes in the future?
- What would be the penalties imposed on the private sector if they do not meet the agreed criteria?

The regulatory rules need to be attainable at an affordable cost to the customer, accompanied by regular improvement in the standard of service. This should be the principle goal to be achieved rather than any one-off artificial improvement.

Regulation needs to be in place before the private sector can offer a realistic price.

Repository for 'social benefit' Many State Government-controlled water utilities in India were overstaffed. Existing staff in the water industry would feel threatened by the thought of private sector participation. It was going to be a 'difficult'

245

decision, therefore, to reduce staffing levels to sensible proportions. Careful planning by State Governments <u>and</u> the private sector would be essential to secure support from the workforce. Any rationalisation would have to be undertaken through a planned and humane process.

Need for competent legal representation My role in the Group was to secure water operation contracts for Vivendi lasting up to 25 years. Any contractual arrangement entered into with a State Government, or Water Supply and

Rajiv Luthra

Sewerage Board would need to be carefully worded if we were not to be disadvantaged during our tenure. It was necessary, therefore, to engage a competent law firm, and we approached the Delhi-based firm, Luthra & Luthra. The founder and senior Partner was Rajiv Luthra, and he invited Jean Claude Banon (JCB) and me to his business club, which was a single-storey extension of the Delhi Oberoi hotel where we were both staying.

During lunch, he plied us with his experience. I was surprised his work took him to both London and New York - a truly international lawyer and younger than me! His anecdotes to 'break the ice' were legendary, and we were not in any hurry to stop him in his tracks. He started by telling us of a meeting he had arranged with four Japanese businessmen that took place in the same private room in which we were busy chatting. Rajiv was very keen to conclude a telecommunications contract and was representing an Indian client. He had deliberately sat the Japanese to face the one-way plate glass window overlooking the hotel swimming pool. When they were nearing the end of the meeting, Rajiv noticed they all appeared to be losing concentration. Rajiv told us:

> *"My tactics were working. Immediately outside the window were several Air France hostesses in their swimming costumes, doing what ladies do when they are not aware of being watched."*

The Japanese' eyes were on storks. This was such a distraction that Rajiv had difficulty getting them to put pen to paper to secure their signatures. In retrospect, they might have signed up for any contract wording that day!

Another story in his quiver, which I could quite visualise but had no belief it was true, related to the magic of the legendary Indian small trader. Many shops in India are no wider than fifteen feet and are run as a family business. Shop interiors go back into some darkened space, and the customer is led to believe the store goes on forever. Shopkeepers are proud and believe they are able to meet every customer's request. Rajiv was determined to trick one shopkeeper into an impossible task.

> *"Yes sir, yes sir, can I help you? What is your request today?"* said the shopkeeper, continuously moving his head from left to right and back again in metronomic motion as he spoke.

> *"I need an RB211 engine. Do you have them in stock today?"*

> *"Yes sir, yes sir,"* he replied with all the enthusiasm he could muster and vanished into the depths of his store.

The RB211 Rolls Royce engine was developed for the Lockheed Tristar commercial airliner launched in 1972 and then used by Boeing on their 747, 757 and 767s. We shall never know the content of the shopkeeper's discussion with his family within the dark shadows of his emporium; he returned disappointed but fighting to save his reputation.

> *"I am so sorry, sir, but we sold the last one yesterday. We will be having another batch in tomorrow. Can I reserve one for you?"*

Rajiv replied in the affirmative and made a hasty but dignified retreat, taking care not to embarrass his newly found friend.

By the end of our very enjoyable lunch, JCB and I were convinced not only of Rajiv's competence as a lawyer with a clear understanding of international business but that also he was an anglophile with a sense of humour that would make life for us in India a true enjoyment. His firm was clearly the one for us.

Delhi Jal Board If Vivendi was to make its mark in India, it would do no better than to start in the capital, Delhi. Privatisation of the water industry continued to be misunderstood and, therefore, generally unacceptable throughout the Indian water business. Our line of attack, therefore, needed to gain support from the very top, which meant securing an audience with the Chief Minister for the National Capital Territory of Delhi. Mrs Sheila Dikshit (a bright star in the Indian National Party) had recently been elected. Arranging a meeting required ingenuity and contacting the right people, which is why we engaged Rajiv Luthra to make the necessary approaches.

JCB and I met this formidable lady (*who was to be Chief Minister for 15 years, the longest tenure on record*). My immediate impression of her was a lady of very likeable character, full of charm, highly intelligent and someone who resembled everybody's grandmother. JCB started his presentation with his usual smile that would make any of the opposite sex melt at his every word. He was a superb marketeer and persuaded the Chief Minister that professional help in the water industry was needed throughout the country, not least in Delhi, and maybe we could be given an opportunity to try some pilot scenarios to see how privatisation might work in practice. A very positive meeting. Sheila Dikshit promised to instruct the Delhi Jal Board (DJB) Chief Executive Officer to meet with us so that we could take it from there.

We immediately contacted the DJB and, the next day, found ourselves in the CEO's office. It became very clear anything to do with their distribution system was off-limits. Local politics at every level were far too great for this CEO to contemplate involvement there by an outsider. Not a good start.

We then proposed a different tack. Our preparation for this meeting had established that water resources serving Delhi were limited and relied principally on a single source, the River Yamuna. The CEO was happy for us to visit one of their treatment works to observe the efficiency of their staff in managing the technology.

That afternoon we were escorted by senior management to the Wazirabad water treatment plant. The works was a conventional sedimentation/rapid gravity filtration plant but operated on unconventional lines. We searched for any issue that might provide us with an advantage. The plant had no recovery of either the filter wash water or the sludge liquor from the sedimentation tanks, both such activities being common practice in Europe where water resources are often 'constrained'. This nugget of information needed further investigation, but we were able to throw doubt in the minds of senior management that maybe this could be an important point. The DJB was planning to extend the works from 80 MGD[28] to 120 MGD, so any savings could defer the need to implement this capital investment. We offered to do a free study of the potential volumes of recoverable water at Wazirabad. Such volumes could then lead to lower costs of pumping raw water out of the River Yamuna. The senior managers seemed to accept our proposal, principally because it was free, and they also thought we might just have a point that they were throwing away water unnecessarily (not just at this works, but at the other six treatment plants across Delhi). As an aside, we said we would also look at the possibility of building the proposed extension for them and analyse costs to provide both funding and a plan to privately manage the whole plant (i.e., provide DJB with the cost of running a privatised 120 MGD treatment plant - a BOT option).

[28] MGD – million gallons per day

We were allowed back to secure technical details throughout the plant and immediately had measured evidence that 40% more water was being pumped out of the River Yamuna than was being put into supply. We were also not surprised that the Plant was heavily overmanned. These points gave us confidence we could put forward a sensible BOT proposal for financing the proposed extension and running the whole plant over a 20-year period - ultimately paid for by DJB, who would reimburse Vivendi on the basis of an agreed amount of Rupees per cubic metre of treated water discharged into the City's trunk mains.

The proposal was not dismissed out of hand by DJB management, and we were invited to meet Mrs Sheila Dikshit again to explain our proposal in detail. Our presentation met with a certain amount of success. We were urged to provide further detail on all our facts and figures. We were confident our initial analysis was sufficiently robust to receive more scrutiny. We got a surprise, however, when we next visited Wazirabad, a surprise I had not experienced before or since. There, blocking the traffic to and from the plant, were a hundred or so trade unionists carrying banners that said:

"*Go away Frenchies. Keep your hands off our water.*"

Or that was the gist of what they said[29].

Back at DJB headquarters, once management became aware of the strong grassroots opposition, all of a sudden, they were not prepared to go through the indignity of supporting the Vivendi proposal. The issue was dropped without any hope of it emerging like a beautiful mermaid out of the Yamuna at some time in the not-too-distant future.

Bangalore – the centre of computer know-how in India It doesn't often happen that rival companies decide to join forces, but we were aware the other big French utility company, Lyonnaise des Eaux, was also interested in securing operations contracts in India. The French Embassy requested us both to attend a meeting in their Delhi Embassy. They had learnt Biwater (the British firm based in Dorking and founded by Adrian White) had made a play for running the operation of Bangalore's water supply system. The French Ambassador suggested if our two companies should join forces for a specific 'project' then we could both depend on the full support of the French Government. This was ironic because the two French conglomerates were using two British companies (Vivendi UK and

---

[29] Apologies to "*Take a Pew*" by Alan Bennett

Northumbria Water) to promote their interests in India![30] The combination of these two corporate French entities was probably more than two orders of magnitude larger than Biwater. We would most likely blow them out of the water, so to speak, if we were able to get our foot in the door. We had a fascinating meeting, including a clear demonstration of how the French Government appeared to be considerably more accommodating in support of their national companies abroad when compared to that our experience of the British Government's approach.

Both companies had had their eye on Bangalore (*often called in those days the Silicon Valley of India*) as we perceived the Karnataka State Government would be more progressive in their approach to privatisation. We were directed towards an 'intermediary' based in Bangalore who would lobby both politicians and technocrats to privatise Bangalore's water systems. We tracked him down to an old-fashioned hotel where he had permanent residence in a bungalow-type set of rooms in the depths of the hotel gardens. There were three of us at this meeting – JCB, myself and Fabian Cox, who was a Vivendi engineer representing us in India. First, we explained the existing city water infrastructure was totally inappropriate for a centre that looked to the future as the focal point of computer technology in South-East Asia. We then explained our proposal was to replicate what Paris did a few decades ago – the then Mayor of Paris, Jacques Chirac, was sympathetic to splitting the city's water infrastructure in two. As a result, one-half of the city's water supply system would be operated by Compagnie Générale des Eaux, the other half by Lyonnaise des Eaux.

Our 'intermediary' understood these two groups were world leaders and that this venture had the full support of the French Government. His business brain was impressed by this opportunity (particularly as he had already learnt about the Biwater initiative) and saw no reason why we could not be successful with our venture. His support and suggestions needed to concentrate on how to tackle those in power who might be vehemently opposed to any suggestion of privatisation. The meeting seemed positive, and we came away thinking the whole venture would definitely be worth pursuing.

We had constructive meetings with the Bangalore Water Supply and Sewerage Board (BWSSB) and, at their suggestion, we sent out engineers from the UK to develop a plan of how best to split the City's water supply systems in two, one to be operated by us (Three Valleys Water Company, part of Vivendi UK) and the

---

[30] If the tables had been turned and a request for project support made to the British High Commission in India by the same two English-based companies (but competing one against the other), such a request would have been turned down on the basis the British Government cannot support one while disadvantaging another. This was often the case elsewhere where there were shortlists of international water consultancy contracts. It was not unusual to see 3 or 4 British firms and only one each from the Dutch, France, Germany and Japan on such short lists, because of our strength and experience in this infrastructure sector.

other by Lyonnaise des Eaux (Northumbria Water). When Biwater learnt of our 'intervention', they were livid as they had already invested considerable sums of money towards securing a non-contested contract. We visited lieutenants of industry based in Bangalore to gauge support, or otherwise, for the privatisation of a public utility, including Sudhakar Rao, Chairman & General Manager of Karnataka Urban Infrastructure Development and Finance Corporation, Som Mittal, President & CEO of Digital and K.P. Singh, Chairman of the Karnataka Electricity Board. Our team received full support from R. Vasudevan, Executive Engineer BWSSB, to establish how best to divide the water infrastructure of the city. One week later, we had a plan. This included a definition of the physical division of the city's water supply apparatus; and both the French conglomerates presented tentative financial plans for the operation of their half of the city over the next twenty years.

It was time to present our proposals to the BWSSB Chairman and his advisers. We were well prepared and had chosen to include the regional French Consul in our team to demonstrate the international acceptability of our imaginative proposal. The meeting was going well. JCB was in full flow and very convincing. His focus was not only to demonstrate the project would be good for the citizens of Bangalore but also that the private sector would have viable projects to fully support the city's obligations to provide a continuous supply of wholesome water.

The presentation was over, and we awaited a response from the BWSSB Chairman. His presence spoke volumes, but he said nothing. He may have been embarrassed to listen to this tirade of excellence from the two French conglomerates in the presence of an employee of the French Government. Our 'intermediary' had clearly not paid attention to either the Chairman or one of his political advisers. Rejection was written all over the Chairman's face. Eventually, he got around to a few diplomatic words that might have implied our offer was premature. In any event, we needed to make a hasty retreat, lick our wounds, and think of where next to try our luck.

Mission of Indian infrastructure financiers to the UK I met with many people from all walks of life when attending conferences in India, including staff from the Delhi-based Infrastructure Leasing & Financial Services Limited (IL&FS). In 2000, they had an inward mission to London in search of funding for infrastructure projects in India. We persuaded them to visit the Three Valleys' Iver water treatment plant (which had been designed by Binnie & Partners and JTS back in the early 1970s). The mission was hosted by the Three Valleys chairman Sir John Page, and supported by JCB and myself. There were three of them, Ravi Parthasarathy, Vice Chairman & Managing Director, R.G.Prabhuchimlkar, Head of Water sector projects and Dr Anand Chiplunkar, Project Director (Water Group) and I had met them all at conferences in India, so they knew my stance on water privatisation.

The meeting took place in the works' conference room, followed by a well-prepared sit-down lunch. The meeting started well and included a tour of the plant. We spoke of our aspiration to work in India. The subject then turned to Chennai, which was a city we had targeted. We referred to their acute problem of water resource availability, having to rely on the River Cauvery, some 200 miles from the city. Our guests suddenly became demonstrably attentive because this River was the subject of their own investigations, specifically in relation as to how controlling abstractions could be managed in future. The River passes through three states, Kerala, Karnataka and Tamil Nadu, each State having the power to abstract as much water as they think is appropriate (particularly for agriculture) without any apparent concern for the States downstream.

Immediately Sir John also came alive, well, more than alive, as he suddenly remembered his family connection in relation to the River Cauvery.

> "My father was a High Court judge in India and was appointed to Chair a tribunal related to disputes on how to share the water resources of the River Cauvery." He went on to say, "hanging on my sitting room wall at home is a framed citation thanking my father for having resolved the quantum of how much water each State could reasonably abstract from the River Cauvery, once and for all."

Our guests were aghast at this revelation. The Chairman went on to say:

> "I will phone my wife right away and ask her to bring it in for you all to see."

Sure enough, this precious family heirloom was duly presented with all its fine words spelt out in the old-fashioned script, beautifully coloured in gold and reds to thank this venerated legal 'genius' for having reached a satisfactory conclusion to their many disputes over the years. We all then noticed the date this precious document was signed. It was exactly 80 years ago to the day that we were meeting with them in the Iver water treatment works on 3rd July 2000.

Alas, the dispute continues for all the reasons that existed before 3rd July 1920, even though the issue of such disputes is referred to in the Indian constitution. The main culprits continue to be local farmers with land adjacent to the River who abstract water to meet their needs without any attention to State controls.

Chennai revisited In Bangalore, the two large French firms were collaborators trying to create and win a mega project. Another project emerged, supported by World Bank, for which we would be fierce competitors and most probably the sole bidders. It was the beginning of the new millennium, and the Chennai

Metropolitan Water Supply and Sewerage Board (CMWSSB) in Tamil Nadu State had the vision to make their utility compatible with 21st-century operations using the latest computer technology and manpower requirements. This was far-sighted, and it looked as though Vivendi UK was admirably suited for such an operation (as was Northumbria Water). This was to be a consultancy management contract with a significant number of expatriate staff seconded to CMWSSB. Each 'expert' would have an Indian counterpart to train in his particular discipline, whether engineering, management, or finance. My discussions with JCB made it quite clear we had to win this opportunity. He offered to put forward Three Valleys Water Company staff for this assignment, all of whom had lifetime experiences in managing one of the world's most up-to-date facilities.

The stage was set, and I met with Gautam Shah (Shah Technical Services) to arrange all the local support we might need. We used our worldwide experience to draft an unbeatable proposal, drawing on my experience going back to 1972 and the Tehran and Mauritius projects, and particularly the Malaysian National Water project, where I had so much help from the JTS submissions supremo, David Yaw. It was looking good, and we were getting good feedback from CMWSSB that our proposal was favoured by senior management.

After a month of hearing all the right 'noises' from senior management of this potential client, we learnt that CMWSSB chairman CP Singh, was uneasy about calling us for negotiation. I immediately called our 'team' together in London and had a meeting with JCB to see how we might move the project forward. It transpired Gautam had been unable to make any direct contact with the Chairman and this fact seemed to be the stumbling block to our winning offer. We needed someone locally to approach the Chairman on our behalf. Just such a man was identified, and we instructed Fabian Cox to meet with him to discuss our predicament. This was India, and the man required a fee based on a percentage of our total estimated income for the project (which was to last for five years in the first instance). Needless to say, his 'remuneration' was outrageous, and there was no way our London-based team would sanction this as a one-off payment. We came up with a device we had used elsewhere to engage him as our agent with the express purpose of 'searching for water operational projects in Tamil Nadu State'. His appointment would be for 12-months, and we would pay him twelve equal monthly instalments. He accepted this principle, and JCB emphasised it was imperative to have the necessary paperwork in place to demonstrate to anybody who might enquire that this genuine 'administration cost' was a bona fide consultancy. We prepared an appropriate 'consultancy contract', which he signed so this whole matter could progress to a satisfactory conclusion. There was another 'piece of paper' that needed to be put in place. This 'intermediary' needed to write a report at the end of his 12-month assignment to identify suitable opportunities for the Vivendi Group in Tamil Nadu. Clearly, he was never going to be able to draft such a report without assistance. It just so happened I had written such a document for another client in another country in my previous employment with John Taylor & Sons/Acer Consultants/Hyder Consultants. I downloaded this word document onto my computer and adjusted keywords such that it could be deemed relevant and to have been drafted by our Tamil Nadu agent. This 'confidential' document remains in my desk to this day, never having been called upon to demonstrate the veracity of our Tamil Nadu Agent. All this may appear underhand, but it was necessary to secure the contract and fifteen engineers, administrators and scientists from Three Valleys enjoyed the pleasures of working in Chennai for the next ten years or so.

Postscript. We heard later that Lyonnaise des Eaux were furious when they discovered we had won the contract. Apparently, somewhere along the line, they believed we would play this competition as though it was taking place in the UK. Such a sentiment may have passed our lips, but this was India, and neither of us would have been appointed unless we followed the path set out for us to secure success.

Jamshedpur, Jharkhand State This city is the home of Tata Steel. It was founded in 1919 by Jamshedji Tata, founder of the Tata Group. He had the vision to create a new city on this virgin territory and wrote:

> *"Be sure to lay wide streets planted with shady trees, every other of a quick-growing variety. Be sure that there is plenty of space for lawns and gardens; reserve large areas for football, hockey and parks; earmark areas for Hindu temples, Muslim mosques and Christian churches."*

He sought permission from the ruling Government at the time in Calcutta to exploit the coal and iron reserves in that region, some 300 km to the west. Surprisingly, he received a positive response, so long as the Government had no responsibility or liability for providing the infrastructure and associated facilities for the town. He accepted this caveat and moving forward to 1990, Tata Steel was still responsible for providing all water and sewerage, highways, hospitals, and schools, as well as the provision of all other facilities normally adopted by local authorities for a city that had grown to house 800,000 population. In essence, it had become a private city totally financed off the 'bottom line' of Tata Steel's profit and loss account. Notwithstanding this financial burden, the city was clean, well administered, and in my opinion, was by far the best well-run city in India.

Tata Steel had ambitions of becoming one of the world's top steel producers and retained McKinsey & Co to advise on how this might be achieved. McKinsey examined their business of how they 'make' steel and were convinced the Group had the potential of securing their aims for excellence. However, when they learnt the Group was liable for the running of a city facility, they were horrified. How could a company spend a significant proportion of their profits running a metropolis? Their advice was:

> *This has got to stop. You must investigate how best to offload these responsibilities and liability."*

The first activity to be 'sorted' was the privatisation of all medical facilities in the city, including the main hospital. We were next on the scene and were prepared to meet Tata's senior management in Jamshedpur to take on board the complete operation and maintenance of the city's water supply and sewerage facilities. JCB and I travelled first to Kolkata; the next stage of our journey was to be in a two-passenger plane We sat immediately behind the pilot. Very noisy. We tried to hold a conversation but gave up when it was clear we could not even hear ourselves think. It might have been a small plane, but it was very manoeuvrable, and we watched in awe once the Indian pilot started his descent, using all his skill to drop out of the sky for landing a lot faster than a commercial airliner!

We were well received by this private sector organisation. Our discussions flowed with so much ease compared to those we had experienced with the public sector. Visits to their facilities were also an eye-opener; operational standards were more akin to those we experienced in Europe. This enabled us to prepare our financial models with a great deal more ease, confidence, and reliability. The net result was we were able to quickly achieve support from our potential clients because they understood from where we were coming to secure an improved water utility.

We returned to Delhi the way we had come! After much discussion with the very top Tata management, we were confident as to how to refine our proposals to be acceptable to both parties. We scored a major success on this occasion. It was 2001, and I was due to retire, and this victory justified JCB's decision to have employed me three years earlier in search of operational water activity in the South Asian sub-continent. As I left Old Queen Street for the last time, a good number of Three Valley engineers were posted to Jamshedpur.

I bowed out gracefully from being an international plumber some 38 years after commencing the journey.

Chapter 18: Epilogue

"Too much of water hast thou, poor Ophelia, And therefore I forbid my tears."
William Shakespeare (Hamlet)

I lived a sheltered childhood dominated by ecclesiastical music. Secondary education put me in touch with the classical and operatic world. During these years, I stumbled through the early stages of becoming a Chartered Engineer.

My musical education remained focused until I travelled to Zambia as a young graduate engineer. A whole new world was waiting to be explored; old-time musicals, the theatre as well as the roles of Pooh Bah (*The Mikado*) and the Caliph of Baghdad (*Kismet*).

This new environment taught me one particular song that merged my two loves of music and engineering. Thirty years later, I was chosen as the cabaret for a Firm's get-together at a posh London hotel. I knew there was only one song I could 'utter' to such an assembly of distinguished engineering guests. I introduced the number, with apologies to Thames Water Authority, and this is what I sang[31]:

When you're working in the dark, down below.
Underneath St James's Park, down below.
When you're working I the dark
Oh, it isn't half a lark,
When you're working in the dark, down below.

It isn't hard to tell, down below,
If its Bow or Clerkenwell, down below,
For Bow and Clerkenwell
Have a different kind of smell
And we know it very well, down below.

Over Covent Garden way, down below,
In the merry month of May, down below,
The fragrance of the flowers
Gives us many happy hours
And we sing a roundelay down below.

---

[31] Words and music by Sidney Carter

Now the objects that you find, down below
Help to entertain the mind, down below.
There are watches you can't wind
Wrapped up in bacon rind
And that isn't all you find, down below.

When you're under Floral Street, down below,
With the water round your feet, down below,
'Mid the cabbages and beet
You may find a marguerite
And the thought is very sweet, down below.

Hatton Garden is a spot, down below,
Where we like to go a lot, down below,
Since a bloke in Leather Lane
Dropped a diamond down the drain
We've been waiting but in vain, down below.

When to Billingsgate we come.
When to Billingsgate, we come, down below.
When to Billingsgate we come
Then things begin to hum
And we wish we'd never come down below
There is something in a sewer down below
That has a strange allure down below.

The magic of the drains
Is a thing you can't explain
But it's calling us again down below.

Strangely, I brought the house down in the nicest possible way.

Printed in Great Britain
by Amazon

20863120R00154